Future Connected Technologies
Growing Convergence and Security Implications

Editors

Maanak Gupta

Tennessee Tech University
Cookeville, Tennessee, USA

Ravi Tomar

University of Petroleum & Energy Studies
Dehradun, India

Anuj Kumar Yadav

DIT University
Dehradun, India

Hanumat Sastry G

University of Petroleum and Energy Studies
Dehradun, India

CRC Press
Taylor & Francis Group
Boca Raton London New York

CRC Press is an imprint of the
Taylor & Francis Group, an **informa** business

A SCIENCE PUBLISHERS BOOK

First edition published 2023
by CRC Press
6000 Broken Sound Parkway NW, Suite 300, Boca Raton, FL 33487-2742

and by CRC Press
4 Park Square, Milton Park, Abingdon, Oxon, OX14 4RN

© 2023 Maanak Gupta, Ravi Tomar, Anuj Kumar Yadav and Hanumat Sastry G

CRC Press is an imprint of Taylor & Francis Group, LLC

ISBN: 978-1-032-26307-6 (hbk)
ISBN: 978-1-032-26308-3 (pbk)
ISBN: 978-1-003-28761-2 (ebk)

DOI: 10.1201/9781003287612

Typeset in Palatino
by Radiant Productions

Preface

Cloud Computing, Edge Computing and IoT are important advances, among others, in the field of technology. These technologies have become a major driving force, being adopted by engineers and professionals around the globe. Real world problems can be solved using the mentioned techniques. Security can be a challenge in the adoption of these technologies, but with the use of access control methods and proposed cryptographic solutions they can be overcome.

This book can be treated as a reference guide by students, educators, and those seeking knowledge of cutting-edge technologies in the field of Computer science. It provides sufficient knowledge and information to researchers, which they can use and explore for further enhancements. Target audiences for the book are students from upper-undergraduate and graduate level courses. Not only students but researchers and industry practitioners and academia from various areas of cloud computing security have found it worthwhile.

It is comprised of thirteen chapters and each presenting a complete insight into the chosen problem. Chapter 1 discusses the role of Quantum Computing in Cloud Security. Chapter 2 is about providing security solutions to Cloud and Cyber-Physical Systems using Blockchain technology. Chapter 3 discusses a detailed review of access control methods in Cloud computing. Chapter 4 proposes solutions to enablement of smart city initiatives using different security methods.

Chapter 5 is dedicated to discussions regarding knowledge representation using Deep learning methods. Chapter 6 presents Machine learning techniques and their use in healthcare. The chapter mainly emphasizes heart disease prediction.

Chapters 7 and 8 are based on the Edge computing technique, in which first the architecture is presented and later security concepts in Edge computing are discussed. Chapter 9 discusses the application of Data-Analytics in cardiovascular disease prediction. Chapter 10 presents the role of Edge computing in smart agriculture. Chapters 11 and 12 explain the theoretical background regarding Cloud computing, IoT, and Edge computing.

We wish and hope that readers of this book find it interesting and it helps them understand important topics on Future Connected Technologies and underlying security implications.

Maanak Gupta
Ravi Tomar
Anuj Kumar Yadav
Hanumat Sastry G

Contents

Chapter 1
A Survey of Quantum Computing for Cloud Security

Matthew Brotherton and *Maanak Gupta**

◇◇

The application of quantum mechanics to computation has the potential to overturn the foundations that our existing computers and internet were built on. The unique principles of quantum systems allow us to solve problems, break encryption schemes, and formulate new frameworks for mass communication that would otherwise be impossible with traditional technologies. Likewise, the cloud architecture for computing has brought about a similar revolution. The two concepts, quantum computing and cloud computing, can be unified by implementing unconditional security in the cloud. This is achieved by leveraging the unique properties of quantum mechanical systems. In this chapter, various methods of improving cloud security using quantum computing will be discussed.

1. Introduction

Traditional digital security is heavily reliant on the inherent mathematical difficulty of specific tasks. For example, finding the prime factors of a large composite number requires enormous amounts of computational resources. Similarly, the hardness of computing the discrete logarithm for cyclic groups is the basis for ElGamal encryption [1] and the Elliptic-Curve Digital Signature Algorithm (ECDSA) [2], both of which have found use in many areas. These methods work solely because they assume it is infeasible for an attacker to spend

Tennessee Technological University, Cookeville TN 38505, USA.
Email: msbrothert42@tntech.edu
* Corresponding author: mgupta@tntech.edu

enough time or have access to the necessary computational resources to break the encryption scheme. As technology progresses, the intended amount of time and hardware power required to break the algorithms as set by the encryption scheme creators, may be surpassed, making the algorithms useless. In fact, this already happens and an example is discussed in Section 2.1.

However, the advent of quantum computing has introduced methods of achieving nontrivial unconditional security by taking advantage of entanglement and measurement. An example is covered in Section 4.7. While some of these techniques are unconditionally secure in theory, imperfections in the hardware that implement these techniques make it so that security breaches are possible. One example of this vulnerability is discussed in Section 3.1. Quantum cloud computing seeks to enhance the security of traditional cloud systems in several applications. Database access, smart grids, IoT networks, containers, and key distribution are some of these areas where quantum computing has proven to bolster existing security.

2. Background

Knowledge of general cryptographic (conditional) security is assumed. Familiarity with the mechanisms behind the Rivest-Shamir-Adleman (RSA) cryptosystem [3], Advanced Encryption Standard (AES) [4], and the Secure Hashing Algorithms (SHA) [5] is sufficient. Information-theoretic (unconditional) security will be discussed. A brief mathematical overview of quantum bits, superposition, measurement, entanglement, teleportation, and key distribution can be found in the Appendix. Quantum circuits and general quantum algorithms that may comprise the following techniques are too lengthy to cover, so this knowledge is also assumed.

2.1 Cryptographic Security

As mentioned in Section 1, the effectiveness of conditional security decreases as computational power increases. In other words, the security is conditioned on the presumed lack of sufficient computational resources. Evidence of this can be seen in the deprecation of the SHA-1 algorithm in favor of the more secure SHA-2.

On the other hand, information-theoretic (unconditional) security is effective even if an adversary has unlimited computational resources. Unconditional security can be achieved through specific classical security protocols such as Shamir's Secret Sharing (SSS) [6], but quantum unconditional security is accomplished largely due to the phenomenon of wave function collapse during qubit measurement. If an eavesdropper tries to interfere with the transmission, the qubit falls out of superposition, and the information is reduced to a single bit. This result will manifest as a deviation from the expected outcome during measurement, and it is how an eavesdropper can be detected. Many of the approaches in this paper utilize a protocol that was developed as a result of this consequence. The initial protocol is covered in Appendix E.

3. Quantum Cloud Attacks

3.1 Photon Number Splitting

Physical implementations of the BB84 protocol using photons are vulnerable to the photon number splitting attack (PNS) [7]. Most lasers used to transmit photons are approximations of a single-photon source, as producing a single photon is exceptionally difficult. Because of this, some laser pulses contain no photons, one photon, or multiple. The exact frequency of photons is typically described by a Poisson distribution [8]. In the case of the laser outputting multiple photons, an eavesdropper, Eve, can split the photons and transmit only one to Bob. Then, Eve can wait for Alice to reveal the original encoding basis. Using this information, Eve can measure her photons in the correct basis and glean information without introducing a detectable error. An overview of qubits and bases can be found in Appendix A.

3.2 Analysis and Detection of DoS Attacks in Cloud Computing by Using QSE Algorithm

Denial of Service (DoS) attacks are a threat to the cloud computing architecture, as clients are completely reliant on the cloud service providers to keep the services operational. To assist in heightening the security of cloud computing, Reddy and Bouzefrane propose a Quantum Evolutionary Algorithm (QEA) and Quantum Swarm Evolutionary (QSE) algorithm [9] for application in the public cloud. Their scheme is similar to classical genetic algorithms where information is regarded as chromosomes that undergo random mutations. In this case, the chromosomes are qubits. The population of qubits is denoted

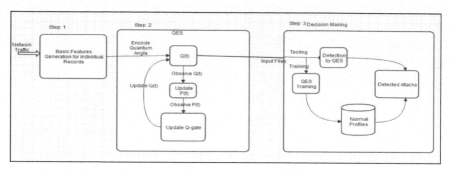

Fig. 1. QiPSO protocol overview as illustrated in [10].

as $Q(t)$, and $P(t)$ is the set of binary solutions resulting from the measurement of the qubits. The best solution is stored, and then $Q(t)$ is updated with quantum gates $U(t)$. Specifically, a modified version of Particle Swarm Optimization (PSO) [10] called Quantum-inspired Particle Swarm Optimization (QiPSO) [11] is used. An overview of the QiPSO process can be seen in Figure 1.

First, the best local quantum angle θ is found as demonstrated by Nicolau et al. [12]. Then, QiPSO is used to increment the angle θ. Each qubit is then encoded using the angle θ. Upon measuring $Q(t)$, $P(t)$ is set to either 0 or 1 depending on the result. Then, $Q(t)$ is updated using the gate $U(t)$.

According to QSE, each particle is assigned a velocity v, the current angle $\theta_{currentangle}$, an individual best θ_{pbest}, and the global best θ_{gbest}. $C1$ and $C2$ are acceleration constants that control the attracting forces. The $rand()$ function ensures diversity of the population, and it reduces the effect of premature convergence to non-optimal solutions [12]. The velocity and angle are updated according to the following equations respectively, from both [9] and [12]:

$$Q(t) = \{q_1(t), q_2(t), \dots, q_n(t)\}$$

$$q_j(t) = [\theta_{j1}(t)|\theta_j 2(t)| \dots |\theta_{jm}(t)|]$$

$$v_{ji}^{t+1} = \chi * \left(\omega * v_{ji}^t + C1 * \mathrm{rand}() * \left(\theta_{ji}^t(pbest) - \theta_{ji}^t\right) \right. $$
$$\left. + C2 * \mathrm{rand}() * \left(\theta_i^t(gbest) - \theta_{ji}^t\right)\right)$$

$$\theta_{ji}^{t+1} = \theta_{ji}^t + v_{ji}^{t+1}$$

The implementation of QiPSO consists of a training and testing phase. First, regular network traffic is captured. Then, particles are

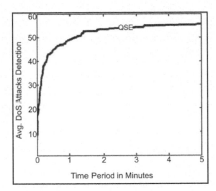

Fig. 2. Effectiveness of QSE DoS attack detection over time as adapted from [12].

Table 1. Percentage of DoS attacks found through QSE as shown in [12].

	Time Period in Minutes				
	1	*2*	*3*	*4*	*5*
QSE per 60	48	52	54	55	56
Average %	80%	86.6%	90%	91.3%	93.3%

moved on the network traffic. Next, the effects of the network traffic on the particles is examined. Lastly, the particles in the swarm are optimized.

For testing, abnormal network traffic needs to be captured. Then, particles are moved through this abnormal traffic, and the effects are recorded. As in the training phase, the particles are then optimized. By doing this, a large percentage of DoS attacks in the public cloud are correctly identified. The behavior and results of QSE detection with respect to time can be seen in Figure 2 and Table 1 respectively.

4. Quantum Cloud Security Implementations

4.1 QEnclave

The cloud gives users access to systems whose specifications often far surpass that of their own. In a similar manner, cloud-based services like IBM Quantum are connected to world-class quantum computers. However, the IBM environment is assumed to be trusted and secure. It is not safe to always make this assumption. For this reason, trusted execution environments (TEE's) are created. Specifically, IBM's service is known as delegated quantum computation (DQC). At the same

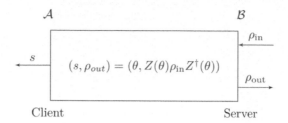

$$\mathcal{A} \qquad\qquad\qquad\qquad \mathcal{B}$$

$$(s, \rho_{out}) = (\theta, Z(\theta)\rho_{in} Z^{\dagger}(\theta))$$

ρ_{in}

s

ρ_{out}

Client   Server

Fig. 3. Remote State Rotation as illustrated in [13].

time, clients using IBM's quantum computers are performing blind quantum computation (BQC). The action is blind because the quantum computer's server does not fully know the client's information. By ensuring this condition, the computation is secure.

QEnclave as proposed by Ma et al. [13] is a quantum equivalent of a classical network enclave. An enclave is an isolated portion of a network that limits internal access. QEnclave can secure the remote execution of quantum operations while only using classical controls. QEnclave performs only single-qubit rotations, but it can secure any quantum computation, even if the qubit itself is controlled by an adversary.

Previously, work has been done on Remote State Preparation (RSP), however it has been proven that there does not exist a describable RSP protocol with composable security [14]. An alternative to RSP is remote state rotation (RSR). Unlike RSP, RSR does not assume a quantum channel exists between the client and server. The viability of RSR-DQC is proven in [13] through the use of the abstract cryptography framework [15]. A diagram of RSR can be seen in Figure 3.

The described mechanism is able to achieve secure delegated quantum computation, however there are some attacks that the QEnclave may be vulnerable to. For example, this scheme assumes that the QEnclave was produced by a certified manufacturer. There is also the possibility of side-channel attacks and counterfeiting the QEnclave.

4.2 Enhancement of Quantum Key Distribution Protocol for Data Security in Cloud Environment

Data privacy in the cloud is a looming concern. Generally, cloud service providers encrypt customer data, however it is recommended

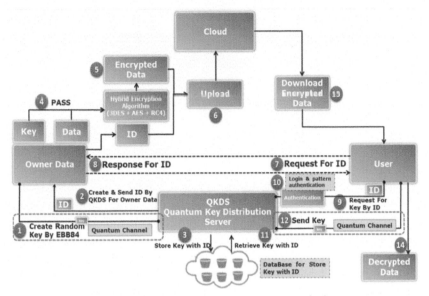

Fig. 4. QKDS protocol as illustrated in [16].

that users encrypt their data before uploading to the cloud as well; this ensures that a cloud provider key leak will not compromise user data. Jassem and Abdullah propose a protocol that allows encryption, uploading, downloading, and decryption [16]. Their protocol has a Data Owner, Triple Data Encryption Algorithm (3DES), AES, Rivest Cipher 4 (RC4), QKD, QKD Server (QKDS), and a Cloud User. The inclusion of QKD ensures that an eavesdropper will not go undetected. An overview of the proposed framework can be seen in Figure 4.

First, the data owner connects to the QKDS to obtain the quantum key. Then, the key is saved in a database for future retrieval. The ID that is stored is agreed upon by the data owner and the QKDS. It is comprised of the QKDS's first ten randomly generated bases. This string is then sent to the data owner. Next, a hybrid of 3DES, AES, and RC4 takes the QKDS key as input and encrypts it. For this protocol, the data is uploaded to the Dropbox cloud using the ID as stored in the database. Then, the user who wishes to access the owner's data needs to get the ID from the data owner over a secure classical channel. After the user has the ID and connects with the QKDS, the key exchange starts. This process uses EBB84 [17] to send a random key to the user. Once the user receives the random key from the QKDS, and they confirm no eavesdropper is present, the

Table 2. Various encryption algorithms and their upload times as in [16].

FILE SIZE	Used Bit Number	Throughput Key Length	3DES ENC + DEC Full Time	AES ENC + DEC Full Time	CR4 ENC + DEC Full Time	3ALG ENC + DEC Full Time	UPLOAD TIME TO DROPBOX
10 k	1024 bits	565 bits	110 ms	110 ms	115 ms	335 ms	5156 ms
1.2 M	1024 bits	582 bits	1507 ms	1026 ms	1187 ms	3720 ms	44101 ms
10 k	512 bits	287 bits	39 ms	30 ms	36 ms	105 ms	2677 ms
1.2 M	512 bits	292 bits	1483 ms	877 ms	834 ms	3195 ms	23929 ms
10 k	256 bits	141 bits	57 ms	31 ms	26 ms	114 ms	2890 ms
1.2 M	256 bits	142 bits	1478 ms	801 ms	771 ms	3051 ms	25691 ms
STANDARD DEVIATION	–	335 bits	779.0 ms	479.1 ms	494.8 ms	1753.3 ms	17407.3 ms

user can download the data and decrypt it. Otherwise, the process is repeated until there is no eavesdropper error. This proposed protocol, due to its layered approach, was found to be much more secure than just implementing AES on the data owner's data. Jassem and Abdullah found that the combination of AES and QKD produced the quickest encryption and decryption times. A comparison of algorithm results can be seen in Table 2.

4.3 Verifiable Quantum Cloud Computation Scheme Based on Blind Computation

One form of BQC is measurement-based BQC (MBQC). A concern with MBQC is detecting misbehavior from one of the clients. Li et al. propose using cluster states in a grid-distributed structure to implement the necessary calculations [18]. The grid topology for delegated calculation can be seen in Figure 5.

Notably, the verification of results is done classically. Cluster states are appropriate for this task as they can perform universal quantum computation; this means it can simulate any quantum operation by single particle measurement. This is possible because MBQC has been proven to be a universal quantum computer [19]. An overview of the protocol in [18] can be seen in Figure 6.

The plaintext input state is denoted as $|\psi_{in}\rangle$, and the encrypted state is denoted $|\psi_{en}\rangle$. The delegated function is denoted as f. The encryption and decryption functions can be written as

$$|\psi_{en}\rangle = \text{Encrypt}\left(|\psi_{\text{in}}\rangle, ek\right)$$
$$|\psi_{\text{in}}\rangle = \text{Decrypt}\left(|\psi_{en}\rangle, dk\right)$$

where ek and dk are the encryption and decryption keys, respectively.

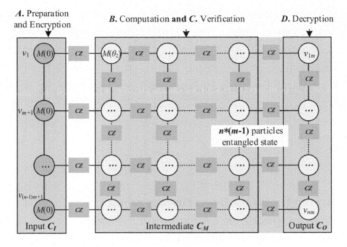

Fig. 5. The proposed lattice structure as shown in [18].

Our Scheme

1. Preparation and Encryption

1.1 For each $i \in C_I$, Alice prepares input state $|\psi_{in}\rangle = \sum_{x \in 2^n} a_x |x\rangle$. Further, Alice generates a string of random numbers $ek = \{(k_{i1}, k_{i2})\}_{i=1,\cdots,n}$ as encryption key to encrypt the input state and gets $|\psi_{ec}\rangle = Encrypt(|\psi_{in}\rangle, ek) = U_{ek}|\psi_{in}\rangle$, where $U_{ek} = \sum_{i=1,\cdots,n} (X^{k_{i1}} Z^{k_{i2}})_i$. Alice sends the encrypted state to Bob.

1.2 Bob prepares $|+\rangle^{\otimes(n \times (m-1))}$, for all $j \in C_M \cup C_O$.and creates an entangled state $|\psi_{en}\rangle$ with CZ operation after receiving all the qubits.

2. Computation

2.1 Alice calculates measurement angle $\theta_2 (r_1)$ for the first measured particle v_2 and sends to Bob.

2.2 Bob measures in the basis $\{|+_{\theta_2}\rangle, |-_{\theta_2}\rangle\}$.

2.3 Bob communicates the result $r_2 \in \{0, 1\}$ to Alice.

2.4 Repeat above process until the measurement on the particle belongs to C_M completed. Bob gets the intermediate state $|\psi_{med}\rangle$

3. Verification

Alice verifies equation (1) and equation (2). If they hold, this calculation continues; otherwise they stop it.

4. Decryption

4.1 Bob performs X-basis measurement $M(0)$ on input particles, and sends outcomes $\{r_j\}_{j \in C_I}$ and output particles to Alice.

4.2 Alice performs Pauli operation U_{dk} to get the final result $f|\psi_{in}\rangle = Decrypt(|\psi_{en}\rangle, dk)$.

Fig. 6. MBQC protocol steps as seen in [18].

Because only Alice knows the random numbers ek, Bob cannot glean any information about the input state, even if he performs entanglement dishonestly. Additionally, because the measurement angles are independent of any given input state, Alice's input state is not disclosed. Also, because Bob measures based on the angle that Alice sends, if Bob measures the incorrect angle, there will be a statistical deviation in verification results. A review of entanglement and measurement can be found in Appendix C and Appendix B respectively.

4.4 Anti-Forging Quantum Data: Cryptographic Verification of Quantum Computational Power

When a client interacts with a quantum computation server, they assume the returned result originated from an authentic quantum source and not a forgery. To formalize this assumption, verification is needed in the form of a cryptographic protocol. The protocol is comprised of two entities. Alice, the sender, takes the role of the verifier, and Bob, the receiver, takes the role of the prover.

Formal decision problems are members of a specific computational complexity class such as P (polynomial time), NP (nondeterministic polynomial time), NP-hard, NP-complete. Similarly, there exist quantum complexity classes such as BQP (bounded-error quantum polynomial time) and IQP (instantaneous quantum polynomial time). Using the model of IQP, Shepherd and Bremner proposed a protocol [20] that seemed to work within near-term quantum computing. However, it was found to have a loophole which made it insecure [21].

To fix this, Yung and Cheng devise an IQP protocol [22] that is immune to the attack that Shepherd and Bremner's scheme fell to. A diagram of the scheme can be seen in Figure 7. This is accomplished both by not relying on error-correcting codes, and an arbitrary number of secret strings can be created instead of a single secret string. In addition to being immune to the attack, Yung and Cheng's protocol is much more secure, as possibly multiple secret strings need to be correctly guessed by a forger instead of just one. It should be noted that this protocol is ideally implemented in the time of quantum supremacy to obtain full security.

The quantum cloud verification protocol:

Step 1. Alice (the verifier) generates one, or multiple, n-bit random string(s) $\mathbf{s} := (s_1, s_2, \cdots, s_n)^T \in \{0, 1\}^n$ kept as a secret, where each string is associated with a Pauli product, $\mathcal{Z}_{\mathbf{s}} := Z^{s_1} \otimes \cdots \otimes Z^{s_n}$.

Step 2. Based on the secret string(s), Alice designs a Hamiltonian H consisting of a linear combination of Pauli-X products.

Step 3. Alice then sends the classical description about the Hamiltonian H to Bob (the prover) and asks him to apply the time evolution of H to the state $|0^n\rangle$, where the angles of each term (i.e. the evolution time) are also determined by Alice.

Step 4. Bob should perform the quantum computation $U_{\text{IQP}}|0^n\rangle$ accordingly and measure in the computational basis multiple times. After that, he returns the output bit strings to Alice.

Step 5. Finally, Alice calculates the correlation function(s) $\langle \mathcal{Z}_{\mathbf{s}} \rangle := \langle 0^n|U_{\text{IQP}}^{\dagger}\mathcal{Z}_{\mathbf{s}}U_{\text{IQP}}|0^n\rangle$ by classical means in Sec. II B, and compares it with the results obtained from the bit strings given by Bob.

Fig. 7. Quantum verification protocol steps as illustrated in [22].

4.5 End-to-End Security Using Quantum Walks in IoT Networks

Current Internet of Things (IoT) technology is lacking in security. If IoT is to become ubiquitous, the protocols implemented need to be hardened. Additionally, with the rapid growth of quantum computational power, current mechanisms deemed safe may not hold for much longer. To improve IoT security, elements of chaotic systems have been tested, however some chaotic systems possess the undesired quality of periodicity and instability.

On the other hand, the behavior of quantum walks (QW) can be used to generate keys as demonstrated by Abd El-Latif et al. in [23]. Unlike other chaotic sources, QW are non-periodic, and they are stable. QW are inherently nonlinear and chaotically dynamic. This makes them an ideal source for producing randomness. The following description of a QW can be found in [23].

A QW has two types: continuous-time and discrete-time. For the purposes of this survey, only discrete-time will be considered. The elementary components of running one-walker QW acting on a circle have two quantum systems: a particle $|\psi\rangle_p$ known as a walker living in a p-dimensional Hilbert space H_p and a 2-dimensional quantum system $|\psi\rangle_c = \cos\alpha|0\rangle + \sin\alpha|1\rangle$ known as a coin living in Hilbert space H_c. Total Hilbert space of the QW is $H = H_p \otimes H_c$. In every step r of running QW on a circle, the unitary transformation $\hat{R}$ is executed on the whole quantum system $|Q\rangle$. The unitary transformation $\hat{R}$ can be expressed as

$$\hat{R} = \hat{F}(\hat{I} \otimes \hat{U})$$

where $\hat{F}$ points to the shift operator and can be stated for running QW on a circle with T vertices as

$$\hat{F} = \sum_{i=0}^{T-1}(|(i+1) \bmod T, 0\rangle\langle i, 0| + |(i-1) \bmod T, 0\rangle\langle i, 1|)$$

After r steps, the final state $|Q\rangle_r$ can be stated as

$$|Q\rangle_r = (\hat{R})^r|Q\rangle_0$$

and after r steps, the probability of locating the particle at location i can be expressed as

$$P(i,r) = \left|\left\langle i, 0\left|(\hat{R})^r\right|Q\right\rangle_0\right|^2 + \left|\left\langle i, 1\left|(\hat{R})^r\right|Q\right\rangle_0\right|^2$$

The proposed encryption scheme obfuscates an image using a QW. First, the image is broken up into 16x16 blocks, and then each block is further broken up into a right and left sub-block. To do this, the QW-generated probability distribution is used to create two permutation boxes as in Figure 9. The two permutation boxes are combined and then XORed with another PRNG sequence to construct the cipher image [23]. This process can be seen in Figure 8.

Simulations and statistical analysis of correlation coefficients, information entropy, and histograms confirms that this scheme is highly efficient and suitably random. For example, QW-encrypted image data approximates a uniform distribution; it is much more difficult to identify the image by its pixel frequency when encrypted. An excerpt of these results can be seen in Figure 10. This makes it ideal and suitable for implementation in cloud-based IoT networks.

4.6 Protecting Privacy in the Cloud using a Quantum-based Database Query Scheme

Privacy is one of the primary concerns with cloud applications. In particular, outsourced databases storing sensitive data such as financial transactions and health records must be kept confidential.

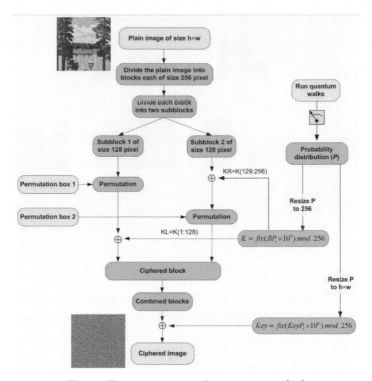

Fig. 8. Encryption procedure as seen in [23].

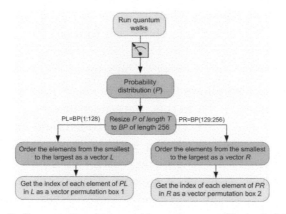

Fig. 9. Permutation box creation process as illustrated in [23].

To do this, a privacy preserving database query scheme (PPDQ) is needed. A PPDQ ensures that the database itself is secure and that the client's information is private. However, traditional PPDQ's are vulnerable to quantum computers employing techniques such as

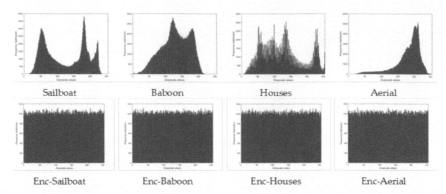

| Sailboat | Baboon | Houses | Aerial |

| Enc-Sailboat | Enc-Baboon | Enc-Houses | Enc-Aerial |

Fig. 10. Effect of QW encryption on pixel frequency distributions as shown in [23]: top row is unencrypted image data which shows unique frequencies for each image; bottom row is encrypted image data.

Grover's algorithm and Shor's algorithm. To counter this, a quantum-based database query scheme (QBDQ) is proposed by Liu et al. in [24]. In it, clients are only allowed to query for one data item.

As a preliminary, oblivious transfer (OT) in cryptography is the idea that the sender can transmit one of many pieces of information to a receiver, but the sender does not know specifically which piece has been sent. In other words, they are oblivious to the information sent.

As an example, consider Charlie as the owner of a database, and both Alice and Bob are clients that wish to query the database. For detailed steps in the protocol and a full security analysis, refer to [24]. A diagram of the entire process can be seen in Figure 11.

This protocol also allows the client to check for an eavesdropper through decoy photons. To do this, the sender inserts random photons in the qubit sequence, and each decoy is encoded randomly with either the Z or X basis. Once the receiver gets the transmission, the sender reveals the correct bases. Then, the receiver measures their photons in those bases and reports the measurements to the sender. When comparing the results between sender and receiver, if the error rate exceeds the set threshold, it can be inferred that an eavesdropper was likely present. If this happens, then the process is restarted until the error rate is within the threshold as defined by the noise level. The proposed scheme ensures correctness, privacy, and improves the efficiency of querying. Evidence of this can be seen in Figure 12.

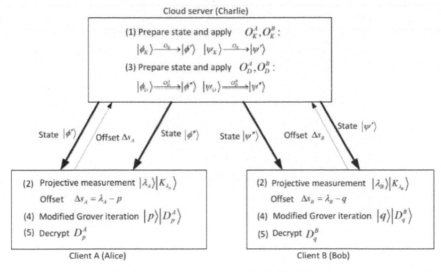

Fig. 11. PPDQ protocol as seen in [24]. The thick (thin) lines are quantum and (classic) channels.

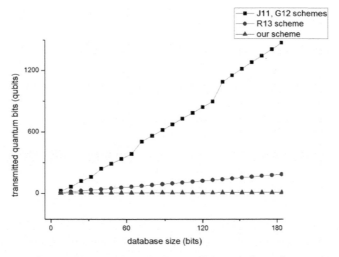

Fig. 12. Complexity comparison in terms of the number of transmitted qubits using QBDQ, J11, G12, and R13 as seen in [24].

4.7 A Novel Scheme for Data Security in Cloud Computing Using Quantum Cryptography

One-time pads (OTP) are a classical implementation of unconditional security. In a sense, OTP are trivial because they are unconditionally secure solely because the key is only used once. Moreover, OTP has restrictions that are not always desirable. For example, the length of the key must match the length of the plaintext. This means that the required key length scales with the size of data to be encrypted. Also, OTPs require a unique key for each transmission.

Thus, OTP is not the best choice for quick secure transmission in the cloud environment. Sharm and Kalra propose a protocol using Quantum AES [25]; this scheme combines QKD and AES. In it, a key k is generated by a quantum key generator and sent through a quantum channel using BB84. The receiver measures the bits received over the quantum channel in their own selected bases. The receiver then announces the selected bases to the sender over the public channel. This is similar to the traditional BB84 protocol.

In this scheme, a key length of 128 bits is chosen. The key is used to encrypt and decrypt the data using AES.

First, the key generated by the quantum key generator is sent through a quantum channel using BB84. Then, the receiver measures the bits received with their own random bases. The receiver announces their bases to the sender to verify generated-key compatibility.

Next, the final key k_{q_n} generated by round r_n is used to encrypt the blocks of data. A diagram of an AES round can be seen in Figure 13. There can be 10, 12, or 14 rounds. They are computed as

$$\mathrm{E}\left(\mathrm{D_1} \bigoplus \mathrm{k_{q_n}}\right) = \mathrm{M_n} \tag{1}$$

Lastly, the receiver can decrypt the encrypted message using

$$\mathrm{D}\left(\mathrm{M_n} \bigoplus \mathrm{k_{q_a}}\right) = \mathrm{D_n} \tag{2}$$

In comparison to regular AES run times, Quantum AES is slower by only a few more millseconds, but it is more secure than traditional AES by itself. Run time analysis for various forms of AES and QAES can be seen in Figure 14.

4.8 Securing Cloud Containers Using Quantum Networking Channels

Containers are a lightweight and portable solution for sharing applications across platforms. It should be noted that containers are untrusted by default. Running the applications or containers through

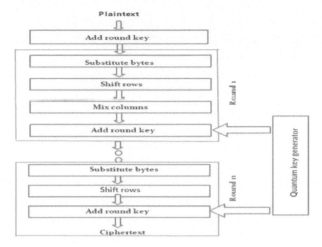

Fig. 13. Round of Quantum AES as seen in [25].

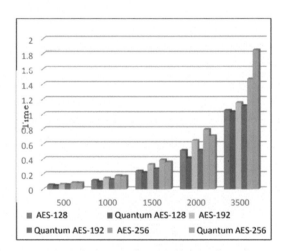

Fig. 14. A run time analysis comparison between AES and QAES for different key sizes as seen in [25].

container engines requires root privileges on the host. Containers are managed by a container daemon. The daemon is exposed to various outlets such as HTTP, REST API's, and disk images. Disruption of the daemon can affect other applications being managed by the daemon. For this reason, container security is extremely important. Kelley et al. propose an unconditionally secure protocol and network for cloud-based container management [26].

Their framework utilizes the E91 protocol [27] to teleport qubits securely. The mechanics of teleportation are covered in detail in Ap-

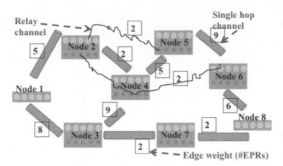

Fig. 15. Topology of a quantum network with path costs and token numbers as seen in [26].

pendix D. The structure of their network consists of eight servers. These nodes are connected through virtual entangled links, and each link is secured through Bell pairs; these pairs are also called tokens. Each node generates a fixed number of pairs. It is important to note that quantum entangled links work on a teleport-once policy. Every entanglement-link reduces the establishing node's token count by one. This process repeats until no more tokens are left, and more tokens need to be generated.

If a node wants to establish a connection, it first sends out a route request (RREQ) message. The message is received by neighboring nodes, and they then check the destination IP address of the broadcasting node. If the IP does not match, reverse routing tables are generated.

The proposed quantum routing protocol is stated to be a modification of Dijkstra's algorithm [28], as the quantum algorithm selects the path with the highest number of tokens available, instead of the lowest cost. A diagram of this technique can be seen in Figure 15. An example of the arithmetic used to decide the optimal route can be seen in Figure 16.

These schemes come into effect when an application requests root privileges. When this happens, a request is sent to the quantum server through a classical channel between the host server and the quantum server. Then, a Bell pair source is introduced on the quantum server to generate Bell pairs. Once the pair is generated, half of the pair is sent to the host, and the other half stays with the quantum server.

Then, the qubit's secure key can be used to securely communicate between a containerized application and the container daemon. In this way, only containers that have secure keys will be allowed access to

$$N_{tn}(r_1) = 1/5 + 1/2 + 1/5 + 1/9 + 1/6 = 53/45$$
$$N_{tn}(r_2) = 1/5 + 1/2 + 1/6 = 13/15$$
$$N_{tn}(r_3) = 1/8 + 1/9 + 1/5 + 1/9 + 1/6 = 257/360$$
$$N_{tn}(r_4) = 1/8 + 1/2 + 1/2 = 7/8$$
$$N_{tn}(r_5) = 1/5 + 1/2 + 1/9 + 1/6 - 11/15$$

Fig. 16. Example calculation of all Node 8 route costs in using normalized EPR numbers to find the optimal route in [26], Eq. 2, as first proposed by Xiaofei et al. [29].

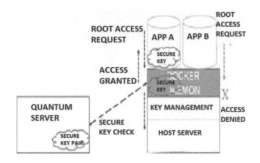

Fig. 17. Container Access Control via QKD as illustrated in [26].

the daemon. An overview of the entire access control process can be seen in Figure 17.

4.9 Quantum Searchable Encryption for Cloud Data Based on Full-Blind Quantum Computation

One of the biggest concerns with cloud-based consumer data is privacy preservation, as the data could be physically stored on a disk in a different country. To protect users, the data is heavily encrypted. However, most encryption schemes require the data to be decrypted first before any query over it can be made. Decrypting exposes the data for a brief moment, so this should be avoided if possible. Thankfully, searchable encryption (SE) allows data to be queried without decryption. Unfortunately, most SE uses public key encryption [30]; it can potentially be broken with quantum computers. To counter this, Liu et al. propose a quantum searchable encryption scheme for cloud data based on full-blind quantum computation (QSE-FBQC) [31] and the assumption of a trusted key center (TKC) and data center (DC). It is important to note that this protocol allows for multiple clients. A diagram of the protocol can be seen in Figure 18.

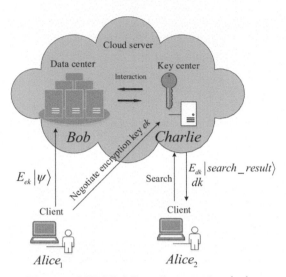

Fig. 18. QSE-FBQC as illustrated in [31].

In it, clients first encrypt their data with the X and Z gates using the keys generated by the TKC. After the data is encrypted, it is uploaded to the DC. Here, the DC conducts the search using a universal set of quantum gates $(X, Z, H, S, T, CNOT, CZ, Toffoli)$. However, the data center constructs these gates using only $\pi/8$ rotations from the set $\{R_z(\pi/4), R_y(\pi/4), CR_z(\pi/4), CR_y(\pi/4), CCR_z(\pi/4), CCR_y(\pi/4)\}$. It then performs these rotations on each qubit sent by the key center. After rotating, it then sends the qubits back to the key center. Repeating this process can compose any gate out of the described rotations. By doing this, the data center is blind; it does not know what gate is being constructed. After the search, the TKC generates a decryption key. Lastly, the client can use the decryption key to apply the X and Z gates and get back the search result.

For example, suppose $Alice_1$ has a set $\{00, 01, 10, 11\}$ and $Alice_2$ wants to find item $\{01\}$ from the set. This is equivalent to using Grover's search algorithm [32] to find $\{|0\rangle|1\rangle\}$ from $\{|+\rangle|+\rangle\}$.

The protocol begins with $Alice_1$ sending a number 2 to $Charlie$. Then, Charlie sends a string of 4 random binary bits (act as ek) back to $Alice_1$ via the BB84 protocol in [E]. Then, $Alice_1$ encrypts her data $|\psi\rangle = |+\rangle_1|+\rangle_2$ with X and Z gates according to ek. Next, $Alice_2$ wants to get $|0\rangle_1|1\rangle_2$ from $E_{ek}|\psi\rangle$, and $Charlie$ interacts with Bob according to the circuit in [32]. First, $Charlie$ needs to insert an auxiliary qubit $|1\rangle$ into $|\psi\rangle$. After the search is finished, *Charlie* sends the search result state and decryption key to $Alice_2$ as

$$\left(X_1^{x_1} Z_1^{z_1}\right) \otimes \left(X_2^{z_1} Z_2^0\right) \otimes \left(X_3^0 Z_3^0\right) \mid \text{result} \rangle_{1,2,3} \, dk =$$
$$\{(x_1, z_1)_1 , (z_1, 0)_2 , (0, 0)_3\}$$

Lastly, $Alice_2$ uses dk to decrypt the state $\left(X_1^{x_1} Z_1^{z_1}\right) \otimes \left(X_2^{z_1} Z_2^0\right) \otimes \left(X_3^0 Z_3^0\right) \mid \text{result} \rangle_{1,2,3}$, and abandons the auxiliary third qubit to get $|0\rangle_1|1\rangle_2$. This is the requested item in the set, and the transaction is complete.

4.10 CloudQKDP: Quantum Key Distribution Protocol for Cloud Computing

Currently, cloud services are secured using conditional security. However, it is possible to integrate quantum unconditional security into the cloud by using QKD, as shown by Murali and Prasad in their proposed CloudQKDP framework [33]. Their architecture consists of a QKD layer, key management (KML) layer, cloud data security layer (CDSL), and cloud layer (CL). A diagram of the architecture can be seen in Figure 19. The CDSL handles encryption and decryption through both classical and quantum cryptography. The CL simply

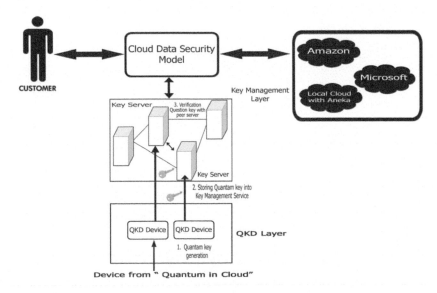

Fig. 19. CloudQKDP framework as illustrated in [33].

provides cloud services. Classical cryptography is used to secure the data, while QKD is used to securely distribute the classical keys. The generated keys are stored in the KML.

To implement this protocol, the Quantum in Cloud platform was used. Murali and Prasad found that there were distance issues when testing their protocol on the public cloud. However, the private cloud on Aneka achieved a 98% key generation success rate, and Quantum in Cloud returned a 100% key generation success rate. For the future, they intend on resolving the issues when testing their protocol on the public cloud.

4.11 Secure Data Access Control for Multi-authority Quantum Based Cloud Storage

The proposed architecture by Vidya and Abinaya, Quantum Ciphertext-Policy Attribute Based Encryption (QCP-ABE) [34], is a scheme that involves a certificate authority (CA), attribute authority (AA), data owners, data consumers, and a cloud server. The CA can accept multiple user registrations and AA's. Each user is assigned a unique user ID (UID), and each AA is assigned a unique AA ID (AID). The AA transmits the UID and key through a quantum gate encoder to obtain the quantum-encoded key (QEK). Each AA must also generate its own public key. A diagram of the architecture can be seen in Figure 20.

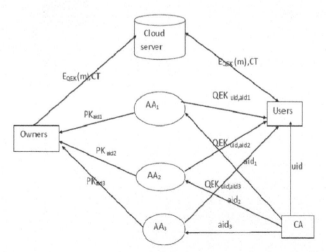

Fig. 20. QCP-ABE architecture as illustrated in [34].

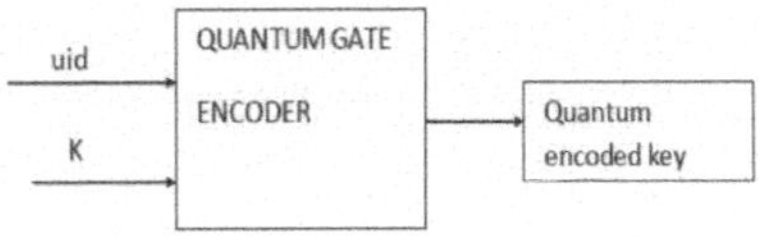

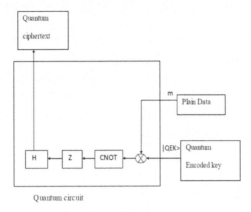

Fig. 21. QCP-ABE encoded-key generation as seen in [34].

Fig. 22. QCP-ABE encryption scheme as illustrated in [34].

To obtain the quantum-encoded key, the AA must pass the UID and content key K into the encoder, as seen in Figure 21. During encryption, each data owner passes their plaintext into the quantum circuit along with the QEK. Specifically, the user must split their data into chunks. Then, each chunk is encrypted with a different key QEK_n using symmetric encryption. The output is the quantum-encrypted ciphertext. A diagram of this encryption into ciphertext can be seen in Figure 22. In this way, only users possessing a valid private key are able to decrypt the data.

There are no results of this protocol in practice, as it has yet to be implemented. However, the theory behind it is sound. Vidya and Abinaya plan to use a virtual machine workstation to test it.

4.12 Enhancing the Security of a Cloud-based Smart Grid AMI Network by Leveraging on the Features of Quantum Key Distribution

Smart grid advanced metering infrastructure (SG AMI) is a technology that allows power grids to intelligently load balance and distribute electricity. A potential implementation of SG AMI could utilize the cloud to distribute hardware resources among multiple regional stations. Naturally, securing this type of infrastructure is essential. While conditional security is sufficient for now, quantum unconditional security is a possible improvement. Diovu and Agee propose a cloud-based SG AMI that uses homomorphic encryption (HE), hashed message authentication codes (HMAC), one-time pads (OTP), and BB84-based QKD to ensure unconditional security [35]. Data in this protocol could either be for billing or for grid control.

In their scheme, a hierarchical cloud is used. It is comprised of a root cloud, regional cloud, top cloud, and communication channels. The root cloud hosts the smart meters, in-home displays (IHDs), intelligent electronic devices (IEDs), root cloud key management server (RCKMS), and data aggregators. The regional cloud contains NAN gateways (NAN GWs) and the regional key management servers (RKMSs). The top cloud is comprised of the top cloud server, Open-Flow firewall, and the AMI master station. Lastly, the communication channels are a mix of quantum and classical. There is a quantum channel between the RCKMS and the RKMSs for quantum key generation. Communication between the top cloud and the regional clouds is done via a quantum channel with QKD-generated keys. Classical channels are needed to transmit measurement results from QKD. A diagram of the protocol can be seen in Figure 23. The steps are as follows [35]:

To send a message, every smart meter encrypts its metering data m_i to obtain the corresponding ciphertext. For i smart meter nodes connected to a given aggregator, the symmetric encryption key, K_{QKD} is generated. The generated key is shared with the closest NAN_{GW} to the data aggregator. The identity of each smart meter, ID_i, is then concatenated with ciphertext computed in the previous equation

$$C_{m_t} = \text{Enc}\,(m_i, K_{QKD}, M)$$
$$ID_i \| C_{m_i} \to DATA \quad AGG$$

where M is a message space (set of all possible messages), which needs to be large enough to prevent overflow. The smart meter then forwards C_{m_i} to the aggregator, which then aggregates C_{m_i} for all smart meters within its domain by performing the addition of modulo M. The aggregated value will then be forwarded to the nearest N_{GW}

$$AGG \text{ Value } \to NAN_{GW} : C_{m_i} = \sum_{ID-1}^{n} C_{m_i}(\text{mod}\,M),$$

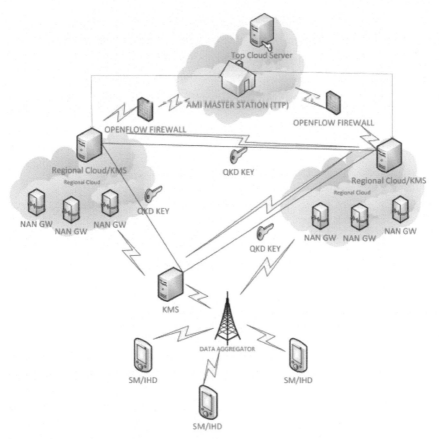

Fig. 23. SG AMI framework as seen in [35].

where n is the number of ciphers added. Given C_{m_1} and K_{QKD}, m_i can be recovered from the decryption algorithm by

$$m_i = \text{Dec}\left(C_{m_i}, K_{QKD}, M\right)$$

Using the smart meters identities, ID_i, the respective metering data can be attributed to the smart meters by the v_{GW}. For onward transmission or to upload data from NAN_{GW} to the upper cloud, additional security measures are then applied by the NAN_{GW}.

To transmit M_i from the NAN_{GW} to a regional cloud server $KMS_{REGIONALCLOUD}$, the NAN_{GW} generates a message authentication code (MAC) by using the generated K_{QKD} key. The time-based message M_i containing the consumption data from the smart meters (or control information) is passed to the $HMACK_{QKD}$. This generates the MAC for the message M_i. The NAN_{GW} then concatenates the message M_i, its time stamp TS^{t_n}, and the $HMACK_{QKD}$. This entire packet is then encrypted using AES. Then, the NAN_{GW} sends this encrypted packet to $KMS\_REGIONAL\_CLOUD$. The time stamp is included to deter replay attacks on the message. The process is as follows:

$$NAN_{GW} \rightarrow KMS\_REGIONAL\_CLOUD :$$

$$\text{Enc} \left(M_i \left\| TS^\ell \right\| HMACK_{QKD}(M_i) \right),$$

Once the $KMS\_REGIONAL\_CLOUD$ receives the packet from the NAN_{GW}, it decrypts it using the K_{QKD} key

$$\text{Dec} \left(M_i \left\| TS^{t_n} \right\| HMACK_{QKD}(M_i) \right)$$

Once decrypted, the $KMS\_REGIONAL\_CLOUD$ checks the time stamp; if the time step is fresh, the $KMS\_REGIONAL\_CLOUD$ verifies the integrity of the message by calculating $HMACK_{QKD}$ of the message, and it then forwards the authenticated message to the AMI master station. If the message cannot be verified, the session is aborted.

During the OTP encryption process at the $KMS\_REGIONAL\_CLOUD$, the ciphertext C can be recovered given the message M_i and the generated key K_{QKD}. Similarly, the message M_i can be retrieved given the ciphertext C and the generated key K_{QKD}. The relationships are

$$\text{Ciphertext} : C = M_i \otimes K_{QKD}$$
$$\text{Message} : M_i = C \otimes K_{QKD}$$

Diovu and Agee found that the optimal bias probabilities (bias ratios between key length in bits and the basis choice bias for Alice) to be utilized by the sending party (Alice), to generate the final key length for symmetric encryption algorithms in the cloud-based SG AMI, lie in the range of 0.1–0.2 and 0.8–0.9. From this observation, the sender can ensure proper security by selecting the correct bias ratio. These bias ranges can be seen in Figure 24.

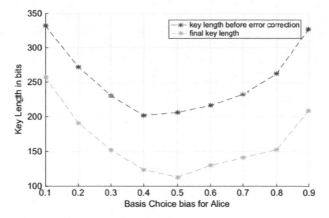

Fig. 24. Bias ratios for Alice against key length as seen in [35].

5. Conclusion

This survey has presented recent applications of quantum computing in the domain of cloud computing. Cloud architecture is incredibly convenient, however proper security precautions must be taken with cryptographic keys. Quantum computing provides an alternative that relies on a fundamentally different method of securing data through entanglement and measurement. Many of the quantum protocols in use today were developed decades ago. As quantum computing technology progresses, more complex and robust protocols will be developed that will further enhance the security of cloud computing.

Appendix

A. Qubit Representation and Superposition

A convenient method for representing quantum states is the bra-ket notation, where $\langle \cdot |$ denotes a "bra", or row vector. $| \cdot \rangle$ denotes a "ket", or column vector. Together, the bra-ket form an inner product $\langle \cdot | \cdot \rangle$. Qubits can be described by a unit vector within the state space. The unit vector is comprised of two orthonormal basis vectors $|0\rangle$ and $|1\rangle$, where $|0\rangle = \left[\begin{smallmatrix} 1 \\ 0 \end{smallmatrix}\right]$, $|1\rangle = \left[\begin{smallmatrix} 0 \\ 1 \end{smallmatrix}\right]$. Geometrically, this can be shown with the Bloch sphere, as depicted in Figure 25, [36]. A pure state $|\psi\rangle$ can be represented by a point on the surface of the sphere using spherical coordinates, where θ is the polar angle that relates to the Z-axis,

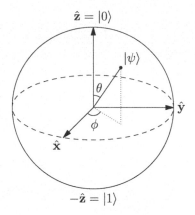

Fig. 25. Using the Bloch sphere representation, a valid qubit state $|\psi\rangle$ is a point that lies on the surface of the sphere. The principal axes (x,y,z) are all orthogonal to each other. The computational basis states $\{|0\rangle, |1\rangle\}$ reside on the poles along the Z-axis.

and ϕ is the azimuthal angle that relates to the X-axis. A general expression for a pure state qubit is:

$$|\psi\rangle = \cos\left(\frac{\theta}{2}\right)|0\rangle + e^{i\phi}\sin\left(\frac{\theta}{2}\right)|1\rangle \tag{3}$$

where $|\psi\rangle$ is the state and $\{|0\rangle, |1\rangle\}$ are orthogonal basis vectors. The angle ϕ corresponds to the phase of the state $|\psi\rangle$. The expression for a qubit can be condensed into the form:

$$|\psi\rangle = \alpha|0\rangle + \beta|1\rangle \tag{4}$$

where $\alpha = \cos\left(\frac{\theta}{2}\right)$ and $\beta = e^{i\phi}\sin\left(\frac{\theta}{2}\right)$. Thus, a qubit can take the form of any linear combination of basis states that satisfy the condition $|\alpha|^2 + |\beta|^2 = 1$.

In classical computing, bits of information are conveyed definitively as either 0 or 1. Because qubits are composed of a combination of basis states, they are not always a definite 0 or 1. This is the property of *superposition*. Instead, they are presented as amplitudes which can be measured to yield probabilities.

B. Measurement

Although a qubit can be in superposition, it must be measured to obtain a definite result. *Measurement* is the act of projecting the qubit's state vector along a specific axis, such as the Z-axis or X-axis. The Z-axis is also known as the standard basis, as it consists of the states $\{|0\rangle, |1\rangle\}$. The probability of measuring $|\psi\rangle$ in the state $|x\rangle$ is defined by:

$$p(|x\rangle) = |\langle x \mid \psi\rangle|^2 \tag{5}$$

For example, given the state $|q_0\rangle = \frac{1}{\sqrt{2}}|0\rangle + \frac{i}{\sqrt{2}}|1\rangle$, the probability of measuring $|0\rangle$ is found by squaring the magnitude of the inner product between the state and axis of measurement:

$$\langle 0 \mid q_0\rangle = \frac{1}{\sqrt{2}}\langle 0 \mid 0\rangle + \frac{i}{\sqrt{2}}\langle 0 \mid 1\rangle$$

$$= \frac{1}{\sqrt{2}} \cdot 1 + \frac{i}{\sqrt{2}} \cdot 0$$

$$= \frac{1}{\sqrt{2}}$$

$$|\langle 0 \mid q_0\rangle|^2 = \frac{1}{2}$$

This result demonstrates the probabilistic nature of qubits. Upon measurement, the wave function collapses to a definite state with idempotence. Measuring the collapsed state repeatedly will always yield the same result. Measurement can be thought of as a transition function between complex values to the set of classical bit values [0,1]. Because of this, measurement is usually reserved for the very end of quantum operations.

C. Entanglement

Qubits are said to be *entangled* if they are inseparable by the tensor product. Any attempt at separation will lead to loss of information. The four *Bell states* $|\Phi^{\pm}\rangle$, $|\Psi^{\pm}\rangle$ are the simplest maximally entangled systems, and they can be created using only X, H, and CX gates. The $|\Phi^{+}\rangle$ state and the circuit that generates it is shown.

The phenomenon of entanglement is not restricted to just two-qubit systems. The Greenberger-Horne-Zeilinger (GHZ) state [37] is one of the two forms of three-qubit entanglement. When one of the entangled qubits is measured, the remaining two are fully separable.

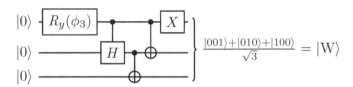

$$\frac{|000\rangle + |111\rangle}{\sqrt{2}} = |\text{GHZ}\rangle$$

The other type of three-qubit entanglement is the W state [38]. Unlike the GHZ state, when one qubit of the W state is measured, the remaining qubits are still entangled.

$$\frac{|001\rangle + |010\rangle + |100\rangle}{\sqrt{3}} = |\text{W}\rangle$$

D. Quantum Teleportation

Teleportation is a bit of a misnomer. Due to the *no-cloning theorem*, which states we cannot copy the unknown state of a qubit to another qubit, the best we can hope for is a transfer of state from one qubit to another. During this transfer, the original qubit's state is lost. To teleport one qubit, we need a total of three qubits and two classical bits. We also need a third party to create an entangled pair that will be distributed to the sender and receiver. Figure 26 depicts a conceptual teleportation circuit that handles the four cases a teleported state can be in, and it successfully recovers the input using the X and Z gates. It is important to note that physical implementations require a slightly different circuit, as *deferred measurement* is required.

E. Quantum Key Distribution

One of the biggest open issues in cryptography is securely distributing the keys that encrypt the sensitive data. Quantum computing permits a tamper-proof method of distributing keys via entanglement. There are many protocols that accomplish this; BB84 and B92 were some of the first. BB84 is an iterative process that establishes a secret

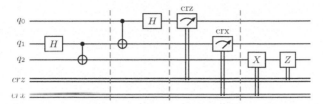

Fig. 26. Teleportation circuit that sends Alice's state, and conditionally recovers Alice's state on Bob's side. Circuit format is in accordance with Qiskit's example.

Alice's message	0	1	1	0	1	0	0	1
Alice's basis	Z	Z	X	Z	X	X	X	Z
Alice's result	$\lvert 0\rangle$	$\lvert 1\rangle$	$\lvert -\rangle$	$\lvert 0\rangle$	$\lvert -\rangle$	$\lvert +\rangle$	$\lvert +\rangle$	$\lvert 1\rangle$
Bob's basis	Z	X	X	X	Z	X	Z	Z
Bob's result	$\lvert 0\rangle$	$\lvert -\rangle$	$\lvert -\rangle$	$\lvert +\rangle$	$\lvert 1\rangle$	$\lvert +\rangle$	$\lvert +\rangle$	$\lvert 1\rangle$
Secret key	0		1			0	0	1

Fig. 27. Alice and Bob randomly select bases and then compare their results. Matching bases in the secret key are colored in green, and differing bases are colored in red. The matching bases will comprise the secret key.

key between Alice and Bob by comparing results on a random string of qubits; each qubit is measured in a randomly selected basis. Typically, photons and their polarizations are used to encode the states. However, any orthonormal bases can also be used to demonstrate the protocol. A visual of the principle used to establish a secret key, such as in the BB84 protocol, can be seen in Figure 27.

Acknowledgment

The author would like to thank Dr. Muhammad Ismail for his teaching of quantum computing theory and concepts as they are extremely relevant to the field of quantum cloud security, and they were directly applicable to the topics covered in this chapter. Thank you to Dr. Maanak Gupta for both providing the context for quantum computing within a cloud computing course and for guiding me on formatting and submitting this chapter. Thank you to the Qiskit textbook for providing example calculations for many of the quantum computing concepts covered in the Appendix.

References

[1]   Taher ElGamal. (1985). A public key cryptosystem and a signature scheme based on discrete logarithms. pp. 10–18. *In*: George Robert Blakley and David Chaum (eds.). Advances in Cryptology. Berlin, Heidelberg. Springer Berlin Heidelberg.

[2]   Don Johnson, Alfred Menezes and Scott A. Vanstone. (2001). The Elliptic Curve Digital Signature Algorithm (ECDSA). Int. J. Inf. Sec. 1(1): 36–63.

[3]   Rivest, R.L., Shamir, A. and Adleman, L. (Feb 1978). A method for obtaining digital signatures and public-key cryptosystems. Commun. ACM 21(2): 120–126.

[4]   Morris Dworkin, Elaine Barker, James Nechvatal, James Foti, Lawrence Bassham, Roback, E. and James Dray. (2001). Advanced Encryption Standard (AES), 2001-11-26.

[5]   Quynh Dang. (2015). Secure Hash Standard, 2015-08-04.

[6]   Adi Shamir. (Nov 1979). How to share a secret. Commun. ACM 22(11): 612–613.

[7]   Norbert Lütkenhaus and Mika Jahma. (Jul 2002). Quantum key distribution with realistic states: Photon-number statistics in the photon-number splitting attack. New Journal of Physics 4: 44–44.

[8]   Amelia Carolina Sparavigna. (Jan 2021). Poissonian Distributions in Physics: Counting Electrons and Photons. Working Paper or Preprint, January 2021.

[9]   Pallavali Radha Krishna Reddy and Samia Bouzefrane. (2014). Analysis and Detection of DoS Attacks in Cloud Computing by Using QSE Algorithm. In 2014 IEEE Intl Conf on High Performance Computing and Communications, 2014 IEEE 6th Intl Symp on Cyberspace Safety and Security, 2014 IEEE 11th Intl. Conf. on Embedded Software and Syst. (HPCC, CSS, ICESS), pp. 1089–1096.

[10] Kennedy, J. and Eberhart, R. (1995). Particle swarm optimization. In Proceedings of ICNN'95 - International Conference on Neural Networks, volume 4, pp. 1942–1948.

[11] Kuk-Hyun Han and Jong-Hwan Kim. (2002). Introduction of Quantum-inspired Evolutionary Algorithm.

[12] Andressa Nicolau, Roberto Schirru and Jose Medeiros. (2022). Quantum Computation and Swarm Intelligence Applied in the Optimization of Identification of Accidents in a PWR Nuclear Power Plant. 04.

[13] Yao Ma, Elham Kashefi, Myrto Arapinis, Kaushik Chakraborty and Marc Kaplan. (2021). Qenclave – A Practical Solution for Secure Quantum Cloud Computing.

[14] Christian Badertscher, Alexandru Cojocaru, Léo Colisson, Elham Kashefi, Dominik Leichtle, Atul Mantri and Petros Wallden. (2020). Security Limitations of Classical-Client Delegated Quantum Computing. In Advances in Cryptology – ASIACRYPT 2020, pp. 667–696. Springer International Publishing.

[15] Ueli Maurer and Renato Renner. (2011). Abstract cryptography. *In*: Bernard Chazelle (ed.). The Second Symposium on Innovations in Computer Science, ICS 2011, page 1.

[16] Yasser Jassem and Alharith Abdullah. (2020). Enhancement of quantum key distribution protocol for data security in cloud environment. 11: 279–288, 03.

[17] Alharith Abdullah and Yasser Jassem. (2019). Enhancement of quantum key distribution protocol bb84. Journal of Computational and Theoretical Nanoscience 16: 1138–1154, 03.

[18] Jing Li, Yang Zhao, Yubo Yang and Yongjun Lin. (2020). Verifiable quantum cloud computation scheme based on blind computation. IEEE Access 8: 56921–56926.

[19] Robert Raussendorf, Daniel E. Browne and Hans J. Briegel. (Aug 2003). Measurement-based quantum computation on cluster states. Physical Review A 68(2).

[20] Dan Shepherd and Michael J. Bremner. (2009). Temporally unstructured quantum computation. Proceedings of the Royal Society A: Mathematical, Physical and Engineering Sciences 465(2105): 1413–1439.

[21] Gregory D. Kahanamoku-Meyer. (2019). Forging quantum data: Classically defeating an iqp-based quantum test.

[??] Man-Hong Yung and Bin Cheng. (2020). Anti-Forging Quantum Data: Cryptographic Verification of Quantum Computational Power.

[23] Ahmed A. Abd El-Latif, Bassem Abd-El-Atty, Salvador E. Venegas-Andraca, Haitham Elwahsh, Md. Jalil Piran, Ali Kashif Bashir, Oh-Young Song and Wojciech Mazurczyk. (2020). Providing end-to-end security using quantum walks in IoT networks. IEEE Access 8: 92687–92696.

[24] Wenjie Liu, Peipei Gao, Zhihao Liu, Hanwu Chen and Maojun Zhang. (Apr 2019). A quantum-based database query scheme for privacy preservation in cloud environment. Security and Communication Networks 2019: 1–14.

[25] Geeta Sharma and Sheetal Kalra. (2016). A Novel Scheme for Data Security in Cloud Computing Using Quantum Cryptography. In Proceedings of the International Conference on Advances in Information Communication Technology Computing, AICTC '16, New York, NY, USA. Association for Computing Machinery.

[26] Brian Kelley, John J. Prevost, Paul Rad and Aqsa Fatima. (2016). Securing cloud containers using quantum networking channels. In 2016 IEEE International Conference on Smart Cloud (SmartCloud), pp. 103–111.

[27] Ekert. (1991). Quantum cryptography based on bell's theorem. Physical Review Letters 67(6): 661–663.

[28] Edsger W. Dijkstra. (1959). A note on two problems in connexion with graphs. Numerische Mathematik 1(1): 269–271.

[29] Xiaofei Cai, Xutao Yu, Xiaoxiang Shi, Jin Qian, Lihui Shi and Youxun Cai. (2013). Ad hoc quantum network routing protocol based on quantum teleportation. In 2013 Proceedings of the International Symposium on Antennas Propagation, volume 02, pp. 1052–1055.

[30] Zhangjie Fu, Kui Ren, Jiangang Shu, Xingming Sun and Fengxiao Huang. (2016). Enabling personalized search over encrypted outsourced data with efficiency improvement. IEEE Transactions on Parallel and Distributed Systems 27(9): 2546–2559.

[31] Wenjie Liu, Yinsong Xu, Wen Liu, Haibin Wang and Zhibin Lei. (2019). Quantum searchable encryption for cloud data based on full-blind quantum computation. IEEE Access 7: 186284–186295.

[32] Lov K. Grover. (1996). A fast quantum mechanical algorithm for database search. In Proceedings of the Twenty-Eighth Annual ACM Symposium on Theory of 34 Future Connected Technologies: Growing Convergence and Security Implications Computing, STOC '96, pp. 212–219, New York, NY, USA. Association for Computing Machinery.

[33] Murali, G. and Sivaram Prasad, R. (2016). CloudQKDP: Quantum key distribution protocol for cloud computing. In 2016 International Conference on Information Communication and Embedded Systems (ICICES), pp. 1–6.

[34] Vidya, K. and Abinaya, A. (2015). Secure data access control for multi-authority Quantum based cloud storage. In 2015 International Conference on Computing and Communications Technologies (ICCCT), pp. 387–391.

[35] Diovu, R.C. and Agee, J.T. (2019). Enhancing the security of a cloud-based smart grid AMI network by leveraging on the features of quantum key distribution. Transactions on Emerging Telecommunications Technologies 30(6): e3587. e3587 ett.3587.

[36] Glosser.ca. (2012). Bloch Sphere. https://commons.wikimedia.org/wiki/File:Bloch Sphere .svg/media/ File:Bloch Sphere.svg, CC-BY SA 3.0.

[37] Daniel M. Greenberger, Michael A. Horne and Anton Zeilinger. (2007). Going Beyond Bell's Theorem.

[38] Dür, W., Vidal, G. and Cirac, J.I. (Nov 2000). Three qubits can be entangled in two inequivalent ways. Physical Review A 62(6).

Chapter 2

Understanding Blockchain Based Solutions for Cloud and Cyber Physical Systems

*Trey Burks** and *Maanak Gupta*

◇◇

This chapter is about the use of blockchains in correlation with cloud infrastructure. Several papers are summarized and compared in their use cases of storing medical health records, as shadows for IoT infrastructures, and to provide security in cloud storage.

1. Introduction and Motivation

Blockchain technology has exploded in recent history due to the cryptocurrency market gaining traction. Several popular cryptocurrencies include BitCoin, Ethereum, and Monero. However, this new technology is useful for more than just cryptocurrency. Blockchains consist of immutable ledgers that provide integrity about transactions that occur between nodes in the network in a decentralized fashion. In addition to integrity, blockchains also provide nonrepudiation, which means it is not possible for anyone to commit a transaction to the ledger and claim it was not them. This level of integrity can be utilized in other domains, including storing medical health records and for use as shadows in IoT infrastructure.

Cloud computing is a computing infrastructure in which resources are provisioned based on a service model. Cloud Service Providers (CSPs)

Tennessee Technological University, Cookeville TN 38505, USA.
Email: mgupta@tntech.edu
* Corresponding author: tmburks42@tntech.edu

have several services which can be used by customers for many different tasks. Some of these tasks include storage, general computation, and machine learning. The role of security falls on both the providers and the customers, depending on the service used, and the policies the data being used requires.

Several research papers have been published about utilizing blockchain technologies with cloud architecture to provide additional privacy for many use cases. One of these use cases includes medical records. Medical records in the United States must follow the policy called HIPPA which states that any medical information about a patient must not be shared without the patient's consent. The additional privacy of blockchain can be utilized with cloud computing to get the benefits of a cloud while still maintaining the confidentiality of the patient's health records.

1.1 Relevant Research Challenges

There are many use cases for blockchain in cloud infrastructure. Two of the main use cases discussed in this chapter are sharing of medical and health records, and using a blockchain based shadow in IoT infrastructures. In the case of medical records, the blockchain must be a permissioned blockchain, and includes methods to verify who is allowed to connect to the network and view the data on the blockchain. The second problem is with how the information is actually shared. The blockchain must be implemented to provide the proper integrity and non-repudiation on the data that is expected from blockchain based systems. An attacker must not be able to modify or delete data from the chain by compromising a single node.

2. Preliminaries

2.1 Blockchain Technology

Blockchains are decentralized databases that store information between several different nodes in the network. One of the key components of a blockchain is that it provides trust without the need for a third party [1]. The way a blockchain stores data is different from traditional databases. In a blockchain, information is stored in groups called blocks, and when a block is filled, it is added to a chain of all the previously filled blocks [1]. As blocks are added to the chain, they are locked so no new transactions are added or deleted from them, making them immutable. Figure 1 illustrates the overall infrastructure and flow of a blockchain. First, a new transaction is created from one of the nodes. Next, the transaction is sent to all the nodes in the blockchain network which perform validity checks to ensure it is a legitimate transaction. Once the checks are completed, the transaction is put into a block. Once the block is full, it is added to the chain, and the transaction is completed.

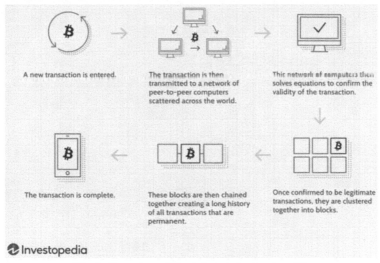

A new transaction is entered.

The transaction is then transmitted to a network of peer-to-peer computers scattered across the world.

This network of computers then solves equations to confirm the validity of the transaction.

The transaction is complete.

These blocks are then chained together creating a long history of all transactions that are permanent.

Once confirmed to be legitimate transactions, they are clustered together into blocks.

Investopedia

Fig. 1. Overview of blockchain infrastructure [1].

One of the key components of a blockchain is the decentralization aspect. It helps to prevent a single point of failure, and allows organizations to store their data across multiple nodes which can be at any location. All the nodes communicate with each other, which prevents an attacker from making a change to or disabling a node, and effecting the rest. All the nodes would also know which node the attacker is tampering with, allowing administrators to take proper action at the right location. Additionally, all these nodes hold a copy of the blockchain, so it is impossible for an attacker to erase a transaction from the blockchain without having control over the entire network.

In order to view the history of transactions, a user must be a node in the network. One type of blockchain is the permissioned blockchain, which means only invited users are capable of being nodes in the network, providing confidentiality to the data in the blockchain. Because of this, most of the solutions discussed in this chapter relating to medical health care records utilize permissioned blockchains.

3. Proposed Approaches

3.1 Medical and Health Care Records

Xia et al. introduced a solution designed to allow medical professionals to securely share data with one another to advance medical science and fight diseases [11]. Their solutions aim to provide a way for researchers to

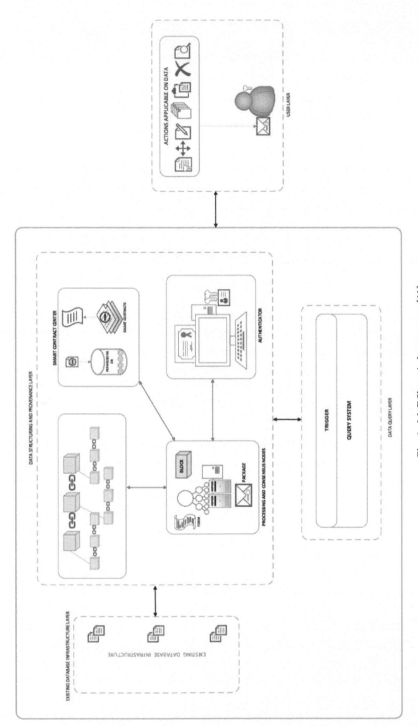

Fig. 2. MeDShare infrastructure [11].

securely access data in cloud storage. Their solution is divided into four sections which are listed below and visualized in Figure 2:

1. *User Layer*: The user layer contains anyone who may need to access the data, including hospitals, research centers, and universities.

2. *Data Query Layer*: The data query layer is what users interact with to receive data from the database. This layer interfaces directly with the third layer. Because of this, users are not able to have direct access to the data.

3. *Data Structuring and Provenance Layer*: The data structuring and provenance layer holds all the components that process the requests from the Data Query Layer. It also monitors every action that happens to the data, and is capable of performing actions on it if a trigger trips.

4. *Existing Database Infrastructure Layer*: This layer consists of all the data infrastructure that already exists from parties in the network. If data is requested from one of these databases, it is sent through a series of algorithms to remove any confidential information before it can be accessed.

The MeDShare infrastructure relies on smart contracts to perform predefined instructions whenever an action is performed. The authors use smart contracts to report actions performed on a piece of data that was requested from the system. This enables the owners of the data to monitor everything that has happened to it since it was requested, which gives them control over its provenance. Data that is sent from the smart contract is stored in a blockchain, which provides an immutable history of the actions performed on it. The actions the smart contract monitors are: read, write, delete, duplicate, move, and copy. The data can also be classified as high or low sensitivity, which allows its owners to change the smart contracts to perform actions based on its classification.

In MeDShare, the sharing of data between the existing infrastructure and the consensus node is critical for sharing it with untrusted parties. Data that is requested from the existing databases is duplicated and shared with the consensus node, which can then apply the smart contracts and ensure its security. Multiple nodes are included in this step to ensure the validity of the data that is taken from the existing database before it is passed to the smart contract generator.

Blocks in MeDShare consist of the block ID and the size of the block followed by the block headers. The block headers are hashed using Sha256 which prevents an attacker from being able to modify them. In order for an attacker to modify the headers, they would have to do so from the very first block in the chain, so by hashing them all with Sha256, data provenance can be assured.

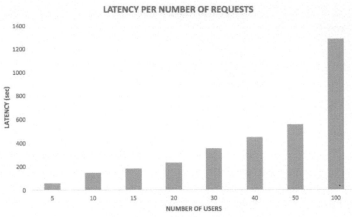

Fig. 3. MeDShare latency [11].

To evaluate their solution, the authors performed requests from several users from a cloud service provider. They found that with 100 users, the latency was 1300 seconds, which can be seen in Figure 3. While this can be argued as being slow, this implementation is not meant for use cases where fast communication is required. The authors claim that by implementing their model, cloud service providers are able to achieve data provenance and auditing when sharing medical data with other cloud providers or researchers without risking the privacy of the data.

Xia et al. proposed a system called BBDS to share private medical data from an institution's cloud to outside users [12]. Their solution relies on a permissioned blockchain, which means only invited and trusted users can access the information. Logs of all the user actions are also kept on the blockchain, providing more accountability.

Unlike their previous publication, this implementation relies on three entities instead of four. The three entities are listed below and visualized in Figure 4:

1. *User*: A user is any person or organization that wants to retrieve data from the closed system. Similar to their previous work, users consist of hospitals, research institutions, and universities.

2. *System Management*: System management consists of the components that are responsible for the secure establishment, efficient running, and optimization of the scheme. There are three additional entities in the System Management entity: Issuer, Verifier, and Consensus nodes.

3. *Storage*: The storage entity consists of the cloud storage and processing infrastructure.

In BBDS, the issuer generates two sets of keys, the membership issuing keys and the membership verification keys. The membership verification

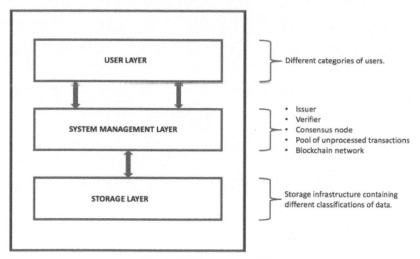

Fig. 4. BBDS ecosystem [12].

keys are then shared with the verifier. To join the network, a user must send a request to the issuer who decides if they should be added to the network or not. If the issuer decides to add the user to the network, it gives the user a membership issuing key. The user then sends that key and the time when they were added to the network back to the issuer, after verifying its authenticity, the issuer sends the user their verification key and other parameters to the user. The user then uses the other parameters to generate its public and private transaction keys. After this, the user sends a verification request to the verifier. The verifier sends the user a challenge which they must successfully answer. After the user is verified, the verifier sends the user its private membership key, and the user sends the verifier the private transaction key. Now the user has been successfully added to the network.

The first step to accessing data from the network is for the users to send a request file to the system. The request file is created from the private membership key. The private membership key creates the block, and the private transaction key is used to sign the request, which is then sent to a list of unprocessed requests. After the request is granted, the user gains access to the data it was requesting, and the block is closed and added to the chain. The entire process is visualized in Figure 5.

In the evaluation for BBDS, the authors were focused on testing the scalability of their system. To do this, numbers were generated from the fastest growing Bitcoin network and plugged into formulas to calculate how much throughput their solution would be able to handle. They found that for 2000 transactions at a time, the throughput would be 1.29 MB per second, and with 2,100,000 transactions the throughput would

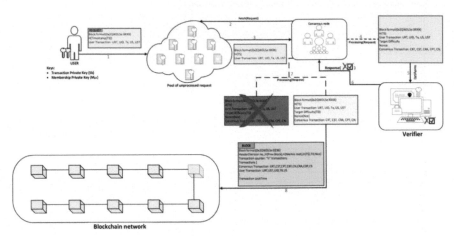

Fig. 5. BBDS system logic [12].

	Data Generated Per Period in Relation to Designed Block			
Transaction	Per Second	Per Day	Per Year	Per 10 Years
2000	1.29 MB	108.84 GB	38.79 TB	387.90 TB
10,000	6.47 MB	545.91 GB	194.59 TB	1.95 PB
15,000	9.71 MB	819.28 GB	292.03 TB	2.92 PB
500,000	323.77 MB	26.68 TB	9.74 PB	97.40 PB
2,100,000	1.33 GB	112.22 TB	40.96 PB	409.60 PB

Fig. 6. BBDS evaluation network growth [12].

be 1.33 GB per second. All the results can be seen in Figure 6. The authors claim that they created a scalable and lightweight blockchain solution which can be used to share private medical information from the cloud storage to trusted and authorized parties. Unlike their previous work, it is not clear how fast the system actually is because they only evaluated the network growth and throughput, but not the transaction latency. It would be good to include latency evaluations support their claim that the system is fast.

Al Omar et al. introduced a solution they call the MediBchain protocol [2] to protect patient medical data using blockchain technology. There are five main components to the MediBchain architecture that are described below:

1. *Data sender*: The data sender is the patient who inputs its medical data into the system. Encryption of this data is handled before it ever reaches the MediBchain system, meaning that it is secure from the moment the patient inputs the data.

2. *Data receiver*: The data receiver is the entity that requests the data from the system after being authenticated.

3. *Registration unit*: The registration unit acts as the authenticator in the system. Whenever a user wants to send or receive data, they must register with the system using an ID and password. Once registered, the users just have to login using their ID and password.

4. *Private Accessible Unit (PAU)*: The PAU is the component that users interact with when they are submitting data to the system. The channel used to interact with the PAU must be secure.

5. *Blockchain*: The blockchain stores the data of the users after submission. There are two levels to the blockchain, Level-1 is a GUI that the users will interact with the blockchain, and Level-2 is the actual blockchain itself.

In addition to these components, the authors also define the ten steps of the protocol in detail. The steps are as follows:

1. *Step-1*: Data sender sends a request to authenticate with the system using their ID and password.

2. *Step-2*: The data sender sends data to the PAU.

3. *Step-3 & 4*: The PAU sends the ID to the blockchain and returns the ID used to access the data at a later time.

4. *Step-5*: The ID generated by the blockchain is sent back to the user.

5. *Step-6*: Data receiver signs into the system.

6. *Step-7*: Data receiver sends a request to the PAU to access the data using the ID generated by the blockchain.

7. *Steps 8 & 9*: PAU sends request to blockchain to receive the data, blockchain returns the data.

8. *Step-10*: PAU sends the data to the receiver.

This solution differs from the previous two solutions because the authors of MediBchain developed a GUI that the users can interact with. The other two works only developed the blockchain implementation and described the process that is needed to store and access data. Because of this, the MediBchain implementation is further developed and closer to production use than the other two solutions described so far.

In their evaluation of MediBchain, the authors tested the computational cost of the system based on the size of input being sent to the blockchain. They found that as the size of the data increased, so does the encryption time, which is to be expected in any implementation using it, as it is the cost of using it. With a data size of five kilobytes, the encryption time is less than ninety milliseconds, but with a data size of thirty kilobytes, the encryption time is over ninety-eight milliseconds. In testing the computational cost of the smart contract, the authors found that the cost steadily increases until the string length reaches thirty, sixty, and ninety characters. The cost is measured in GAS, which is the resources used by the Ethereum blockchain to execute transactions. The full results of this experiment can be seen in Figure 7.

Nguyen et al. implemented a blockchain solution to secure EHR data of patients using the Ethereum blockchain [6]. The overall architecture of the system is based on a use case where patient records are gathered on a mobile cloud platform and stored on a public cloud for the data to be shared with medical professionals. All patients have their own ID which is used to associate them with the transactions in the blockchain, and it is assumed the EHRs can be collected from body sensors on the patient by an application on the patient's smartphone. It is also assumed that each healthcare provider has a smartphone that they can use to retrieve the EHRs on the cloud.

There are five components in this blockchain implementation, listed below:

1. *EHRs Manager*: The EHR manager is required for all transactions on the blockchain network, including the storage and data access.

2. *Admin*: The admins manage transactions and operations on the cloud by managing permissions. They also deploy smart contracts and update smart contracts as needed.

3. *Smart Contracts*: Smart contracts define all operations allowed in the access control system. They can "identify, validate requests and grant permissions for medical users by triggering transactions or messages." All smart contract operations are available to each user on the blockchain.

4. *Decentralized Storage*: A decentralized peer-to-peer file system called Inter Planetary File System (IPFS) is used. With this system, there is no need for a centralized data server. Due to the decentralized nature of IPFS, it provides a way for users to store their data in a system without a single point of failure.

5. *Data Block Structure*: The data block consists of two main components, the first is the transaction record. The records are formatted in a Merkle tree structure. The patient must provide an area ID and a patient ID to make a data request. The second component of the data block is the block header. The block header contains the hash of the current block, the hash of the previous block, the Merkle root, a nonce, and a timestamp.

This solution also includes a user interface that allows the users to interact with the data in the blockchain. A request handler is also implemented to process the user requests. The authors of the paper implemented this solution as a proof of the concept in AWS. In their evaluations, the authors tested the amount of time it takes to access an

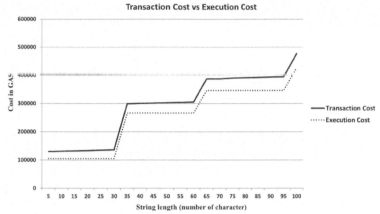

Fig. 7. Computation cost of transaction and execution of smart contract [2].

EHR on the cloud with using centralized storage versus their blockchain implementation. They found that the distributed solution was much faster than the centralized solution by less than half a second for a file of fifty kilobytes, and almost one and a half seconds for a file size of 300 kilobytes. In the conclusions, the authors state that they believe their solution is a step forward for storing EHR records in the cloud.

Kaur et al. proposed a blockchain based platform for heterogeneous medical data [3]. Their proposal is similar to what was implemented by the previously discussed works. The user sends a request to make a transaction to the system, and the request is sent to the blockchain where the identity of the user is verified with cryptographic keys. Once the user is verified, the transaction is executed, and a new block is added to the blockchain. The user then receives a confirmation that the transaction was successful. Heterogeneous data cannot be stored on the blockchain itself, but rather is stored off chain by providing an address to the information in the blockchain.

The authors did not implement their proposed solution in any cloud service provider, so no evaluations can be gathered from this work. However, this proposed method could potentially lay the ground work for other researchers to implement this solution. This work is different from the other works discussed thus far because it is related to heterogeneous data, and not standard EHR data.

3.2 Data Storage in Cloud Based Blockchain Solutions

Zhou et al. implemented a solution to provide secured cloud storage using blockchains called ChainFS [9]. The system implementation relies on three components: a client and server hosted on a cloud that is considered to be untrusted, and a blockchain. The blockchain is used as a trusted third party to prevent forking attacks, which is an attack where a cloud server can present different results for the same query to different users. Due to the nature of blockchain, forking attacks can be detected and prevented.

Every time a new query is created, a log is created and sent to the blockchain. Whenever users attempt to read some data, they can verify if it is correct by checking the logs in the blockchain. The authors state that the only way to bypass this protection is to fork the blockchain itself, which is very difficult to achieve.

The authors implement a proof of concept in the paper based on the S3FS project. The authors added an authentication layer on top of S3FS by using a hash function to digest the file content and use a Merkle tree to digest metadata and the content hash. The Merkle tree is stored off-chain in a cloud, and also as a shadow file in the blockchain. For read operations, the transaction is verified against data in the blockchain, and for write operations, the results from the cloud are verified and a new root hash is generated then sent to the blockchain.

The authors performed performance evaluation on their implementation using AWS S3 instances. The authors randomly generated small files to use for testing with varying data, so there will not be an issue of data being skewed by caching. They found that with smaller files, the system becomes unstable performance wise. They also repeat the experiment with large files, and found that the blockchain performance drops due to Internet speeds. They also tested the performance of reading files with ChainFS, and found that as files grow larger, the time to read the files increases at a constant rate.

The authors implemented a solution to prevent forking attacks in cloud storage by implementing S3FS and the Ethereum blockchain. ChainFS was shown to provide users with a way to securely share data with the cloud. This solution is different from the works described in the medical health records section because it focuses on the integrity of the data instead of its confidentiality.

Wang et al. implemented a framework to provide secure cloud storage with access control using a blockchain [10]. Its implementation relies on smart contracts to store information about encrypted files. Ethereum smart contracts are used by data users and owners to store and retrieve ciphertext data in order to run the encryption and decryption algorithms. Each contact call is stored in the blockchain to provide non-repudiation and to ensure that the data has not been tampered with. The system is comprised of four components which are described below:

1. *Cloud server*: Stores the encrypted files uploaded by the data owners.
2. *Ethereum blockchain*: Deploys the smart contracts to interface with themselves.

3. *Data Owner*: Creates and deploys smart contracts, uploads encrypted files, defines access control polices, and appends valid data access points to data users.

4. *Data User*: Accesses an encrypted file in the cloud server. If the attributes set matches the access structure embedded in a ciphertext object, the user can decrypt the ciphertext using the content key.

There are four phases in the overall system implementation. The first is the system initialization. This phase is when the data owners and users create their accounts in the Etherum blockchain. In this phase, the cryptographic keys are also generated for the data owner. The second phase is the file encryption phase. This phase includes the whole setup that is needed by the data owners before they can encrypt and upload the data. Once the setup is done, then each data owner can encrypt the file. The third phase is key generation. This phase includes the data user sending a request to the data owner which includes the Ethereum account public key and the account address, along with other metadata. The data owner then runs the key generation algorithm which uses the Diffie-Hellman protocol to exchange the secret key with the data user. The fourth phase is the file decryption phase. When in this phase, the data user sends the file hash they want to decrypt to the server, and the server checks if the file exists. The data user then executes a smart contract to get the file access permissions. Once all this has been obtained, the data users can decrypt the file if they have the proper permissions.

In the evaluation, the authors compared their runtime with that of a similar implementation from the literature. Their solution was much slower than the one found in the literature by over 6000 milliseconds. The authors claim that their solution is more efficient than the one found in the literature, however as a reader, it appears that their chart contradicts their claims. The full chart of their evaluations can be seen in Figure 8. The authors also state that additional research work is still on-going, and they claim that cloud storage platforms may be replaced by decentralized storages such as IPFS in the future.

Li et al. introduced a solution to provide a secure peer-to-peer (P2P) blockchain based storage in the cloud called Block-Secure [4]. The high-level overview of the architecture can be described as dividing user files into blocks of the same size, then encrypting and digitally signing them before they are uploaded to the P2P network. Blockchain is then used to allow users to share their vacant storage space with users who need storage. A file replica placement strategy is then used so users can retrieve their files from the cloud. Data integrity is also used by implementing a Merkle tree.

For the evaluation, the authors tested the transmission time of their solution with different numbers of users. Figure 9 shows the full results

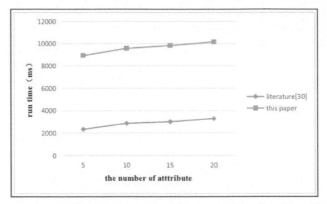

Fig. 8. Runtime of algorithm under different number of attributes [10].

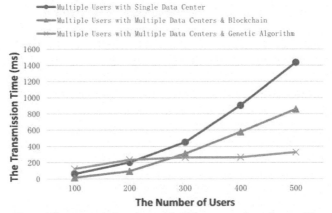

Fig. 9. The transmission time with different number of users [4].

from this experiment. The fastest implementation with the greatest number of users is that with Multiple users using multiple data centers and a genetic algorithm. The next fastest is that with multiple users using multiple data centers and blockchains. The slowest implementation is with multiple users using a single data center. However, when the number of users is small, the implementation proposed in this paper with blockchain is the fastest. The implementation that is the slowest when the number of users is low is that with the genetic algorithm. This is due to the fact that this implementation has to calculate the genetic algorithm and the others do not.

3.3 *IoT and Manufacturing*

Sharma et al. implemented a solution for software defined fog nodes using blockchain for IoT [8]. The architecture is divided into three different components: the device, fog, and the cloud. The device layer is used to

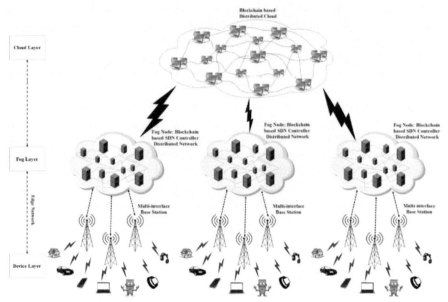

Fig. 10. Overview of the distributed blockchain cloud architecture [8].

monitor infrastructure environments and sends that data to the fog layer. The fog layer consists of a number of different nodes that are in charge of managing the data for different communities. The fog layer communicates the results of its computations to the cloud and device layers if needed. Essentially, the cloud layer is used for wide-spread monitoring, while the fog layer is used for a more localized analysis. Figure 10 shows the full design of the architecture.

The distributed blockchain cloud architecture has three main components that comprise the system. The first is the proof of service. The Proof-of-Service component is similar to a Proof-of-Work in Ethereum. It is in place to ensure that transactions occur in an accurate and flawless manner. The security of the implementation requires that the legitimate user controls a greater proportion of resources, including stakes and computation power. The second component is the matchmaking algorithm. The matchmaking algorithm is used to provision resources. Smart contracts are stored that determine the requirements for performing a task. The third component is the Scheduling Algorithm. The scheduling algorithm is used to make sure applications run efficiently, so it is a very important component in the architecture. The authors used an algorithm called CLOUDRB and customized it to match their own needs.

The next component of the overall architecture is the Edge Computing Network Architecture. This component consists of five different entities. The first is the Packets Parser. This component is used to identify abnormal behavior by catching each piece of network data. Attackers typically use Flow Mod packets in their attacks, and the proposed system also uses them, so in order to detect abnormal network behavior, the Packet Parser dynamically looks at each of these packets to decide if they are abnormal or not. The next component is the Flow Topology Graph Builder. The graphs analyze the network data to create flow diagrams based on it. Security strategies are then used to determine if any data is malicious or not. The third component is the Verifier. The verifier is used to generate reactive flow rules needed by the system. The fourth component is the Migration Agent. The migration agent is used to decide whether an attack is occurring and what to do. If a flood attack is detected, it will hold all the malicious packets and forward the legitimate packets, so the controller is not overloaded. The fifth component is the Data Plan Cache. The Data Plan Cache is used to cache missing packets in the event of a saturation attack. When the cache receives packets, it parses the headers to determine which queue they should be stored in so they can be sent to the appropriate location during an attack.

In the evaluation the authors tested their implementation by looking at the throughput, response time, and delay-incurred performance metrics. In their evaluation they found that their solution was more efficient in every aspect compared to the core model. The only evaluation where their solution was slower was in the throughput as the number of requests increased. The full results are shown in Figure 11.

Li et al. implemented a solution for a blockchain cloud manufacturing system as a P2P distributed network platform they called BCmfg [5]. The proposed architecture is a combination of two related works: BC and mfg. The main architecture consists of five components listed below:

1. *Resource layer*: This consists of the physical manufacturing resource and its capabilities. The resources can be either hardware or software. Manufacturing capabilities are formed with resources, people, and knowledge.

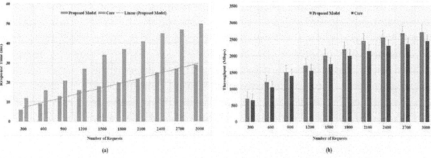

Fig. 11. With regard to the number of requests: (a) the variation in response time; (b) the variation in throughput [8].

2. *Perception layer*: This layer senses the physical manufacturing resources and virtualization. This layer forms a connection in the network by utilizing IoT.

3. *Manufacturing Service Provider Layer (MSPL)*: This layer contains the blockchain client which is responsible for connecting with the note and block. The blockchain establishes P2P communication between other components of the manufacturing system and changes data formats to hashes then encapsulates the hashes to form blocks.

4. *Infrastructure layer*: Provides the infrastructure that supports the different layers. This layer consists of cloud manufacturing and the BCN. Cloud manufacturing is responsible for providing the core functions and services for the manufacturing system and customers.

5. *Application layer*: It is responsible for providing different application interfaces and related end-interaction equipment. The applications can be the PLC and the end-user application. Both these applications are web based and use BCN and cloud service providers for provisioning.

The proposed solution also provides on-demand secure services, secure data exchange, and service execution. On-demand secure services are achieved by the fact that originality of data is defined in a deterministic way and symmetric encryption is used to share data on the network. Because of this, it is known which user sent data to the network and where the user is. Secure data exchange is handled in a manner similar to how the other papers discussed their solution implementation. Smart contracts are used as agreements between end users. There are two types of service executions provided by this implementation, the first is OnCloud and OffCloud services. OnCloud services are handled completely by the proposed implementation, and OffCloud services require some operations to be performed by humans. User verification is needed for the service execution portion of the implementation.

To test their implementation, the authors created a network of five controller nodes and 1000 request nodes. Figure 12 shows a representation of what this network looks like. The request nodes are blue and the controller nodes are red. For performance evaluation, the authors tested the time it took to create wallets, blocks, miners, the time is takes for distribution to users, and the time it takes for the network to connect, stop, and delete. The results can be seen in Figure 13. The time it takes to perform most operations increased as expected, but the Network delete and Miners create operations dropped in time based on the number of users. The authors stated, because Miners create dropped with the number of users in a linear fashion, it was proved that the proposed solution is highly scalable.

Rehman et al. proposed a solution to provide secure service providing for IoTs using blockchain [7]. The architecture of this solution is broken

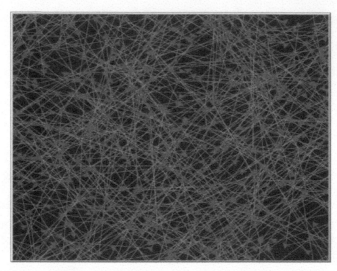

Fig. 12. Schematic of Blockchain Network with five controller nodes and 1000 request nodes [5].

Test time	End user 5	End user 10	End user 15
Wallet create	2.1	3.8	6.87
Block create	0.18	0.23	0.29
Miners create	1.5	1.46	1.42
Distribute to users	1.88	2.22	3.62
Network connect	0.21	0.35	0.58
Network stop	1.3	1.9	2.77
Network delete	3.4	3.3	3.2

Fig. 13. Average time based on seconds, three test was done by considering 5, 10 and 15 end users [5].

down into four main layers: cloud servers, edge servers, LWC, and the blockchain mechanism. LWC is described as "resource constrained devices with limited computation, storage, and power resources." The cloud servers provide trusted service codes to the edge servers without involving the blockchain. The blockchain is used to distribute service codes among different cloud servers. The edge servers are used to provide trusted service codes to the LWC with minimum delay. An incentive mechanism is given to the edge servers in this implementation. If the service code provided by an edge server to a LWC is valid then an incentive will be given, but if it is invalid then a set amount of cryptocurrency will be deducted from the edge server. A reputation system is also provided to the edge servers. If the user is happy with the service code, they can give positive feedback to the server, but if they are not happy, they can give negative feedback, hurting the edge server's reputation.

There are two main entities in the blockchain system, Cloud Nodes and the Lightweight nodes. The Cloud Nodes (CNs) are privileged nodes in the blockchain network which maintain the ledger, and those which have enough computational power to do so. They are also responsible for adding blocks into the blockchain, validating transactions, and executing smart contracts. The lightweight nodes (LNs) are less privileged nodes in the network and can only read from the blockchain and verify edge service providers and service codes. LWCs also act as LNs in the implementation.

The overall workflow of the implementation is summarized as follows: first a LWC requests a service code from the nearest edge server. Service codes can be stored in the cache memory of an edge server if it is frequently used. If the edge server does not have the service code in its cache memory, then it makes a request to the cloud server for it. All cloud servers have the blockchain implemented, and it is used for the consensus mechanism to determine if the service code is valid. The reputation and validity of edge servers are also stored in the blockchain. Smart contracts are used to determine the validity of edge servers. Validity of service codes are acquired by LWCs communicating with the cloud servers to get the hash of the service code. LWCs then compare the hash of these service codes to those that are provided by the edge servers. If the results are valid the LWC will give incentives and a reputation to the edge server, and if it is not valid, it will take some cryptocurrency from the edge server and give it a negative reputation.

In their evaluation, the authors looked at the amount of GAS taken to perform a number of transactions. GAS, like in a previously discussed work is used to determine the overall time spent on an operation and is taken from the Ethereum blockchain. One of the results can be seen in Figure 14. This evaluation looked at different service codes and measured the amount of GAS they took to perform. The amount of GAS consumed correlates directly to the length of the service code and the difficulty of the hash. These results can be related to every experiment performed by the authors and shows that the efficiency depends mostly on these two factors.

4. Conclusions and Future Research Directions

The papers discussed in this chapter all used blockchain combined with cloud architecture for two main domains: healthcare and IoT/manufacturing. There is one main difference between the two domains, the healthcare implementations are more concerned with the confidentiality of the data, and the IoT domain is more concerned with the integrity of the data. For the healthcare domain, it would be critical to see more work done in using blockchains in different novel ways. These

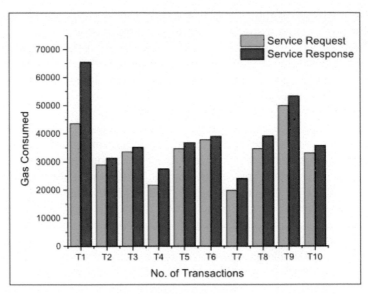

Fig. 14. Gas consumed with respect to service response and service request [7].

papers implement blockchain as is, and do not do much to change the behavior of this technology. The implementations are good, but they all rely on the immutability of the blockchain and how it naturally provides data integrity. A comparison of several papers from each domain can be found in Tables 1, 2, 3.

Table 1. Medical record implementations compared.

Reference	Core Idea	Strengths	Weaknesses
Xia et al. [11]	Utilize blockchain and smart contracts to securely share medical data to fight diseases and advance medical science	The solution can securely share medical information using blockchain technology	It can be argued that the proposed solution is slow, with transactions involving 100 users taking 1300 seconds
Xia et al. [12]	Use a blockchain solution to share private medical data from institutions with external users	The solution is very scalable and has room for growth in the network	They do not clearly evaluate the performance of their system in the publication
Al Omar et al. [2]	Protect patient medical data using blockchain technology	Implemented a GUI and proposed a solution that is more user friendly than the other works	As the string length of the data increases, the cost of GAS increases substantially at certain intervals

Table 2. Data storage in cloud based blockchain implementations compared.

Reference	Core Idea	Strengths	Weaknesses
Zhou et al. [9]	Provide secured cloud storage using blockchain	This solution is capable of preventing forking attacks in cloud-based storage	The performance of the system becomes very unstable with small data sizes
Wang et al. [10]	Provide access control using blockchain technology in cloud storage	The solution uses an Ethereum blockchain and smart contracts to provide access control in cloud storage	Their solution is much slower than other related works and they show it in a graph during evaluation, but claim that their solution is very efficient because of the blockchain implementation

Table 3. IoT and manufacturing implementations compared.

Reference	Core Idea	Strengths	Weaknesses
Sharma et al. [8]	Software defined fox nodes using blockchain for IoT	Their solution is more efficient than the core model in every aspect	The throughput is lower than the core model when the number of requests increases
Li et al. [5]	Solution for blockchain cloud manufacturing system as a P2P distributed network	The solution provides on-demand secure services, secure data exchange, and service execution. Their solution is highly scalable	The times for wallets to create increases linearly as more users are added to the system

References

[1] Blockchain explained (2022), https://www.investopedia.com/terms/b/blockchain. asp, accessed: March 12, 2022.

[2] Al Omar, A., Bhuiyan, M.Z.A., Basu, A., Kiyomoto, S., Rahman, M.S. et al. (2019). Privacyfriendly platform for healthcare data in cloud based on blockchain environment. Future Generation Computer Systems 95: 511–521.

[3] Kaur, H., Alam, M.A., Jameel, R., Mourya, A.K., Chang, V. et al. (2018). A proposed solution and future direction for blockchain-based heterogeneous medicare data in cloud environment. Journal of Medical Systems 42(8): 1–11.

[4] Li, J., Wu, J. and Chen, L. (2018). Block-secure: Blockchain based scheme for secure p2p cloud storage. Information Sciences 465: 219–231.

[5] Li, Z., Barenji, A.V. and Huang, G.Q. (2018). Toward a blockchain cloud manufacturing system as a peer to peer distributed network platform. Robotics and Computer Integrated Manufacturing 54: 133–144.

[6] Nguyen, D.C., Pathirana, P.N., Ding, M. and Seneviratne, A. (2019). Blockchain for secure ehrs sharing of mobile cloud based e-health systems. IEEE Access 7: 66792–66806.

[7] Rehman, M., Javaid, N., Awais, M., Imran, M., Naseer, N. et al. (2019). Cloud based secure service providing for iots using blockchain. pp. 1–7. *In*: 2019 IEEE Global Communications Conference (GLOBECOM). IEEE.

[8] Sharma, P.K., Chen, M.Y. and Park, J.H. (2017). A software defined fog node based distributed blockchain cloud architecture for iot. IEEE Access 6: 115–124.

[9] Tang, Y., Zou, Q., Chen, J., Li, K., Kamhoua, C.A. et al. (2018). Chainfs: Blockchain-secured cloud storage. pp. 987–990. *In*: 2018 IEEE 11th International Conference on Cloud Computing (CLOUD). IEEE.

[10] Wang, S., Wang, X. and Zhang, Y. (2019). A secure cloud storage framework with access control based on blockchain. IEEE Access 7: 112713–112725.

[11] Xia, Q., Sifah, E.B., Asamoah, K.O., Gao, J., Du, X. et al. (2017). Medshare: Trust-less medical data sharing among cloud service providers via blockchain. IEEE Access 5: 14757–14767.

[12] Xia, Q., Sifah, E.B., Smahi, A., Amofa, S., Zhang, X. et al. (2017). Bbds: Blockchain-based data sharing for electronic medical records in cloud environments. Information 8(2): 44.

Chapter 3

A Systematic Review of Access Control in Cloud Computing

Lopamudra Praharaj* and *Maanak Gupta*

As services offered by cloud computing increase, control access to these facilities turns out to be more complex, and more security breaches are created. This is because of the development of new needs and constraints in the open, dynamic, diverse, and distributed cloud environment. There is a need to design more robust, secure access control models. This literature review identifies the articles that have dealt with cloud access control requirements and techniques. We answer the following research questions: What cloud access control security model is needed for the cloud services provided by the provider? What access control mechanisms should propose to fulfill them? What are the pros and cons of the access control model? This review yielded the service requirements and access control mechanisms. The study in this review will help researchers, academics and practitioners evaluate the efficiency of cloud access control models and proposed gaps that are not addressed in the proposed solutions.

1. Introduction

Cloud computing is a paradigm that offers cost-effective, on-demand services such as Software as a Service (SaaS), Platform as a Service (PaaS), and Infrastructure as a Service (IaaS). Despite these advantages, the cloud

---

Tennessee Technological University, Cookeville TN 38505, USA.
Email: mgupta@tntech.edu
* Corresponding author: lpraharaj42@tntech.edu

computing paradigm encounters several challenges, such as data security and privacy, cyber-attacks, and exploitation of cloud services. Among all cloud computing security methods, access control (AC) plays a crucial role in keeping the integrity of the information by restricting resources only to legitimate users. Access control also protects confidentiality by ensuring that the data is revealed only to customers who have been authorized to access it.

The formal model [1] that expresses access control is the "Access Control Model" (ACM) which describes the relations between permissions, operations, objects, and subjects. According to National Institute for Standards and Technology (NIST), cloud computing is defined as "a model for enabling convenient, on-demand network access to a shared pool of configurable computing resources that can be quickly provisioned and released without much effort or service provider interaction". According to this definition, the cloud computing paradigm is identified as a service working in distributed, open, dynamic heterogeneous environments. As the functionality and services, offered by cloud computing expand, access control to these services turns more complex, and more security breaches are generated. This is because of the new requirements such as multi-tenant hosting, the unidentified users, the heterogeneity of users, security policies, resources, rules, and domains. These conditions were not considered in the design of traditional access control models such as the mandatory access control (MAC), discretionary access control (DAC), and role-based access control (RBAC). Therefore, to add these new requirements, it is essential to design an effective access control model for the cloud environment. Despite the importance of cloud-based access control models, there are very few studies that define ACM requirements in a cloud environment, compared to many proposed ACMs.

Due to these reasons, the purpose of this chapter is to present an integrative review of the research related to the requirements of ACMs in the cloud environment and to detect crucial gaps that are not encountered by conventional access control models.

This article is structured as follows: Section 2 describes the performance matrix of access control models; Section 3 describes the different access control models in the cloud. Challenges and future directions are discussed in Section 4, and the conclusion is described in Section 5.

2. Characteristics of a Good Access Control Model

According to NIST [2] the capability of an organization to implement its access policies shows the degree to which its data is protected and shared between its user groups. The effort on sharing and protecting information is intense in organizations. The properties to evaluate good access control models depend on these performance criteria.

Privacy: The user's privacy in the cloud should be protected because the user's location and identity should be kept confidential as the user moves around the cloud. Cloud cryptography-based solutions are applied to protect data without user identity or attribute information. As a result, the identities and attributes of cloud users remained unidentified in the system at the time of the request. Therefore, controlling access to cloud services is vital, while preserving user privacy.

User's heterogeneity: Users of cloud environments have several attributes. They can access cloud services at any point in time from any location. The cloud user's roles also vary frequently in the companies that use cloud services. Therefore, managing them against many secure resources becomes extremely challenging, and an access control system should be able to efficiently deal with the authorizations and authentication of these types of users.

Resources heterogeneity: As the size of the cloud gets bigger, the number of heterogeneous resources from different domains increases. Service providers of—ten offer several types of resources, such as interfaces, applications, APIs, and infrastructures. Due to this, the number of threats increases. Moreover, in the cloud, some objects and resources are unknown. Therefore, security management concerns turn out to be very challenging. Thus, access control should be able to support access to various resources of any kind.

Fine-Grained Policy: Traditional access control models cannot represent various access situations and scenarios because these models offer only coarse-grained security policies such as in Open Stack. This gap can be utilized by attackers to gain access to protected resources. Thus, access control models in cloud computing environments should have the capability to specify a fine-grained policy, which is capable of representing different access scenarios such as in AWS.

Resource Pooling: The computing resources of a cloud system are assembled to be provided to multiple users via a multi-tenant model through a varied range of virtual and physical resources that are dynamically allocated and reallocated. Information may be released if the resource allocated to a user can be accessed by another co-located user. The user should have been unaware of the location of the allocated resources. Location may be specified at a higher degree of abstraction (e.g., data center, country, state) which leads to security problems. Therefore, the methods of applying resource pooling while confirming the isolation of shared resources should be considered in the AC design.

Rapid Elasticity: Cloud services can be elastically provided and released (automatically, in some cases) to quickly scale inward and outward with demands. For the consumer, provisioning resources usually appears to be unlimited and can be applied at any time and are compatible with the addition of new virtual machines (VMs) with computing resources. However, the capability to quickly assess the security of new VMs and verify whether the newly added VMs are competent to carry out a particular activity is a task for AC design.

Table 1. Administrative properties for access control model evaluation.

Performance criteria	Description	Research
The privacy	The identities and attributes of cloud users must be unknown to the system at the time of request	[3, 4]
User's heterogeneity	An AC system should be able to efficiently deal with the authorizations and authentication of various users with different attributes	[5, 3]
Resource's heterogeneity	AC should be able to support many resources	[3, 6]
Contextual Information	All Constraints should be considered while taking AC decision	[7, 4]
Fine grained policy	AC model should provide fine grained policy which is suitable for various access scenarios	[8, 9]
AC for network access	AC allows heterogeneous client devices to have access to a broad range of networks and through standard protocols	[7]
Resource pooling	AC must implement the method of resource pooling while confirming the isolation of shared resources	[7, 4]
Rapid elasticity	AC must have the ability to provide the security of new VMs	[7, 10]
Least privilege principle	Every subject in the cloud should be allocated the essential permissions required to fulfill the responsibilities	[7, 10]
Separation of duties	SOD should be consider in designing AC models	[7]
Scalability	The maintenance, operation, and administration expenses should not raise as the number of applications and users rises	[7, 4]
Confidentiality	The model should ensure confidentiality and user's privacy	[4]
Functionality	AC implements various types of SoD without impacting the functionality of the system	[5, 3]
Auditing	In AC systems, the audit is responsible for keeping track of the state of the system, recording any failure, and reporting any attempt to change access policies	[7, 4]
Safety	AC system should offer safety check capabilities to avoid leaking of permission	[5, 3]

Least Privilege Principle: In cloud computing, the design of any ACM should be supported, such that every subject in the cloud should be allocated the basic permissions required to accomplish responsibilities. Service providers in the cloud often handle access to data and services based on service or system perspectives without considering the least privilege principle. This causes numerous threats to organizations that adopt these services. For example, users in both AWS and Open Stack are always combined with full permissions instead of only the permissions necessary for their tasks. Once users have access to a resource, they might misuse their permission to configure or delete the protected resources to which they are not authorized to access. Therefore, accomplishing this principle is an important requirement in the access control model to protect resources effectively against misuse and malicious insider attacks.

Separation of Duties: This maintains privacy and prevents conflicts, abuses, frauds, and errors such that SoD should be considered in the design of the cloud access control model. SoD splits permissions of a critical task between different roles.

Confidentiality: When access control is implemented in the cloud, the system should protect data confidentiality and user privacy, for example, when most access controls are assigned to the service provider.

Auditing: Auditing is a vital element in protecting cloud computing and the access control systems that complement it. In access control systems, the audit is useful for keeping track of the recent state of the system, recording any failure to decide, either by authorizing or denying access, and reporting the attempts to avoid the access policy or change privileges. It must also track and record the capabilities assigned to subjects, and also changes made to objects, such as renaming, copying, and deleting the records.

3. Different Access Control Models in Cloud

As cloud computing offers on-demand access to resources and services, there should be proper security arrangements in terms of authentication and authorization. The access control model monitors, controls and limits the access to cloud users on the set of resources and services. Access control improves the security of a system and delivers predefined access to the resources. Access control is a policy or procedure that allows, denies, or restricts access to a system. Access control in the cloud depends on cloud storage and data security. Access control is a very significant part of the data center of government and businesses. DAC (Discretionary Access Control), MAC (Mandatory Access Control), RBAC (Role-Based Access Control), and Attribute-Based Access Control (ABAC) [11–14] are traditional formal access control models while Attribute-Based encryption (ABE) schemes are represented access control implementation which introduces the concept of encryption. Access control mechanisms are used to restrict users based on the access privileges provided by the system. All these mechanisms are discussed below.

3.1 Discretionary Access Control

DAC is an access control method where the owner of the organization sets policies defining who can access it. DAC is useful for an organization that has a limited number of users, and the user set will remain relatively stable. DAC [15] is implemented using an Access control list or capability list. The administrator of the organization defines a profile for each object and updates the access control list for the profile.

Advantage of DAC: flexibility in usage by providing the authorization database which contains several authorized users.

The disadvantage of DAC: The feature may be exploited by a third party by abusing the owner's permission and malware may be injected into the system. DAC incurs substantial management costs in the cloud environment. Therefore, it is normally, only used by legacy systems.

3.2 Mandatory Access Control

In MAC, a central authority makes the access decision. Thus, it offers a high level of security and a low level of flexibility, since the subject has no control over object permissions, and the users do not have absolute privacy [16]. It is therefore utilized in government and military systems.

The security of a cloud system IaaS is related closely to virtualization (hypervisor). As a result, new solutions are being implemented to enforce

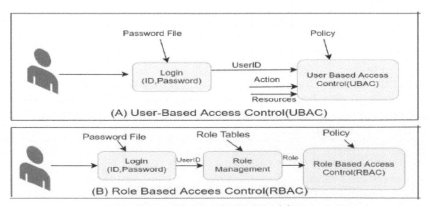

Fig. 1. UBAC and RBAC model.

access control on virtual machines and hypervisors, where MAC is being applied to isolate various virtual machines and to impose AC on both hypervisors and virtual machines. This will protect the hypervisor from prohibited access and different types of attacks, such as a denial-of-service attack (DOS) on a virtual machine (VM) and hijacking attacks on a hypervisor [17].

3.3 Role-based Access Control

The central purpose of RBAC [7] is to deal with security management complexities in large organizations by roles and separately allocating each subject to a role. This means that access control decisions are made based on the user's role. RBAC utilizes security principles such as least privilege and static and dynamic separation of duties. This model has a centralized administration by applying a centrally protected base managed by a single authority, which contains all the security policies for the organization. When a user is assigned a role, that user immediately has all the rights and privileges of that role. Although this approach diminishes the cost, complexity, and errors, it cannot be scaled for many unknown users, especially in a federated environment where organizations that collaborate in the cloud have no reliable centralized authority [7]. In RBAC, subjects are assigned roles and permissions to objects by the administrator. Due to many users and resources in the cloud, the RBAC becomes cumbersome and expensive [5]. The conventional operation–object form is applied to represent the authorization in RBAC. However, this model makes security management worse with many objects, different operations, and object hierarchy.

In [18] a proposed model called RBE (Role Based Encryption) integrates the cryptographic technique with RBAC. RBE scheme allows RBAC policies to be applied to the encrypted data stored in public clouds. Based on the proposed scheme, a secure RBE-based hybrid cloud storage architecture is proposed that allows an organization to store data securely in a public cloud while preserving the sensitive information related to the organization's structure in a private cloud. A common disadvantage of

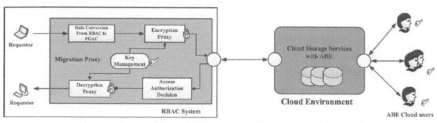

Fig. 2. ABE-AH model [19].

RBAC is that it is a coarse-grained access control model that is incapable of dynamically adapting permissions through environment information, such as time and location. However, such factors are utilized partially in RBAC extensions. Most of the current cloud platforms do not support allocating users to roles. Instead, each user in the cloud separates from others and is allocated a root privilege to access resources [20]. In IaaS platforms such as Amazon's EC2, Eucalyptus provides restricted support for the RBAC mechanism.

3.4 Attribute-Based Access Control

The ABAC model is used to overcome the constraints of traditional access control models and has been implemented in a lot of cloud providers. The basic objective of ABAC is to use the attributes of involved entities as a basis to make the access control decision [12, 13, 16]. In the user's access profile, ABAC uses a combination of the attributes associated with the subject's identity such as role, and department; the attributes associated with the resource such as owner, type, and creation time, and the attributes of the environment in which the authorization process happens as a time, location [12, 13, 16]. Thus, ABAC offers a fine-grained representation of the authorization policy rules. Such a feature is important in dynamic and open environments such as the cloud and the use of various attributes in ABAC instead of one "role" as in RBAC, which is expected to fulfill the flexibility needs of the cloud paradigm. AWS utilizes this characteristic [14] and offers such an authorization based on context information such as location, time, and address which is embodied in ABAC authorization policies [21]. Many researchers have created the cloud computing access control models by combining the flexible administration feature of RBAC and the dynamic features of ABAC. RBAC was expanded by including attributes of the subject, object, and the cloud context environment in a dynamic authorization process and used the roles in RBAC [2]. Yan Zhu [19] proposed how to create an RBAC-compatible reliable cloud storage service with a user-friendly and easy-to-manage attribute-based access control (ABAC) mechanism. Like role hierarchies in RBAC, attribute hierarchies are introduced into attribute-based encryption (ABE) to define a seniority relation among all values of an attribute, whereby a user carrying senior attribute values acquires permissions of his/her juniors. Based on these notations, a new ABE scheme called attribute-based encryption with attribute hierarchies (ABE-AH) is presented to provide an effective approach to execute comparison operations between attribute values on a poset originated from an attribute lattice. By using bilinear groups of composite order, the practical construction of ABE-AH is presented based on forward and backward derivation functions. In [22] a Multi-Level Security Attribute-Based Access Control (MLS-ABAC) scheme

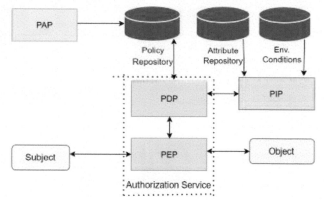

Fig. 3. NIST architecture of ABAC model.

is proposed which ensures that a data user has to show all the necessary static and dynamic attributes that can retrieve the information for which it can satisfy the security level features. MLS-ABAC is lightweight and can be utilized in the IoT environment. By utilizing the attribute token and access token, only the user who fulfills the security level embedded inside the access token and meets the required policies can get access to the ciphertext labeled with this security level. The proposed access control model demonstrates that it can be used in real-world applications and is compatible with the NIST's distributed ABAC model [23].

As shown in Figure 4, there are five main entities, which include Attribute Authority Server (AAS), a trusted party that produces the system parameters and the secret keys for the data users. The Identity and Access Management Server (IAMS) creates tokens for users according to their access security level. AAS generates, removes, and updates the secret keys and then submits them to the IAMS. Cloud Server (CS) is a repository that stores the ciphertext. CS also verifies the validity of the received tokens from another IoT device as a data consumer. Then CS determines whether access should be granted or denied based on the defined predicate functions. Data Owner (DO) is an IoT data producer who wants to share a sensitive message among users by specifying a security level. It produces a ciphertext that carries some metadata. Therefore, to avoid data leakage, the DO selects the security level for the ciphertext and uploads both ciphertext and associated security level to the CS. Data User (DU) is a lightweight IoT device that intends to read data from the CS utilizing its credentials (i.e., data consumer). If the DU passes the verification phase, it can get the ciphertext. Finally, if the DU's attributes fulfill the access policy, the DU can decrypt the ciphertext to learn the entire message; otherwise, it learns nothing. As described in the Figure, in the proposed MLS-ABAC model, the PAP component depends on the AAS and DO, and

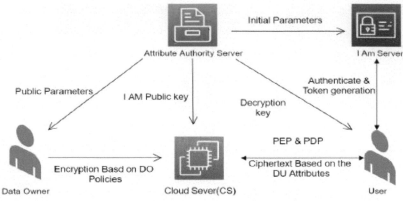

Fig. 4. MLS-ABAC model.

the PIP component relies upon DO, CS, DU, and ultimately, IAMS, CS, and DO act as PEP and PDP components that are fully consistent with the standard ABAC model.

3.5 *Attribute-Based Encryption Access Control (ABEAC)*

In cloud computing to protect data privacy, either symmetric or asymmetric encryption technology can be used to get more protection against threats. However, these authorization mechanisms are not scalable and flexible, because of the use of shared secret keys or public keys by the data owner to distribute his data to the cloud. To add new users to the cloud a flexible and scalable attribute-based encryption algorithm based on an identity-based encryption algorithm (IBE) [8] was proposed. The flexibility this model gets is from the public key encryption mechanism in ABE where user attributes are used instead of user identity in IBE. The encryption algorithm in ABE produces encryption keys and the ciphertext depends on the user's attributes. Scalability in ABE is enabled because the ciphertext can be decrypted based on the receiver's attributes, which must assure the encryption policy.

ABE has two methods, that is the ciphertext-policy ABE (CP-ABE) and the key-policy ABE (KP-ABE). In CP-ABE, a user's attribute is correlated with the private key, and a ciphertext establishes an access policy. The plaintext can only be recovered if the user's attribute matches the access policy of the ciphertext. In KP-ABE, an access policy is delineated with a secret key, and ciphertext is created based on an attribute list. If the user's attribute complies with the access policy together with the secret key, he/she can decrypt the ciphertext. On the contrary, CP-ABE is better than KP-ABE because the data owner decides the access policy.

Table 2. Administrative properties for access control model evaluation.

Performance criteria	DAC	MAC	RBAC	ABAC	ABEBAC	MTAC	TBAC
The privacy	YES	NO	YES	YES	YES	YES	YES
User's heterogeneity	YES	NO	YES	YES	YES	YES	YES
Resource's heterogeneity	NO	NO	NO	YES	YES	YES	YES
Fine grained AC	NO	NO	NO	NO	YES	NO	NO
AC for network access	NO	NO	NO	NO	NO	YES	NO
Resource pooling	YES	NO	NO	NO	NO	YES	YES
Rapid elasticity	NO	NO	YES	YES	YES	YES	YES
Least privilege	NO	NO	YES	YES	YES	YES	YES
Separation of duty	YES	NO	YES	YES	YES	YES	YES
Scalability	NO	NO	YES	YES	YES	YES	YES
Confidentiality	NO	NO	YES	YES	YES	YES	YES
Auditing	NO	NO	YES	YES	YES	YES	YES
Functionality	NO	NO	NO	YES	YES	YES	YES
Safety	NO	NO	NO	YES	YES	YES	YES

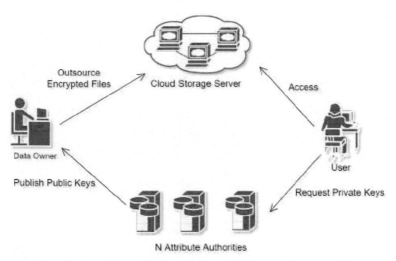

Fig. 5. CP-ABE model.

For fine-grained access control, the ciphertext policy attribute-based encryption (CP-ABE) scheme has been broadly used in the cloud storage system. As the CPABE scheme is outsourced to the cloud storage server, it causes the disclosure of access policy privacy. In addition, there are multiple authorities, and each authority is capable of issuing attributes independently in the cloud storage system. However, existing CP-ABE schemes cannot be directly used for data access control for the multi-authority cloud storage system, due to the inefficiency of user cancellations. In this paper [24], to overcome these challenges, a decentralized multi-authority CP-ABE access control scheme is proposed, which is more efficient for maintaining user revocation. In addition, this scheme can ensure data privacy and access policy privacy with the policy hidden in the cloud storage system. Here, the access policy is accomplished by the linear secret sharing scheme. Finally, the security and performance analyses determine that the proposed scheme has high security in terms of access policy privacy and efficiency in terms of the cost of user revocation.

A new secure cloud storage framework was proposed by [25] with access control by using the Ethereum blockchain technology. The new method is a combination of Ethereum blockchain and ciphertext-policy attribute-based encryption (CP-ABE). The proposed cloud storage framework is decentralized, that is there is no need for a trusted party. The proposed scheme has three main aspects. First, as the Ethereum blockchain technology is applied, the data owner can store data ciphertext through smart contracts in a blockchain network. Second, the data owner can establish valid access periods for data usage so that the ciphertext can only be decrypted during legitimate access periods. Finally, as the design and invocation of each smart contract can be accumulated in the blockchain, thus, the function of the trace is accomplished. This chapter [26] proposes an efficient traceable attribute-based encryption with a dynamic access control (TABE-DAC) scheme based on blockchain for fine-grained sharing of encrypted private data on the cloud. The proposed TABE-DAC scheme supports traceability for the accountability of malicious users

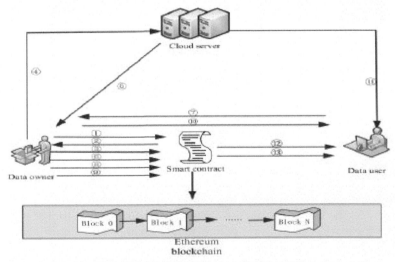

Fig. 6. Etherium block-chain technology [25].

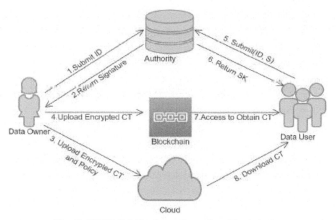

Fig. 7. TABE-DAC scheme based on blockchain.

who leak their private keys. The proposed solution also does dynamic access control where data owners have the elasticity to update the access control policy. The proposed system contains five entities: data owner, data users, cloud platform, authority, and blockchain. Figure 7 shows the interaction between each entity in the proposed system. Authority: The authority initializes the public parameter PK and the master private key MSK of the system. The authority creates PK publicly and keeps MSK secret. Data Owner (DO): The data owner first forwards his/her ID to the authority. The authority produces the signature of the ID and reverts it to the data owner. DO then utilizes symmetric key k to encrypt the message m to the message ciphertext CTM, and then uploads CTM and access policy to the cloud. DO also encrypts the symmetric key k using ciphertext-policy attribute-based encryption. The generated ciphertext CT is divided into CT1 and CT2 and stored in the blockchain as a transaction block TX and access policy block A, respectively. Cloud Platform: The ciphertext CTM and access policy are stored in the cloud. Only the user who meets the access policy can obtain the CTM from the cloud. Blockchain: The blockchain is used to store the encrypted k and access policy, which can get tamper-proof data and the dynamic modification of the access control policy. Data User (DU): The data user proposes his/her identity ID and attributes set S to the authority, which creates the corresponding key and returns it to the data user. The DU can get the encrypted key and access policy from the blockchain through the CT. When the attribute set S of the DU fulfills the access policy in the cipher-text CT, he/she can decrypt it to acquire the symmetric key k. The DU then downloads the message ciphertext CTM from the subsequent location on the cloud and decrypts the CTM to get the private data M using the symmetric key k. This paper [27] defines and enforces access policies based on data attributes and lets the data owner assign most of the computation tasks involved in fine-grained data access control to untrusted cloud servers without revealing the underlying data contents. This goal is achieved by utilizing and uniquely merging techniques of attribute-based encryption (ABE), proxy re-encryption, and lazy re-encryption. The proposed scheme also has relevant properties of user access privilege confidentiality and user secret key accountability.

To assign each user an expressive access structure that is defined over these attributes of access control, KP-ABE is utilized to construct data encryption keys of data files. Such construction facilitates quick access to the fine graininess of access control. However, this construction, if deployed alone, would create heavy computation overheads and a cumbersome online burden on the data owner, because he oversees all the operations of data/user management. Specifically, this problem is mainly caused by the operation of user withdrawal, which inevitably requires the data owner to re-encrypt all the data files accessible to the leaving user, or even requires the data owner to remain online to update secret keys for users. To solve this challenging issue and make the construction appropriate for cloud computing, PRE with KP-ABE is uniquely combined and enables the data owner to allocate most of the computation-intensive operations to Cloud Servers without revealing the underlying file contents.

Such a construction allows the data owner to control access to his data files with minimum overheads in terms of computation effort and online time, and thus suits well into the cloud environment. Data confidentiality is also accomplished since Cloud Servers are not able to understand the plaintext of any data file in the construction. To further decrease the computation overhead on Cloud Servers, the lazy re-encryption technique is used which allows Cloud Servers to cumulate computation tasks of

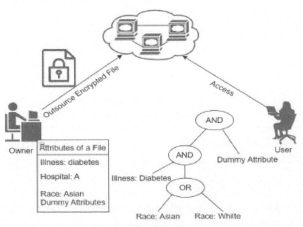

Fig. 8. KP-ABE scheme.

multiple system operations. The proposed construction also protects user access privilege information against Cloud Servers. Accountability of user secret keys can also be accomplished by using an enhanced scheme of KP-ABE.

3.6 Multi-Tenant Access Control (MTAC)

Multi-tenancy is a cloud architecture, which is used for SaaS, PaaS, and IaaS. When many tenants share the same resources in the cloud, multi-tenancy access control becomes vital. Each tenant utilizes its configuration independently based on the hardware or software required, with no impact on the privacy and security of other users [9]. Preserving the privacy and security of the customer's data is vital in a multi-tenancy cloud environment, particularly to prevent a tenant from accessing other's resources. Therefore, tenants can share a single application without violating the security of the others. Several access control models in cloud computing have been proposed for multi-tenancy architecture. Some of them utilized the security features in the traditional access control models to support a multi-tenancy environment. To manage individual tenants in a cloud environment, RBAC was expanded by using users' roles and an identity management scheme. But, to manage resource sharing in a multi-tenant environment, an extended RBAC and task access control model was proposed [28]. An ABAC model was proposed for cloud IaaS where the access decision depends on the attributes of tenants, networks, storage, and other resources in the cloud [10]. To enable the management of access control in federated multi-cloud applications, a new mechanism was proposed. This approach utilized the Representational State Transfer (REST) services interfaces for managing access to various XACML component functionality. To manage a wide range of access control policies, a cloud access control model was suggested for heterogeneous multi-tenancy architectures. The proposed model applied the concepts of RBAC, TRBAC, and ABAC.

3.7 Trust-Based Access Control Model (TBAC)

Utilizing roles and attributes in designing cloud access control models creates challenges like the waste of resources and the dynamic changing in attributes which requires additional calculations that may be misused by the attackers [29]. To get rid of these issues, researchers proposed the trust concept in the access control model. This paper proposes an access control model by a mixture of trusted mechanisms and roles. The roles are allocated to users based on their trust value. However, attackers can gain access to the system by developing trust values. This paper introduced an access control model based on trust. This model assigns permission based on the various trust properties of users. However, this mechanism becomes more complicated in the cloud computing environment, where the users have several trust attributes. This paper utilizes user behavior trust to assign permissions and roles to the cloud users. However, there are two steps to authorize the user, that is, initiating the role and authorizing the role [31]. However, the access control decision process is not flexible. A fine-grained cloud access control model was proposed to impose access based on the user trust values and roles. Once a user accesses a cloud service, he/she will get an initial trust value, and then roles and permissions are assigned to him/her based on the initial trust value.

3.8 Risk-Based Access Control

Due to the ambiguity in cloud access control models risks are created by a non-dynamic access control system policy, or by a non-compliant access control decision support mechanism. Therefore, numerous ACMs were suggested to mitigate these risk factors in access control. A novel approach to managing the user risk in RiskBAC was suggested by [16].

In this model, statistical ways are applied to verify and calculate factors contributing to risk in a user inquiry. However, this model does not examine the risk of objects and permissions, which are the basic elements in the RiskBAC model. To get more risk factors in the access decision-making process, a dynamic mechanism was proposed to get an access control decision based on a risk assessment associated with the environment, object, and user. However, implementing this model needs a mechanism to measure and collect the necessary information to assess the risk. To improve the access control decision, more risk factors are included in the decision-making process. For example, in the case of the Fuzzy Multi-Level Security model [16], the risk of negative effects is considered in the access decision. However, massive work is required to calculate the risk of unauthorized detection. In the same direction, new fuzzy risk values were included in the access decision process in the cloud [32]. These attributes are the data sensitivity, chronological risk information, and the significance of the process. However, this model requires an obvious mechanism to measure the risk value.

4. Challenges and Future Directions

This chapter aims to review the requirements and access control mechanisms used by researchers designing ACMs for the cloud computing environment. These requirements help us to identify in designing ACMs. Researchers and designers of security should have complete knowledge of the dynamic and complex nature of cloud computing. For example, cloud service can be elastically provisioned and released (in some cases

Table 3. Performance evaluation cloud based access control model.

References	Application	Problem considered	AC model	Limitation
Secure cloud Framework Using Block Chain [25]	Cloud Storage	Elimination of Access key distributed by a third party	CP-ABE	The model lacks data integrity that is document uploaded by the data-owner may be tampered by unauthorized user
Efficient Multi-Level Security Scheme [22]	Internet of Things	Secure data transmission of data to a cloud in the Internet of Things	ABAC	No real world scenarios of IoT model
Constructing Flexible Data Access Control for Cloud Storage [19]	Cloud storage service	To improve ABE for implementing cloud data encryption in the existing RBAC systems	ABE	Not applicable to the organisation that have no role hierarchy
Secure Cloud Computing [29]	Cloud Storage	To outsource the shared data to the cloud server	IBE	No data Integrity imposed in the model
Multi-authority attribute-based encryption [24]	Cloud storage system	Existing CP-ABE schemes cannot be directly applied to data access control for multi-authority cloud storage system	CP-ABE	Depends on the third-party for encryption and decryption
Multi-tenant attribute-based access control [30]	Storage and Network cloud resources	To enforce consistent security services operating in virtualized multi-provider cloud environment	ABAC	Lack of key management model for Intercloud using combining public-key and symmetric cryptography
Efficient Traceable Attribute-Based Encryption Scheme [26]	Cloud data storage	To improve inefficient, key abuse, and inflexibility of access control policy ABE	ABE	Dishonest authorities may be accountable for distributing keys to illegal users

automatically) according to demands. The user can add limitless resources that can be used in any amount at any time and are compatible with the addition of new virtual machines (VMs). The capability to instantly assess the security of new VMs and to determine whether newly added VMs are competent to carry out a specific activity is a challenge to the design of ACMs. Despite the importance of this requirement, some points are not considered in the design of ACMs.

For example, the multi-tenancy cloud architecture requirement. The importance of this cloud architecture requirement is exemplified when numerous tenants share the same resources. In addition, this requirement is directly linked to the privacy and security of the customer's data requirement, which blocks a tenant from gaining access to the other's resources in a multi-tenancy cloud environment. Therefore, multiple tenants can share an application without violating the security of the others. Another requirement of the cloud architecture is data sharing and resource isolation. To enable data sharing trust and risk models are used. Risk, for example, was used as a mechanism to mitigate ambiguity in cloud access control models created by a non-dynamic access control system policy.

The current review showed that some researchers have not considered the essential requirements of the cloud environment while designing the ACMs. Some researchers, for example, estimated privacy, while others focused on data protection without considering the elastic nature of the cloud. There are several possible reasons why an ACM has not been evaluated according to all criteria. Such reasons are a shortage of time and resources and a focus of researchers on solving one of the ACM issues. This review showed that the evaluation criteria used by most researchers are not clearly mentioned or not stated at all. This may reduce the efficiency of the proposed ACMs. Researchers should therefore be urged to publish more detailed information on the evaluation process while evaluating their proposed ACMs.

5. Conclusion

The role of access control techniques in cloud computing is critical and has developed in recent years. The key contribution of this review is to deliver a clear picture that summarizes what has already been researched about requirements and mechanisms of access control. The review discovered the most important studies in the field, delivering details on the topics that have more academic attention and describe access control requirements in a cloud computing context.

References

[1] Maanak Gupta and Ravi Sandhu. (2016). The GURAG administrative model for user and group attribute assignment. pp. 318–332. *In*: International Conference on Network and System Security. Springer International Publishing.
[2] Vincent C. Hu and Karen Ann Kent. (2012). Guidelines for Access Control System Evaluation Metrics. Citeseer.
[3] Muhammad Rizwan Ghori and Abdulghani Ali Ahmed. (2018). Review of access control mechanisms in cloud computing. *In*: Journal of Physics: Conference Series, volume 1049, page 012092. IOP Publishing.

[4] Praveen S. Challagidad and Mahantesh N. Birje. (2020). Efficient multi-authority access control using attribute-based encryption in cloud storage. Procedia Computer Science 167: 840–849.

[5] Ravi S. Sandhu, Edward J. Coyne, Hal L. Feinstein and Charles E. Youman. (1996). Role-based access control models. Computer 29(2): 38–47.

[6] Angelos D. Keromytis and Jonathan M. Smith. (2007). Requirements for scalable access control and security management architectures. ACM Transactions on Internet Technology (ToIT) 7(2): 8–es.

[7] Vincent C. Hu, Rick Kuhn and Dylan Yaga. (2017). Verification and test methods for access control policies/models. NIST Special Publication 800: 192.

[8] Wei Teng, Geng Yang, Yang Xiang, Ting Zhang, Dongyang Wang et al. (2015). Attribute-based access control with constant-size ciphertext in cloud computing. IEEE Transactions on Cloud Computing 5(4): 617–627.

[9] Yinghui Zhang, Robert H. Deng, Shengmin Xu, Jianfei Sun, Qi Li et al. (2020). Attribute-based encryption for cloud computing access control: A survey. ACM Computing Surveys (CSUR) 53(4): 1–41.

[10] Redia Houssein and Younis A. Younis. (2021). Deploying risk access models in a cloud environment: Possibilities and challenges. pp. 234–238. *In*: 2021 IEEE 1st International Maghreb Meeting of the Conference on Sciences and Techniques of Automatic Control and Computer Engineering MI-STA. IEEE.

[11] Maanak Gupta, Farhan Patwa and Ravi Sandhu. (2018). An attribute-based access control model for secure big data processing in hadoop ecosystem. pp. 13–24. *In*: Proceedings of the Third ACM Workshop on Attribute-Based Access Control.

[12] Maanak Gupta, James Benson, Farhan Patwa and Ravi Sandhu. (2019). Dynamic groups and attribute-based access control for next-generation smart cars. pp. 61–72. *In*: Proceedings of the Ninth ACM Conference on Data and Application Security and Privacy.

[13] Maanak Gupta, Feras M. Awaysheh, James Benson, Mamoun Al Azab et al. (2021). An attribute-based access control for cloud-enabled industrial smart vehicles. IEEE Transactions on Industrial Informatics (10.1109/TII.2020.3022759).

[14] Smriti Bhatt, Thanh Kim Pham, Maanak Gupta, James Benson, Jaehong Park et al. (2021). Attribute-based access control for AWS internet of things and secure industries of the future. IEEE Access 9: 107200–107223.

[15] Maanak Gupta, Farhan Patwa and Ravi Sandhu. (2017). Access control model for the hadoop ecosystem. pp. 125–127. *In*: Proceedings of the 22nd ACM on Symposium on Access Control Models and Technologies. ACM.

[16] Li Chunge, Ma Mingji, Li Bingxu and Chen Shuxin. (2021). Design and implementation of trust-based access control model for cloud computing. pp. 1934–1938. *In*: 2021 IEEE 5th Advanced Information Technology, Electronic and Automation Control Conference (IAEAC), volume 5. IEEE.

[17] Rohit Ahuja and Sraban Kumar Mohanty. (2017). A scalable attribute-based access control scheme with flexible delegation cum sharing of access privileges for cloud storage. IEEE Transactions on Cloud Computing 8(1): 32–44.

[18] Lan Zhou, Vijay Varadharajan and Michael Hitchens. (2013). Achieving secure role-based access control on encrypted data in cloud storage. IEEE Transactions on Information Forensics and Security 8(12): 1947–1960.

[19] Yan Zhu, Dijiang Huang, Chang-Jyun Hu and Xin Wang. (2015). From RBAC to ABAC: Constructing flexible data access control for cloud storage services. IEEE Transactions on Services Computing 8(4): 601–616.

[20] Vishwas Patil, Alessandro Mei and Luigi V. Mancini. (2007). Addressing interoperability issues in access control models. pp. 389–391. *In*: Proceedings of the 2nd ACM Symposium on Information, Computer and Communications Security.

[21] Saiyu Qi and Yuanqing Zheng. (2019). Crypt-DAC: cryptographically enforced dynamic access control in the Cloud. IEEE Transactions on Dependable and Secure Computing 18(2): 765–779.

[22] Seyed Farhad Aghili, Mahdi Sedaghat, Dave Singel´ee and Maanak Gupta. (2022). MLS-ABAC: Efficient multi-level security attribute-based access control scheme. Future Generation Computer Systems 131: 75–90.

[23] Vincent C. Hu, David Ferraiolo, Rick Kuhn, Arthur R. Friedman, Alan J. Lang et al. (2013). Guide to attribute based access control (ABAC) definition and considerations (draft). NIST Special Publication 800(162): 1–54.

[24] Hong Zhong, Wenlong Zhu, Yan Xu and Jie Cui. (2018). Multi-authority attribute-based encryption access control scheme with policy hidden for cloud storage. Soft Computing 22(1): 243–251.

[25] Shangping Wang, Xu Wang and Yaling Zhang. (2019). A secure cloud storage framework with access control based on blockchain. IEEE Access 7: 112713–112725.

[26] Lifeng Guo, Xiaoli Yang and Wei-Chuen Yau. (2021). TABE-DAC: Efficient traceable attribute-based encryption scheme with dynamic access control based on blockchain. IEEE Access 9: 8479–8490.

[27] Shucheng Yu, Cong Wang, Kui Ren and Wenjing Lou. (2010). Achieving secure, scalable, and fine-grained data access control in cloud computing. pp. 1–9. *In*: 2010 Proceedings IEEE INFOCOM. IEEE.

[28] Shin-Jer Yang, Pei-Ci Lai and Jyhjong Lin. (2013). Design role-based multi-tenancy access control scheme for cloud services. pp. 273–279. *In*: 2013 International Symposium on Biometrics and Security Technologies. IEEE.

[29] Jianghong Wei, Wenfen Liu and Xuexian Hu. (2016). Secure data sharing in cloud computing using revocable-storage identity-based encryption. IEEE Transactions on Cloud Computing 6(4): 1136–1148.

[30] Canh Ngo, Yuri Demchenko and Cees de Laat. (2016). Multi-tenant attribute-based access control for cloud infrastructure services. Journal of Information Security and Applications 27: 65–84.

[31] Gozde Karatas and Akhan Akbulut. (2018). Survey on access control mechanisms in cloud computing. Journal of Cyber Security and Mobility, pp. 1–36.

[32] Bhuvaneswari, C., Malini, T., Anupriya Giri and Sushmita Mahato. (2021). Biometric and IOT technology based safety transactions in ATM. pp. 949–952. *In*: 2021 7th International Conference on Advanced Computing and Communication Systems (ICACCS), volume 1. IEEE.

Chapter 4

A Secure and Efficient Approach to Smart City Initiative

Muskan Sawa,[1] *Niharika Singh*[1,*] and *Ravi Tomar*[2]

In order to efficiently manage the resources in an urban city and provide a better quality of life to citizens, the concept of smart cities has been adopted by various governments around the world to create a more sustainable and liveable environment for them. Some of the most successful real-world implementations of smart cities have been discussed in this paper. A smart city integrates a wide variety of technologies like big data, Machine learning, Blockchain, Cloud and Edge computing under a single umbrella. Security is often overlooked while providing intelligent solutions to modern problems. In this chapter, various possible technologies and security threats in a smart city scenario have been highlighted by looking into the vulnerabilities of each of the technological components of the smart city separately.

1. Introduction

Modern Cities have been observing an exponential growth in population, which is worsened by the depletion of natural resources [1], necessitating more efficient municipal management. As a result, a smart and automated approach to municipal administration is required. The concept of smart cities has become increasingly popular during the last decade. The government

---
[1] School of Computer Science, University of Petroleum and Energy Studies, Dehradun 248007.
[2] Senior Architect, Persistent Systems, India.
Emails: muskaan.sawa@gmail.com; ravitomar7@gmail.com
* Corresponding author: niharika1519@gmail.com

and business sectors have started a number of smart city initiatives to find long-term solutions to the developing difficulties by making conscious investments in information and communication technology. A solution based on IoT infrastructure creates an interconnected environment which shares data and environmental information through the network to an external cloud data centre, where data analytics is employed on the gathered data to empower us with the expertise to effectively deal with the difficulties that Smart Cities face. There are 50 billion gadgets connected to the Internet, which means the network has more sensors to collect data from the surroundings. A substantial portion of these devices are gadgets used in day-to-day life, that may collect data about the user and the surroundings, as a result huge volumes of data can be gathered for analytics [2].

IOT devices are known to have less power consumption and a long battery life which makes them ideal for remote deployment to collect environmental data through sensors. In order to extract any value from the data collected, we need to perform some data crunching and machine learning to provide intelligent feedbacks and automated insights, for which, we need some computing power at hand. However, cost and power have some limitations in IoT devices and so, they cannot afford to waste battery life to execute such intensive operations [3, 4]. By utilising edge computing to deliver relevant insights into the data, deep learning may be leveraged to advance IoT technologies. Although the raw data gathered from IoT devices is exposed to a lot of noise from the surroundings, deep learning may be used to extract real-world data from it [3].

Because a smart network is interlinked by design, there could be repercussions in the entire system due to security flaws in one part of the system. Therefore, we need to make sure that Every IoT device on the network is protected. Cybercriminals attacked an unidentified casino in London using a digital thermometer connected to the internet which was integrated with an aquarium. The aquarium was a legitimate entity of the casino's network. The hackers leveraged the weakness in the security of the thermostat to gain network access through it. After they got into the network, they got access to the high-roller database as well. Finally, they pulled sensitive data through the device in the thermostat into the cloud. Security is often neglected when building IOT applications, this incident being a good example of vectoring where attackers get access to sensitive information in the network by gaining access to one unsecured system [5]. Clearly, IoT will penetrate daily life in a lot of different ways with its implementation in smart cities. A survey conducted by VDC Research Group Inc. concluded that security concerns account for 60% of the hindrance in developing reliable networks of connected devices [6], thus, it's critical that we identify and address security concerns at all levels of the IoT ecosystem [7].

1.1 Smart Cities

A smart city is one in which various environmental, social and economic parameters are managed in an efficient manner with the assistance of technology. This can be achieved through sincere administrative panning and collaboration. This facilitates better management of resources for real-time activities. Social and urban interconnectivity are enhanced in a smart city by integrating its infrastructure with ITC which facilitates the use of Internet of Things (IoT) devices. The concept of smart cities increases public engagement and government efficiency in the management of modern cities [8, 9]. Countless smart gadgets will be present in smart cities, all of which will communicate with each other through a gateway which will be used to push the data to a remote server. This process has the potential to generate and collect large amounts of data, some of which will be sensitive and should be protected. Smart cities are expected to use cloud services to store such vast volumes of data [10]. Because each city has its own set of requirements and limitations, it is not practical to create a universal smart city model. However, as seen in Table 1, the following is a general framework for smart cities, which consists of four layers as follows: perception layer, network layer, middleware layer and application layer. The perception layer includes the sensors, actuators and other devices present at the physical level in the smart city environment.

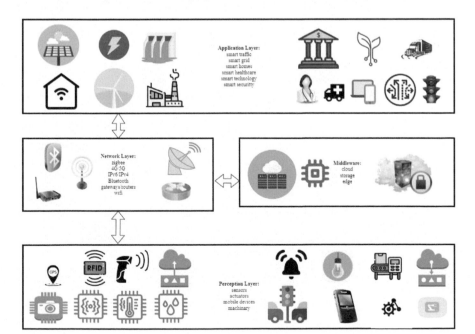

Table 1. Smart city overview ([12, 13]).

Network layer includes devices such as gateways and routers which help in the communication of different devices in the ecosystem; it uses protocols like IPv6/IPv4, Zigbee and RPL for communication. The middleware comprises of the cloud computing databases and other technologies for processing and analysing data. The application layer receives the insights and information from the middleware layer by means of communication protocols like MQTT and CoAP [11–14].

1.1.1 Components of Smart Cities

The development and functioning of smart cities require a lot of technological and hardware components, as seen in Table 2, below, which lists four generalised categories of smart city components:

- *IT infrastructure*: The IT infrastructure comprises of several technologies like RFID, network equipment, public access point and other hardware which are important parts of smart cities. Various ICT technologies, data management and information processing methods are used for providing an interconnected infrastructure for smart cities [15, 16].

- *Physical environment*: Whenever a smart city project is planned, the city infrastructure like roads, bridges and airports and environmental impacts are always studied in detail. The existing city infrastructure is the base on which the smart city is developed. If a city's infrastructure

Table 2. Smart city core components [15, 16].

is old and damaged, then it becomes difficult to integrate the concept of smart cities with it [15, 16].

- *Human resources*: Human capital is an important aspect of a smart city; a relevant knowledge base and skills are required to come up with creative ideas of development in a smart city [15, 16].
- *Government policies*: It is necessary to have administrative support and policy planning to develop a city into a smart one. Without legal and institutional support, infrastructure and human capital are useless. It is very important to have an organised approach for efficient and successful deployment of smart city models [15, 16].

1.1.2 Applications of Smart City

- **Smart citizens:** Smart cities allow more interconnectedness and geo-awareness through which citizens may get cognitive insights into the environment around them and make better decisions thanks to the combination of IOT with smart cities.
- **Smart technology:** Various smart technologies like RFID and WSN have been integrated to build smart systems and intelligent infrastructures in smart cities.
- **Smart energy:** In a heterogeneous smart city environment, it is vital that energy resources are monitored and managed efficiently. Smart cities comprise of smart grids, which provide an excellent support for efficient decision making and process optimization in a smart environment [17, 18].
- **Smart infrastructure:** Various infrastructures like buildings, factories and parking systems are combined with an IOT environment in a smart city setting to give additional interconnectivity to them and facilitate an improved quality of life for its citizens [17].
- **Smart healthcare:** It is agreed that healthcare is a vital part of any city. Thus, a smart and more efficient approach to healthcare is ideally required. A patient oriented and intelligent approach in healthcare can help to offer better living standards to people [19].
- **Smart governance:** Due to increasing urbanisation there is a need for intelligent ways to manage and govern modern cities, therefore a smart city is incomplete without its judiciary working in a connected environment as well [20].
- **Smart education:** In the world of modern computing, it is essential that we make use of technology to provide better education to smart learners who need to learn in and adapt to a fast-changing world [21].
- **Smart security:** The security of the city infrastructure and its citizens is an important aspect of smart cities; smart surveillance as well as crime detection can lead to a safer environment in the smart city [17].

1.1.3 Smart City Initiative in India

Asia and Africa are home to countries with fast growing populations. India being one of the most populated countries in Asia, has seen an exponential growth in urbanisation in the recent years. India has realised that in order to develop as a country, it must develop its cities first. In 2015, the Indian government started the 'smart cities mission', a smart city plan for 100 Indian cities aimed at finding innovative solutions to the country's urban problems. Urban cities in developing countries like India often lag behind in terms of the management of its development plans, infrastructure and sector policies. It is known that the government is a crucial component of a smart city. Therefore, it is critical to have effective administrative collaboration in order to ensure the smart city mission's success [22–24]. Apart from governance, India's current infrastructure necessitates consideration of urban realities, which obstruct the development of smart cities in the country. As a result, we must examine local difficulties while adopting popular techniques for smart city implementation in industrialised nations in the past [25].

2. Security

Security is the protection against potential harm to an entity. Computer security is the concept of the protection of sensitive resources against potential threats in a computerised environment. Computer security has various aspects like database, OS and Internet security [26]. Information and communication technology (ICT) is usefully integrated with these computer systems. Information and communication security deals with the protection of ICT resources, that deal with the processing and transmission of data. Information security deals with securing the data held by the resources in the computerized environment. Cyber security expands the concept of information security, deals with protection of data held by the resources in the cyber system but also protects the resources as well as physical assets in the organisation. The 'CIA' triangle is the most fundamental and important aspect of computer security, which has been discussed below with respect to an IOT ecosystem [27].

2.1 Confidentiality and Data Privacy

Confidentiality means that the actual data being transmitted in the network is not visible to unauthorised entities. Encryption techniques are applied to the data so as to maintain user privacy. There are two areas which require maintenance of data privacy. One is during the data collection phase where the entity collecting the data is restricted according to how much and what type of data it can collect. Another way to maintain user privacy is during the data transmission phase where data anonymity and confidentiality have to be maintained. This means that we need to encrypt the data being transmitted for confidentiality as well as hide its relationships. That is, hide the data, to maintain user privacy [6, 28].

2.2 Data Integrity

Integrity means that data received or transmitted by an IOT device has not been tampered with by an attacker during network transmission [6]. IOT data tampering can cause malfunctioning of the complete system. Interference with IoT data is typically used by attackers to inflict harm or financial losses. For example, tampering with medical data by wearable sensors can result in incorrect medical information data collection resulting in an erroneous analysis of the patient's condition. Another example is, tampered data collected by the sensors in a smart city could lead to incorrect control signals. In case of smart cities, if an attacker is able to manipulate the sensor data, then disruption of the street lighting system or the automatic parking system would lead to great system inefficiency. As a result, it would defeat the goal of smart city infrastructure management. Calculating and appending a Message Authentication Code (MAC) to each packet during communication among the IOT devices can provide support for data integrity but this process requires some extra computation power, which might be possible in scenarios where latency is not an issue but for smart cities most of the network devices work with real-world data and this strategy isn't ideal for such applications to ensure data integrity [29].

2.3 Availability

It is important in an IOT network that a device or a node is available to an authorised entity whenever it wants access to it but at the same time unauthorised entities should not get access to it. Dos (denial of service) has become a common type of attack for stopping an authorised user from being able to access a resource in the network [6].

3. Enablers of a Smart City

3.1 SCADA System

SCADA (Supervisory Control and Data Acquisition) systems are intelligently designed mechanisms that allow site operators to remotely monitor various locations and machines. SCADA systems help in saving time and money. Deployment of SCADA systems helps in data acquisition and analysis [30]. They enable the monitoring of industrial processes and machines. SCADA systems are used in a wide range of industries, including electrical distribution systems, food manufacturing and facility security alarms [31].

Various components like Human–Machine Interface (HMI) displays, database servers and Programmable Logic Controllers (PLCs), are integrated to create a SCADA system. SCADA systems can be considered as forerunners to IoT. IoT is a mix of SCADA and other new technologies that have emerged since, they both have characteristics in common, such as communication, visualisation, data access and manipulation, among others. SCADA has already existed in industries long before IOT and hence, it adds up several decades of knowledge to deal with applications in industries that function with high-velocity and high-volume data. It provides support for interoperability and hardware-agnostic integration of multiple data systems and has developed security standards for communication. All this has led to easier integration of IOT in industries. Integral IOT concepts like machine-to-machine communication and visualisation of data in real time came from SCADA in the first place. To sum it up SCADA is a combination of automation and computers in industries and when it is combined with the power of the internet an IOT ecosystem is created [32, 33].

3.2 *Internet of Things*

The Internet of Things is a network of interconnected objects that can include sensors, actuators, controllers, and computer devices with unique identities. Devices in an IOT ecosystem have specific functionalities to perform in an IOT environment with varied levels of access to the network. WSN, RF identification, cloud computing, middleware systems, and end-user applications are some of the technologies that already exist and have become an important part of the IoT [1, 34, 35]. Sensors and actuators are integrated with embedded systems to perform a specific functionality in IOT devices; various such devices are interconnected to form an IOT network. An embedded system consists of field programmable gate arrays (FPGAs) or microprocessors, communication modules, memory, and input/output interfaces. Various environmental characteristics are tracked and measured using sensors in an IOT ecosystem. There can be different types of sensors for different purposes, such as electrochemical, optical, mechanical, location and airflow sensors. Sensors gather information from the environment, which is then used by the actuators present in that IOT environment to perform certain actions for example: switching on a water pump when a soil moisture sensor detects soil moisture content has gone below a threshold value or switching on the lights of a room automatically whenever a motion detector sensor like an ultrasonic sensor detects someone [1, 36].

IoT in smart cities aims to create an infrastructure of interconnected physical devices, vehicles, buildings, and electrical devices that communicate with one another in order to make the internet even more pervasive and provide an immersive experience of automation and the ability to monitor and control remote objects, saving time and money while improving quality of life. Smart housing, smart grid, smart street lights and parking systems, smart weather and water systems are some of the IOT applications in smart cities. Some of the IOT technologies crucial in creating such infrastructure are listed below [17, 35].

3.2.1 IOT Ecosystem

The IOT ecosystem combines different IOT components in a unified framework to create a well managed and coordinated environment. Mentioned below are some important components of an IOT ecosystem [13].

3.2.1.1 IOT Devices

A network of IOT devices make up an IOT ecosystem. IOT devices differ in their computing power, storage and other resource capabilities and using this differentiation they can be classified as low end, middle end and high end devices. Low end devices comprise IOT devices with low memory, lightweight operating systems and lower computing capabilities; they can include sensors and actuators deployed at the physical level of the ecosystem. Middle end devices have a slightly higher computing capability and memory; these devices monitor and communicate with low end devices; they include microcontroller boards like Arduino, ESP2866 and gateways. High end devices comprise single board computers with a 64-bit architecture, having enough computing and memory resources to run traditional operating systems like LINUX and UNIX. These devices support the integration of machine learning and other technologies which are leveraged by IOT ecosystems in order to facilitate a smart environment. They include devices like Raspberry pie, beagleboard and controllers [13, 37].

3.2.1.2 Addressing

The total count of devices connected to the internet and the IoT ecosystem is growing exponentially. Therefore, it is important that we have an established system that can handle addressing the large number of devices present in the environment. Addressing means providing the devices with unique labels so that they can be efficiently addressed in an IOT ecosystem [17, 38].

3.2.1.3 Middleware

Middleware bridges the gap between the network and application layers. It provides various features like intelligence, storage, security and privacy to the complete ecosystem. It brings together and integrates all the technologies in one single layer to provide support to the IOT ecosystem in terms of processing and storage. In the middleware layer we are able to integrate various technologies like machine learning, big data, cryptography, which otherwise could not have been implemented by low end devices of the ecosystem [13, 17].

3.2.1.4 IOT Communication Protocols

IOT devices do not have a very high computational, storage and network capacity, moreover, they require low latency for real time applications. IOT devices cannot support traditional IP communications which creates a need for specially designed lightweight and efficient protocols for IOT devices at each layer of communication. There are different protocols used for different use cases in IOT. NFC is a protocol that connects a network of sensors and devices in close proximity, whereas WSN is a widely used protocol for connecting thousands of devices through IPs. Low power devices make up a majority of the IOT ecosystem, so there are protocols like Bluetooth, low power Wi-Fi, low power wide area networks (LPWANs), NB-IoT and Zigbee for support. Figure 3 lists some protocols designed for different layers in the IOT communication model [13, 39].

Table 3. Communication technologies in IOT [12, 13, 39].

IOT layer	Communication protocol used
Physical	IEEE 802.15.4, RFID, Wi-Fi, BLE, NFC
Datalink	IEEE 802.15.4, RFID, Wi-Fi, 6LowPAN, BLE, NFC
Network	IPv6, RPL, Zigbee
Transport	TCP, UDP, ZigBee
Application	DDS, XMPP, AMQP, HTPP, CoAP

3.2.2 Standard Bodies for Smart Cities

It is important to ensure device compatibility when working with large-scale applications in a smart city which includes various types of heterogeneous IoT devices. Mentioned below are a few major governing bodies tasked with creating standards which support large-scale applications for smart cities [40, 41]:

- The Internet Engineering Task Force (IETF)
- The Third Generation Partnership Project (3GPP)
- Open Mobile Alliance (OMA)
- The European Telecommunications Standards Institute (ETSI)
- IEEE
- oneM2M

3.3 Cloud Computing

Cloud computing is a technology which facilitates a set of shared resources such as servers, storage, and networks in a scalable and customizable manner in accordance with a pay-as-you-go architecture. This means the users are charged just for the services they actually utilize. On-demand service, broad network access, resource pooling, rapid flexibility, and measured service are the five primary qualities of cloud computing. Moreover, it has 3 general service models: Infrastructure as a service (Iaas), Software as a service (Saas), Platform as a service (Pass). It provides great flexibility with different deployment models: public, private and hybrid clouds [42, 43].

IoT devices are installed remotely for a variety of activities like monitoring, data collection and relaying the data to a gateway; they also serve as the controller and coordinator. The battery driven embedded devices have limited resources for performing specific tasks and therefore have limited computational capabilities with low power and clock speed CPUs. Certain IOT services like data analytics performance on the data collected from sensors require much complex computation activities which can be offloaded to the cloud for practical IOT applications [44].

3.4 Edge Computing and Its Requirement

While moving all data and computing tasks to the cloud has been a huge benefit because cloud data centres have more computing power than a typical local computer, it still falls short in practical areas where real-time analysis and decision making are required. Cloud data centres are not suitable for computational purposes in real time IOT applications due to network bandwidth limitations and the presence of multiple routers and gateways between the cloud data centre and the local device [45]. Along with its benefits of elasticity, mobility and flexibility [42], cloud computing brings its own set of challenges like latency, scalability and privacy threats. To deal with all these edge computing has been presented [46].

Edge computing helps to decentralize the system by bringing the computational resources closer to the client peripheral or the original data source [47]. When so much data is collected by devices all over the world, businesses seek to leverage the data as a resource to perform real-time data analytics. They can act upon the insights extracted from real time data, so that their customers can receive better services, i.e., data must be processed in real time. If the processing power is close to that of the data source then there is relatively low latency experienced due to a reduction in the data transmission time, which allows quicker analysis of the data and facilitates real time insights [48–51].

Conventional Cloud computing is unlikely to fulfil the reaction time expectations of delay-sensitive IoT networks, because of the unsecure public network between the IOT devices and the cloud data centre. As mentioned earlier IOT devices have limited computational capabilities and hence it is prudent to use cloud services for such tasks but certain scenarios require low latency which cannot be provided by the cloud data centres due to low bandwidth and limited network resources. Therefore, edge computing is used to bridge the gap between requirements and efficiency. It not only provides computational power to IOT devices remotely but also offers low latency as they are situated much closer to the devices and handles delay sensitive tasks for the smart device in the network and transfers delay-tolerant services to the cloud data centre. Edge computing helps to reduce bandwidth consumption of the cloud data centre. Edge computing offloads the resource consuming tasks to itself so that it can reduce the power consumption of the IOT device. This allows an increase in the battery life of the device [52–55].

3.5 Big Data Ingestion and Analysis

Volume, variety, and velocity are the three major components that define Big Data. Volume denotes the enormous quantity of data produced, variety denotes its heterogeneity, and velocity is the rate at which it is received [56]. Data ingestion is the systematic and efficient transmission of data acquired from multiple sources to a target source. ETL (Extract, Transform, and Load) is a traditional data input process designed with focus on data warehouses. It is useful where latency is not a concern, however IOT applications require real-time decision making. Therefore, it is important to have a real-time data processing mechanism for IOT applications [57, 58].

It is certain that IOT infrastructure will be the main source of big data in the coming years. Currently there are nearly 50 billion IOT devices which are a part of the internet and already producing massive volumes of heterogeneous data which is analysed in real time, therefore it is crucial to create efficient methods for storing, transferring and recollecting data gathered by the IOT devices in real time [17]. Big data has a plethora of tools and platforms available. MapReduce was the first of these technologies, and it paved the way for others like Pig, Hive, and Cascade. However, the former is suitable for tasks which require high throughput not low latency. Platforms like Hadoop Online, Scribe, S4, HStreaming, Storm, Flume, Spark, Spark Streaming, Kafka, Impala, and others, on the other hand, are built for such tasks [59].

Data analytics has a great potential for designing intelligent tools for understanding human behaviour, predicting future possibilities, visualizing, modelling and more [60]. Big data analytics is agreeably a vital area of research in IoT. With billions of IoT devices, smart cities throughout the world may generate tremendous amounts of data. This data might range from environmental data to a person's personal information (such as medical information, daily activities and personal preferences). Smart grids are a good application area of big data analytics. Big data analytics should be leveraged to improve the power grid performance, safety and decision-making process of power sharing [61, 62]. It is crucial that the actual useful data is separated from redundant data collected due to the noise in the environment; Hadoop framework can be used for this purpose [63]. To leverage the big data available through IOT devices, we need to use intelligent techniques and sophisticated algorithms to efficiently store and analyse the generated data. It's critical that our infrastructure has the capability to compute and store huge quantities of data. In addition, we must ensure that our IoT ecosystem has the computational resources to extract insights from the data [40, 64].

3.6 Machine Learning in Smart Cities

Machine learning is a branch of computer science that grew out of pattern recognition and computational learning theory, and it studies and builds algorithms that can learn from and predict complex events. It can be divided into three categories: supervised, unsupervised, and reinforcement learning [6, 65]. Machine learning algorithms make it easier to analyse and forecast complex circumstances, and therefore to take the best possible actions in communication protocols and various IOT applications [65].

3.6.1 Machine Learning

Machine learning helps us to not only extract useful information from large volumes of redundant data, but also to draw intelligent insights from it. Machine learning may be used to make intelligent recommendations based on the data gathered from the actual environment through IOT nodes. Machine learning may be leveraged to predict certain events before they can occur so that required steps can be taken to deal with them. For example, it can predict a disease a patient might contract, by using machine learning algorithms such as decision trees, logistic regression, and LibSVM on gathered patient health such as past history, demographics, and archived patient data retrieved from smart wearable devices. After the prediction of a patient's possible future medical condition a mathematical model can be used to make personalised IOT and ML based recommendations [63, 66, 67]. Machine learning can also be used to detect certain activities in smart infrastructures [68].

3.6.2 Deep Learning

Deep learning is a branch of machine learning that entails creating computational models with multiple layers of artificial neural networks. The layers present in a deep learning model consist of several neurons. Activation functions are used after each layer to produce non-linear outputs; this allows the successive layers of a model to communicate with each other. The neuron structure of the human brain is thought to have inspired this technology. It has proven to be useful in applications like language modelling, image recognition, natural language processing, information retrieval and speech synthesis. It has a great leverage over traditional machine learning as it can perform better on large scale data in lesser time durations. IOT ecosystems generate data on a large scale which has to be analysed for providing better intelligent solutions to real world problems [3, 6, 69–72].

3.6.3 Tapping into the Power of Machine and Deep Learning with Cloud and Edge

3.6.3.1 Machine Learning

Machine learning is good for applications such as pattern detection as well as predicting system failures. This makes it useful in various aspects of a smart city. To leverage the benefits of machine learning which requires huge amounts of data for training a central cloud data WAN, increased network bandwidth consumption and scalability issues arise. A better approach would be a distributive machine learning where instead of sending raw data to the cloud, the data could be used to train models locally at the edge near the sensor nodes. Afterwards the parameters obtained from these models can be sent over to the cloud, where parameters from several other edge devices as well can be used to train an adaptive model to get a better accuracy. After training the model in the cloud the global parameters can then be shared with the edge devices. For instance, data from an IOT device, might be acquired at the nearest gateway. After which, machine learning algorithms like K-means clustering could be used to identify patterns in the collected data to provide real time insights [54, 68].

3.6.3.2 Deep Learning

Introducing deep learning in an IOT environment is not an easy task. Deep learning needs hardware and software which can support high parallel computing, which is seldom the case with IOT devices due to their low computing power due to general cost constraints and other requirements like portability. We can use bigdata with cloud or edge computing to solve this issue; the former uses a central data centre for performing computing tasks whereas the latter offloads them from the cloud. Since the cloud has a limited bandwidth it creates scalability issues when it comes to analysing large volumes of data gathered in a smart city. To handle this issue first we train an initial model in the cloud, then the initial data gathered from the IOT nodes present in the physical environment can processed at the edge layer of the IOT ecosystem after which we can use the intermediate data as an input to the lower layer of the initial model at the edge layer itself. After that the output generated by the model, which is much smaller in size is fed as input to the higher layer of the model in the cloud to get the result. Although adding more layers of the model at the edge layer reduces network traffic, we can only employ our edge server with a certain number of layers as it cannot handle similar computational overheads to a cloud server [3].

3.7 Blockchain

Blockchain is the concept of a distributed ledger over a distributed system. Satoshi Nakamoto, the creator of the Bitcoin, was the first to implement blockchain technology. Since its introduction, blockchain has grown in popularity due to its capacity to perform trustworthy transactions with decentralised consensus, as well as the elimination of the requirement for a trusted third party by validating transactions in a mutually distrusted system. The blockchain is made up of a series of blocks that contain transaction data and are linked together using the hashing technique. The genesis block, which is the first block in the chain does not have a preceding block. Every block points to the previous block in the chain with the use of the hash value of the preceding block. Every entity in the network shares a copy of the blockchain. Post every transaction a new block is added to the chain after getting a mutual consensus from the peers in the network; this provides data integrity, immutability, non-repudiation, transparency, traceability and decentralization. Blockchain technology has been leveraged to solve problems in a variety of fields, including risk management and financial services, as well as cryptocurrencies, public and social services. With qualities like interoperability, privacy, security, reliability, and scalability, Blockchain may be integrated into the IOT ecosystem for building secure and efficient smart cities. Some problems In IOT which can be solved with the help of blockchains are listed below [73, 74].

- Scalability issues with the cloud due to limited network bandwidth
- Real time data exchange
- Data analytics and network issues
- Transaction automation and verification
- Data transparency
- Tracing processes from end-to-end

3.8 5G

The fifth generation of communication technology, or 5G, is the next step in the evolution of communication. Its aims to deliver great network connectivity and facilitate fast communication. 5G, IoT, and edge computing as one are capable of creating an extremely fast and efficient communication system. Furthermore, 5G can complement many real time IOT applications brilliantly for providing faster services to the end users in the IOT network [53, 75].

4. Reviewing the Existing Strategies

There are various successful smart city models all around the word with a different implementation of various features of an ideal smart city. While there does not exist any one perfect model of an existing smart city, below are listed some salient features of some of the most successful smart city implementations around the globe.

After reviewing various smart cities implementations across the world, a smart city is viewed as a collection of numerous technologies and frameworks, which work to create a heterogenous and interoperable system. With the integration of AI, big data, data analytics, NLP and other technologies, a smart city infrastructure is designed to enhance the citizens' daily activities by providing better services. Data collection is a huge aspect of all these systems at various stages of the smart city implementation; sensitive data and remotely controlled assets bring security concerns with it. The application and field of smart city implementation is quite vast for coming up with any one security solution or framework but its security is an important factor and cannot be overlooked when dealing with systems of such scale. Hence it is important to closely look at the possible security challenges and threats to the smart city [83–85].

5. Security Challenges in Smart Cities

A smart city prioritises automating its operations to save time and money. Artificial intelligence is a fundamental requirement in the implementation of such automated activities. Data is required by AI models in order to fulfil its basic purpose of providing intelligent inputs into the automatic system. Anything from citizen emergency services to criminal activity recognition inside a smart city requires artificial intelligence to detect abnormal scenarios. AI executes responses at a much faster rate than humans can but all this requires highly sensitive data. If the data is leaked or a vulnerable part of the system gets compromised then it might lead to malfunctioning and disruption of the whole system. Therefore, it is important for us to look into the security of various smart city aspects [10]. There are many IOT enablers discussed above; integrating all of them is what makes a

Table 4. List of smart city implementation [76–82].

City Name	Started In	Initiatives	Technology
Singapore	2014	Digital health system; smart homes; elderly monitoring system, smart transport	SINGAPORE ONE, is a nationwide broadband network was launched to facilitate nationwide broadband network; ICT technology
Copenhagen	2009	Smart economy; smart governance; Copenhagen Connecting.	Smart information system, Hitachi cloud technology.
Helsinki	2014	Helsinki Smart Region; Forum Virium Helsinki a smart mobility initiative launched in 2020, which includes carbon neutrality in logistics, providing remote security and environmental traffic emissions' monitoring; Parking permit chatbot; automated waste collection system	ICT technologies, Smart information system, Artificial intelligence, IBM Watson; Big Data analytics.
London	2013	Automatic traffic signals' control, automated traffic alerts, smart mobility	ICT infrastructure, IoT sensor network, big data t
Zurich	2017	Streetlight project; smart building management system to interconnect the city heating, cooling and electricity systems, smart and sustainable transport.	ZuriTraffic an online tool which shows real time traffic conditions, ICT technology.
Amsterdam	2009	e-health, smart mobility, Goochem a chatbot for the 'I Amsterdam', online portal to report complaints, give feedbacks and receive updates.	Smart information system; NLP; Big Data, Image recognition and AI
Barcelona	2011	Public transport monitoring; smart transportation; smart parking; smart traffic lights; smart street light, smart waste collection	ICT infrastructure, IoT sensor network, GPS tracking system, traffic magnetometer sensors.

smart city. A smart city is a heterogeneous environment where various technologies interoperate to provide seamless services to its citizens. While the environment heterogeneity provides opportunities to provide better services and facilities, it brings with it various unpredictable vulnerabilities which are often overlooked during the development stage and become difficult to handle afterwards [86]. Because of the heterogeneous nature of the smart city system, it is difficult to create any one security framework. Therefore, it is more efficient to take a closer look at each of the enablers separately; various security threats associated with different technologies used in smart cities have been discussed in detail below.

5.1 Types of Security Challenges and Requirements in IOT

Security becomes a hindrance when in the execution of IOT models. The IOT architecture is divided into numerous layers and each layer has its own vulnerabilities, which must be evaluated to design a secure system. A lack of effective security could lead to loss of data, violation of privacy, and unauthorized access to original data and its source [1, 7, 36]. The information collected from the sensors may be utilised to better understand user behaviour and preferences. This in turn might be used by the attacker to attack the victim [2]. If the risks present at different stages of the IOT ecosystem are not addressed properly it would be unfeasible and uneconomical to address them at a later stage amidst a diverse range of technologies which are interdependent on each other [7]. In a nutshell, proper security must be provided at all levels of the IoT ecosystem.

5.1.1 Authentication and Authorization

Authentication means that the identity of the object communicating with the IOT device is valid, and that only authenticated users have access to various network resources like remote actuator controlling an actuator remotely [6]. Public key cryptosystems lack in actual deployment of theoretically feasible schemes due to the lack of a global root certificate authorization entity. In addition the number of IOT objects in a smart city environment is often too huge for the issuance of a certificate to each of them. In the case of IoT, the concepts of entrusted authentication and authorization techniques must be considered [28, 122].

5.1.2 Identification of an IOT Device

Each IOT device is a separate network entity; these devices may have private data as well as network access. As a consequence, each network entity must be uniquely identified [87]. One of the challenges in IOT is to provide a secure naming architecture for the objects in the network. While translational services such as DNS exist, they are vulnerable to cyberattacks such as DNS cache poisoning and man-in-the-middle attacks. Although Domain Name Service Security Extension (DNSSEC, IETFRFC4033) is being used to enhance the security of DNSs for validating the authenticity of a resource record and to distribute public cryptographic keys, it requires tremendous computational power which is a challenge in these IOT devices [28, 88, 89].

5.1.3 Lightweight Cryptography

Computation power for performing cryptography is a concern for IOT devices. IOT devices often do not use encryption while transmitting data to save time and computation power because M2M/IOT devices have a limited battery life and computing resources. In most scenarios security is not given a priority when making IOT applications while top priority is given to data availability. Generally symmetric encryption is used in IOT devices. However, public key encryption is better than symmetric keys as it provides us with data integrity as well as source authentication other than data confidentiality. We need to find ways to reduce computational overheads for public key cryptography and the intricacies of security protocols for IOT. Therefore, lesser resources and time consuming methods and protocols are required for communication among IOT devices [7, 28, 90].

5.1.4 Heterogeneous Nature of the Network

There are almost 50 billion IOT devices present in the world today, off which there are many devices which are not typically an IOT device, the best example being a mobile phone which can be a data collector and a controller in an IOT network. Not just the devices but also the protocols used to communicate between these devices might differ for each device along with the formats of the packets. These devices require interoperability and bring their own set of security issues in an IOT environment. Most of such devices have android which is open source and hence more susceptible to attacks because it is easier for the attacker to find vulnerabilities in such scenarios. Android has its own set of malwares and if any such device gets infected then the whole IOT network is exposed to various security threats as the high computational capabilities of such devices could be used to exploit the network and perform malicious activities. Therefore, it is crucial that all the components in an IOT ecosystem (Operating system, server, database, frameworks) are properly configured with strict security policies [13, 28, 91].

5.1.5 Security Attacks in IOT

The IoT architectures have been subdivided into various levels, One of the most common ways to categorise them into different layers is by dividing them into: perception, network and application layers. Security attacks can also be classified in an IOT architecture as: Perception, Network and Application layer attacks [91–93].

5.1.5.1 Perception Layer Attack

- **Botnet:** Bots are IOT devices that get infected with malware and are captured by the attacker. A collection of these bots for a network is referred to as a botnet. Some of the popular malwares for creating botnets are Qbot, Kaiten and Mirai. After capturing a good amount of IOT devices the attacker misuses the bots devices' network to perform malicious activities like a DDos attack on a server; the power of a botnet lies in the number of bots. Previously botnets used to control the captured IOT devices through a single command and control server but now peer-to-peer communication is commonly used to launch botnet attacks, which are generally more difficult to bring down as compared to a single command and control server which has only one server which could be taken down to secure the network [6].

- **Eavesdropping:** It is an attack against user privacy, in which the communication channel between the devices is compromised and the attacker monitors the data being passed through the channel; RFID is the most vulnerable device for an eavesdropping attack; an antenna can be used to track the conversation between the tag and reader and vice versa [6]. There are two types of eavesdropping attacks:

  i. **Passive eavesdropping:** In a passive eavesdropping attack the attacker quietly monitors the network traffic. The attacker's primary goal here is to jeopardise the network's privacy and gather network information like source, destination and packet size which could be further used by the attacker for a more critical type of attack [94].

  ii. **Active eavesdropping:** In an active eavesdropping attack, the hackers need to decipher the payload, so they try injecting their own messages in the communication channel to decipher the actual message in order to monitor the network communication; for injecting data into the channel, the attacker needs to have transmission access in the network, as well as access to either part of the plain text for example the destination IP address or the entire payload [94, 95].

- **Reverse Engineering:** It is an attack where the attackers actually break down the device and study it's architecture, with an aim to find device vulnerabilities. Once the attackers find device weaknesses, they can use them to exploit the device and the network by replicating the attack on similar devices in the network [91, 96].

- **Tampering:** A tampered IOT node means its hardware has been compromised, generally this happens during or before the manufacturing phase, which means the hardware which was actually intended to be delivered by the manufacturer is partially or fully replaced by a compromised one, using which the attacker can gain access to sensitive information intended for storage in the actual intended hardware [6, 91].

- **Jamming and Radio Interference:** Radio interference is the unintended unavailability of the network due to environmental disturbance. A jamming attack is against the availability service of the IOT device. The attacker aims to interfere with the wireless connectivity by interfering with the same radio frequency with which the device is communicating [6, 91].

- **Sleep Deprivation:** Most IoT devices are battery-powered nodes with limited battery life, as a result, they have a routine of putting the device into sleep mode on a regular basis to extend the device's lifetime. In such cases, an attacker may launch sleep deprivation attacks, with the goal of keeping the device awake for long periods of time and thus shortening the device's lifetime and forcing an early shutdown [6].

5.1.5.2 Network Layer Attack

- **Man in the Middle Attack:** Here, the attacker is able to read, modify and delete the data. They do so by taking possession over the channel of communication between the entities. This attack could be used to hijack credentials exchanged between two legitimate devices [6, 121]. A smart fridge released by Samsung in 2014 was an example of such an attack, the fridge's node failed to validate SSL certificates while implementing SSL because of which it was possible to obtain the user's google account credentials through a man in the middle attack [97, 98]. Few categories of this attack are:

    i. **ARP cache poisoning:** In this fake ARP replies are sent to corrupt the ARP cache by taking misusing stateless properties of ARP caching protocol which updates the cache even if the reply was not for a valid request [97–99].

    ii. **DNS spoofing:** Domain name service (DNS) maps search engine friendly names to the device's real IP address. DNS spoofing, also known as DNS cache poising, is an attack that seeks to store inaccurate name-to-address mapping information in the DNS server. It can be done either by compromising a DNS server or by sending fake replies to recursive DNS queries [6, 97].

    iii. **Session hijacking:** The goal of a session hijacking attack is to steal a user's session token, which may be used to validate a login into a secure network while impersonating the real device whose credentials were taken [6, 97].

- **Middleware Attack:** In the Internet of Things architecture, middleware refers to the components that connect to the network layer, receive data from it, and conduct data processing and storage. While middleware is useful in providing more storage and computing capacity to the IOT ecosystem, the security risks of middleware components such as database and cloud affects the quality of services provided at the application layer [100]. There are various types of authentication attacks in which the attacker impersonates a legitimate user to gain access to the middleware [6].

- **Denail of Service/DDos:** This attack occurs when an attacker floods a network server with connection requests by sending large quantities of requests directly to the server. A Distributed denial of service (DDos) attack is similar, however, the attacker (botmaster) floods the server by leveraging hacked IoT devices (bots). The attacker's aim is to use the server's bandwidth to jeopardise the availability of services to valid users in the network [6, 91, 98].

- **Routing Attack:** The crux of the routing attack is disrupting the routing operations in the network to degrade the network performance. Examples of such attacks are sybil, sinkhole and wormhole attacks [6, 100, 101].

5.1.5.3 Application Layer Attack

- **IOT Malwares:** A malware is an executable code, which when run on a device takes control over it. Mirai malware is a botnet attack in which the virus uses brute force to gain control of its target IoT devices, and then uses multiple compromised devices(bots) to launch a Dos attack in a network. The Dyn assault is a well-known example of this, in which just 10,000 IoT devices were used to conduct a DDos attack on a Dyn server. As a result companies like Netflix, Twitter, PayPal, and Sony PlayStation were unable to render their website to its actual customers [1, 47, 48, 102]. The main difficulty in identifying such malwares in IOT devices is thir low computational capabilities; the antivirus applications designed for x86-architectured PCs is not useful in an IOT environment for the same reason. Moreover, the differences in the hardware architecture of various IOT devices led to confusion in the creation of a general security scheme for protection against different types of malware [33, 38].

- **SQL Injection:** This sort of attack targets vulnerable input sources to the database, allowing the attacker to transmit malicious SQL instructions that are subsequently processed by the SQL database [6, 91].

5.2 *Vulnerabilities in SCADA Systems*

It is useful to rely on SCADA systems for references while evaluating security vulnerabilities in smart cities, which are themselves an ecosystem of networked devices. SCADA networks already contain industrial infrastructure that might integrate with the smart cities in the future, like chemical factories, power stations, manufacturing units, and oil refineries. SCADA systems are the predecessors of smart cities; if an attacker obtains access to one, the entire system may be disrupted. If attackers obtain access to one susceptible infrastructure or building in a smart city, they disrupt the entire network, by jamming the street lights and parking system for example. More than 70% of attacks on SCADA systems are from outside the network; the attackers act through machines with sensors which require interconnectivity and thus make the system vulnerable to cyberthreats and worm attacks. Virtual Private Network (VPN), SQL injection and device threshold manipulation are some examples of attack techniques in SCADA systems. Smart cities could take lessons from them to improve their security [10, 103].

5.3 Security Challenges in Cloud

Since the quantity of heterogenous data produced by IOT devices is high there is a need to involve a third party to process and store it. Traditional cloud data centres, because of their centralised nature are open to many single point attacks like cyber/flooding attacks, Dos, information theft, and malware injection [104].

5.3.1 Man in the Cloud Attack

While using the cloud service for sending and receiving huge volumes of IOT data is efficient, it is also critical to consider the security risk associated with each data transmission session. During each data transfer session, an authentication mechanism would and should be used to verify the data's legitimacy. Consider how inconvenient it would be if each data transfer session required a login process. As a result, session tokens are used to authenticate data originating from a network device that is valid for a set amount of time. While this simplifies data transfer, there's a potential that an attacker may take the session token from the device's local system and use it to get access to the data [97, 105].

5.3.2 Cloud Malware Injection

In this sort of attack, the attacker steals a valid user's login credentials and uses them to obtain unauthorised entry into user's service instance in the cloud. They then inject a malicious code into the server, such as a malicious clone of the user's service instance for processing and analysing the user's service via the malicious instance [6].

5.3.3 Cloud Flooding Attack

Cloud flooding attacks are easy to perform but create the most disturbance. The attacker floods the victim's device with bogus packets, which might be a mix of numerous TCP, UDP, or ICMP packets, by sending a large volume of data through an unsuspecting host on the network. This type of attack inhibits the target device from serving legitimate network users. This sort of denial of service attack might be exacerbated in a cloud setting since the cloud lacks the capacity to discern legitimate versus illegitimate traffic and hence is unable to identify the attack traffic [6].

5.4 Security Challenges with Edge Computing in IoT Network

Edge computing will play a key role in the growth of IoT and smart cities in the coming years, thus it's critical that we build a durable architecture with edge computing [106]. In smart city scenarios, edge brings distributed architecture by allocating diverse applications such as data gathering, model training and control signalling to the local servers. These local servers might be IoT devices with a single CPU core and RAM of less than one megabyte. Such hardware architecture heavily relies on Linux technology, whether it's for the operating system or for server distribution. Virtualization is a concept that is widely employed in edge devices for distributing resources to improve performance and reliability. RTOS are used in edge devices to deliver real time performance; it is a simple light weight kernel which can be vulnerable to attacks the Dos and code injection. Docker is another technology that may be used in conjunction with virtual machines in edge devices, although malicious apps could be present in an untrusted image. While having these technologies can lead to better services, it also exposes devices to attackers and makes them vulnerable to attacks such as remote code execution, unauthorised access, tampering, network-based intrusions, viruses, threats to data privacy, privilege escalation, and denial of service [107].

5.5 Challenges with Blockchain

The adoption of blockchain-based smart city systems poses a significant issue with respect to data privacy and security. Although data anonymity and integrity are unique selling features of blockchains in terms of security, they are excellent solutions for applications that require data security. The identity of a user is kept anonymous by using pseudo addresses to make them untraceable, but data transparency in the blockchain makes all transaction records public, meaning that any participant in the network can access them. This is accomplished by making a copy of the blockchain available to each participant. However, this results in massive storage consumption and latency issues because every new transaction needs to be verified before getting added to the chain. Application of blockchain is questionable in an environment where tons of sensitive information is generated all across the system. Moreover, there needs to be an improvement in the consensus algorithm which is used to validate a transaction in the distributed system of the blockchain environment [74].

6. Security Mechanisms

6.1 Security in IOT Ecosystems

6.1.1 RFID

RFID technology consists of a tag and reader. Tags consists of small chips. The reader communicates with the tags by listening to the signals emitted by them. RFID tags are easily modifiable and can send harmful data to unsecured databases. RFID tags could be put to sleep for a short while with the tag sleeping technique; all this could be reason for concern in terms of security. Custom data coding, repeated retransmissions, and a data integrity check can all be used to mitigate RFID interference. There are lightweight cryptography, re-encryption and relabelling approaches which can be used to keep the data private. Whereas the Hash Lock and Hash Link are methods which use symmetric key distribution for improving the authentication mechanism in RFID communications [10, 108, 119].

6.1.2 Efficient and Lightweight Schemes for Data Security

Many present IoT security mechanisms presume that the IoT device should be equipped with sufficient network and processing capability required for running the traditional cryptography algorithms, which isn't the case in most instances. To safeguard the confidentiality of the information being shared, cryptography is employed to encrypt it. There are two main types of cryptography: symmetric key cryptography and public key cryptography. Symmetric key cryptography includes block cyphers, stream cyphers, and hash functions. RSA (Rivest-Shamir-Adleman) and ECC are two well-known instances of public key cryptography (Elliptic curve cryptography) [109, 110].

The parameters that are considered in the evaluation of a cypher include security, chip area, power and energy consumption, FoM, and latency. The security parameter can be measured in bits and evaluated in terms of the logarithmic value of the fastest known computational attacks against that cipher. The chip area measured in gate equivalence is another important factor in analysing the application of a cipher in a particular hardware and negotiating its suitability. Its performance is linked with the CMOS technology used in the hardware, the lesser the chip area the better. Lightweight cryptography provides a low-cost, low-latency implementation that takes up less chip space and requires less memory (RAM or ROM). Hence, it is proposed as a promising security mechanism. Throughput and latency are also important factors when real-time IOT applications are in consideration. For example, in Unmanned Aerial Vehicles there needs to be a correct balance between security and latency. Certain lightweight ciphers like Lightweight block ciphers

(LWBC), Lightweight stream ciphers (LWSC), Light weight hash functions and ECC have been especially crafted to suit such hardware where there is less RAM and computing power available [123, 124]. The cipher algorithm for a particular hardware must be selected depending upon the hardware parameters like chip area, battery consumption, RAM/ROM capacity of that hardware [111, 120].

6.2 Cloud Computing and Machine Learning

Since IoT devices lack processing capability, functions such as malware detection and encryption cannot be performed locally. A standard IoT cloud server may be used to identify malware and prevent botnet assaults using machine learning. The reports from such attacks could also be used to retrain newer classification models for better performances [112].

6.2.1 Network Behaviour Analysis

We can separate attack situations from typical network behaviour by carefully analysing the network. There are two approaches to analysing the network. The first is network payload analysis, and the second is network traffic analysis, which entails looking at a variety of network parameters such as packet size, the number of ACK and SYN packets per flow, and the flow duration to analyse the network. This approach does not require as much computing power as its counterpart payload analysis, which not only slows down network speed but also raises certain privacy problems. For detecting intrusions such as botnet attacks, network traffic analysis employs a variety of machine learning techniques such as the Naive Bayes classifier, Gaussian based classifier, Artificial neural network, Linear support vector machine and Nearest Neighbours classifier [63, 113].

6.3 Big Data Tools

While it is difficult to provide data confidentiality when it comes to handling huge volumes of data, certain data mining techniques such as Anonymization, Generalization and Randomization can be applied for providing data privacy. None or Probabilistic Results for Queries which help in user de-identification [114]. Moreover, Authentication techniques for Remote Procedure Call (RPC) channels are included in big data platforms like Apache Spark, which can be useful to provide authentication during M2M communication as well as authorization of an IOT device in a network. Data integrity checks are also supported in the Spark Data Frame by Apache Spark. Big data and deep learning when combined together can facilitate detection of different security attacks in a smart network [6].

6.4 Machine learning and Deep Learning Models for Anomaly Detection

Machine models are great tools for pattern recognition and hence they can be used to detect changes in the behaviour of a system and detecting various types of anomalies. Although traditional machine learning models are useful but not scalable in an IOT ecosystem where large quantities of data are produced, the computational power available to the device or the edge is low; machine learning models train the whole model at once assuming the whole data to be present at a single location; although having a huge amount of data is an advantage, the accuracy of a machine learning model decreases with an increase in the dimensionality of the data, one of the reasons why picking an ML model is difficult for an IOT environment. Deep learning on the other hand is quite efficient with handling huge amounts of data, moreover a deep learning model can be trained in stages. Which means we do not have to train a model on any single device, just like we do it with edge devices, we train the lower layer the edge and then the rest can be trained in the cloud data centre with more computing capacity [3, 6, 115, 116]. Therefore, machine learning and deep learning can be used to increase the security and privacy of IOT network in a smart city. Listed below are some machine and deep learning algorithms which tackle different categories of attacks in an IOT network [117]:

Table 5. List of ML and deep models used for different types of attack detection [6, 115, 116].

Type of attack	Machine learning Algorithms used	Deep learning model used
Anomaly detection	k-nearest neighbours	RNN, GANs
Host Intrusion Detection System (HIDS)	SVM, k-nearest neighbours	RNN
Network Intrusion Detection System (NIDS)	SVM, Naïve Bayes, Decision tree	RNN, Restricted Boltzmann machine.
Malware Detection	SVM	CNN, LSTM + Bidirectional Neural Networks (BNN)
Ransomware Detection	-	LSTM + CNN
Intruder Detection	Decision tree, k-nearest neighbours	LSTM + Bi-directional Recurrent Neural Network (BRNN), Evolutionary Deep Network.
IoT Botnet Attack Detection	-	DAE

6.5 Blockchain

Blockchain has a lot of features which might help with implementation in an IOT ecosystem. Because of its secure and reliable attributes blockchain along with smart contracts can be used to improve the security of an IOT ecosystem and hence securing all the smart city applications. Listed below are some of the security issues blockchain can help to solve in an IOT network:

6.5.1 Identity Management Issues

Object identification is a major issue in an IOT network, where there a thousand of IOT devices and each device must be uniquely identified for secure communication and access control. A blockchain has 160-bit address spaces which can make 20 byte blockchain addresses with the help of the Elliptic Curve Digital Signature Algorithm which makes it possible to create an addressing system which can be used to allocate globally unique identities such as the chance of an upcoming address collision 10^48 [118].

6.5.2 Access Control

The unique devices in an IOT network can have different levels of access to an IOT network and these might change over time. Since blockchain provides a distributed ledger to track all the transactions publicly, it makes it difficult to tamper with authorization and ownership to an IOT device in a network [118].

6.5.3 Data Integrity

Each transaction added to a blockchain adds a new block in the blockchain which passes through a hashing function and the hash along with the new block is shared with every member in the network. This makes tampering of data in a blockchain almost impossible. Also, each block added to the blockchain has to get the approval of a consensus algorithm which makes it difficult for attackers to enter false data into the system. Moreover, the data being transmitted by a valid IOT device is signed with a unique public key for authentication [118].

7. Conclusion

The growing population and exponential increase in urbanization has propelled us in the direction of smart cities. A smart city aims to improve the quality of living by providing better infrastructure and services to its citizens. Security is a vital aspect of the services provided in a smart city in terms of both physical security of assets and citizens. It is the convergence of several technologies that makes up a smart city and makes it truly intelligent and efficient. While the different technologies like big data, cloud, machine learning and blockchain provide a lot of benefits in a smart city, each of these bring their own set of vulnerabilities into the system. There are massive volumes of data produced in a smart city. To efficiently process and utilize the data we need to employ the heterogenous technology framework while also maintaining the security of data as well as of each entity in the network.

In this chapter we have studied what makes up a smart city. Then, we have taken a separate look into the technologies that have been used to enhance the services provided by a smart city while also taking some insights from actual smart city implementations around the world. We have also analysed various security threats to a smart city network by diving deep into the security vulnerability of several components of a smart city. Finally, some preventive measures have been discussed for some of the threats and vulnerability issues mentioned.

References

[1] Elijah, O., Rahman, T.A., Orikumhi, I., Leow, C.Y., Hindia, M.N. et al. (2018). An overview of Internet of Things (IoT) and data analytics in agriculture: benefits and challenges. IEEE Internet of Things Journal 5(5): 3758–3773, Oct. 2018, doi: 10.1109/JIOT.2018.2844296.

[2] Perera, C., Zaslavsky, A., Christen, P. and Georgakopoulos, D. (2014). Sensing as a service model for smart cities supported by Internet of Things. Transactions on Emerging Telecommunications Technologies 25(1): 81–93, Jan. 2014, doi: 10.1002/ETT.2704.

[3] Li, H., Ota, K. and Dong, M. (2018). Learning IoT in edge: Deep learning for the Internet of Things with edge computing. IEEE Network 32(1): 96–101, Jan. 2018, doi: 10.1109/MNET.2018.1700202.

[4] Rodrigues, T.G., Suto, K., Nishiyama, H. and Kato, N. (2017). Hybrid method for minimizing service delay in edge cloud computing through VM migration and transmission power control. IEEE Transactions on Computers 66(5): 810–819, May 2017, doi: 10.1109/TC.2016.2620469.

[5] Casino Gets Hacked Through Its Internet-Connected Fish Tank Thermometer. https://thehackernews.com/2018/04/iot-hacking-thermometer.html (accessed Apr. 16, 2022).

[6] Amanullah, M.A. et al. (2020). Deep learning and big data technologies for IoT security. Computer Communications 151: 495–517, Feb. 2020, doi: 10.1016/J.COMCOM.2020.01.016.

[7] Asplund, M. and Nadjm-Tehrani, S. (2016). Attitudes and perceptions of IoT security in critical societal services. IEEE Access 4: 2130–2138, doi: 10.1109/ACCESS.2016.2560919.

[8] Ismagilova, E., Hughes, L., Rana, N.P. and Dwivedi, Y.K. Security, privacy and risks within smart cities: literature review and development of a smart city interaction framework, doi: 10.1007/s10796-020-10044-1.

[9] Yeh, H. (2017). The effects of successful ICT-based smart city services: From citizens' perspectives A R T I C L E I N F O. 824(1), doi: 10.1016/j.giq.2017.05.001.

[10] Braun, T., Fung, B.C.M., Iqbal, F. and Shah, B. (2018). Security and privacy challenges in smart cities. Sustainable Cities and Society 39: 499–507, May 2018, doi: 10.1016/J.SCS.2018.02.039.

[11] Su, K., Li, J. and Fu, H. (2011). Smart city and the applications. 2011 International Conference on Electronics, Communications and Control, ICECC 2011 - Proceedings, pp. 1028–1031, doi: 10.1109/ICECC.2011.6066743.

[12] Silva, B.N., Khan, M. and Han, K. (2018). Towards sustainable smart cities: A review of trends, architectures, components, and open challenges in smart cities. Sustainable Cities and Society 38: 697–713, Apr. 2018, doi: 10.1016/J.SCS.2018.01.053.

[13] Bansal, S. and Kumar, D. (2020). IoT ecosystem: a survey on devices, gateways, operating systems, middleware and communication. International Journal of Wireless Information Networks 27(3): 340–364, Sep. 2020, doi: 10.1007/S10776-020-00483-7.

[14] Kour, V.P. and Arora, S. (2020). Recent developments of the Internet of Things in agriculture: A survey. IEEE Access 8: 129924–129957, 2020, doi: 10.1109/ACCESS.2020.3009298.

[15] Gil-Garcia, J.R., Pardo, T.A. and Nam, T. (2015). What makes a city smart? Identifying core components and proposing an integrative and comprehensive conceptualization. Information Polity 20(1): 61–87, Jan. 2015, doi: 10.3233/IP-150354.

[16] Nam, T. and Pardo, T.A. (2011). Conceptualizing smart city with dimensions of technology, people, and institutions. ACM International Conference Proceeding Series, pp. 282–291, doi: 10.1145/2037556.2037602.

[17] Arasteh, H. et al. (2016). Iot-based smart cities: A survey. EEEIC 2016 - International Conference on Environment and Electrical Engineering, Aug. 2016, doi: 10.1109/EEEIC.2016.7555867.

[18] Tamane, S.C., Dey, N. and Hassanien, A.-E. (eds.). (2021). Security and privacy applications for smart city development. 308, doi: 10.1007/978-3-030-53149-2.

[19] Zhu, H. et al. (2019). Smart healthcare in the era of Internet-of-Things. IEEE Consumer Electronics Magazine 8(5): 26–30, Sep. 2019, doi: 10.1109/MCE.2019.2923929.

[20] Pereira, G.V., Parycek, P., Falco, E. and Kleinhans, R. (2018). Smart governance in the context of smart cities: A literature review. Information Polity 23(2): 143–162, doi: 10.3233/IP-170067.

[21] Zhu, Z.T., Yu, M.H. and Riezebos, P. (2016). A research framework of smart education. Smart Learning Environments 3(1): 1–17, Dec. 2016, doi: 10.1186/S40561-016-0026-2/FIGURES/2.

[22] Praharaj, S., Han, J.H. and Hawken, S. (2018). Urban innovation through policy integration: Critical perspectives from 100 smart cities mission in India. City, Culture and Society 12: 35–43, Mar. 2018, doi: 10.1016/J.CCS.2017.06.004.

[23] Kumar, T.M.V. (2017). E-democracy for smart cities. doi: 10.1007/978-981-10-4035-1.

[24] Al Nuaimi, E., Al Neyadi, H., Mohamed, N. and Al-Jaroodi, J. (2015). Applications of big data to smart cities. Journal of Internet Services and Applications 6(1): 1–15, Aug. 2015, doi: 10.1186/S13174-015-0041-5/FIGURES/3.

[25] Praharaj, S. and Han, H. (2019). Cutting through the clutter of smart city definitions: A reading into the smart city perceptions in India. City, Culture and Society, vol. 18, Sep. 2019, doi: 10.1016/J.CCS.2019.05.005.

[26] Gollmann, D. (2010). Computer security. Wiley Interdisciplinary Reviews: Computational Statistics 2(5): 544–554, Sep. 2010, doi: 10.1002/WICS.106.

[27] von Solms, R. and van Niekerk, J. (2013). From information security to cyber security. Computers and Security 38: 97–102, doi: 10.1016/J.COSE.2013.04.004.

[28] Zhang, Z.K., Cho, M.C.Y., Wang, C.W., Hsu, C.W., Chen, C.K. et al. (2014). IoT security: Ongoing challenges and research opportunities. Proceedings - IEEE 7th International Conference on Service-Oriented Computing and Applications, SOCA 2014, pp. 230–234, Dec. 2014, doi: 10.1109/SOCA.2014.58.

[29] Aman, M.N., Sikdar, B., Chua, K.C. and Ali, A. (2018). Low power data integrity in IoT systems. IEEE Internet of Things Journal 5(4): 3102–3113, doi: 10.1109/JIOT.2018.2833206.

[30] Mishra, R.S. and Goel, A. (2009). Remote Data Acquisition Using Wireless-Scada System Physically Unclonable Function and Side Channel Resistant Circuit View project Security Solution for WSN Using Mobile Agent Technology View project Remote Data Acquisition Using Wireless-Scada System. Accessed: Apr. 22, 2022. [Online]. Available: https://www.researchgate.net/publication/41845945.

[31] Room, A.H.-S.-S.R., Practical, G. and undefined. (2005). Security for critical infrastructure scada systems. controlglobal.com, Accessed: Apr. 22, 2022. [Online]. Available: https://www.controlglobal.com/assets/Media/MediaManager/wp_026_security_sansinstitute.pdf.

[32] Hunzinger, R. (2017). Scada fundamentals and applications in the IoT. Internet of Things and Data Analytics Handbook, pp. 283–293, Feb. 2017, doi: 10.1002/9781119173601.CH17.

[33] Hwaiyu. Geng. (2016). Internet of Things and Data Analytics Handbook. p. 811.

[34] Wu, H. et al. (2021). Survey on Internet of Things and its application in agriculture. Journal of Physics: Conference Series 1714(1): 012025, Jan. 2021, doi: 10.1088/1742-6596/1714/1/012025.

[35] Rajab, H. and Cinkelr, T. (2018). IoT based smart cities. 2018 International Symposium on Networks, Computers and Communications, ISNCC 2018, Nov. 2018, doi: 10.1109/ISNCC.2018.8530997.

[36] Rob, M.A. and Sharifuzzaman, S.A.S.M. (2021). The role of IoT in digitalizing mining sector of Bangladesh. 2021 5th International Conference on Electrical Engineering and Information and Communication Technology, ICEEICT 2021, doi: 10.1109/ICEEICT53905.2021.9667893.

[37] Mahbub, M., Hossain, M.M. and Gazi, M.S.A. (2020). IoT-cognizant cloud-assisted energy efficient embedded system for indoor intelligent lighting, air quality monitoring, and ventilation. Internet of Things 11: 100266, Sep. 2020, doi: 10.1016/J.IOT.2020.100266.

[38] Huseien, G.F. and Shah, K.W. (2022). A review on 5G technology for smart energy management and smart buildings in Singapore. Energy and AI 7: 100116, Jan. 2022, doi: 10.1016/J.EGYAI.2021.100116.

[39] Al-Sarawi, S., Anbar, M., Alieyan, K. and Alzubaidi, M. (2017). Internet of Things (IoT) communication protocols: Review. ICIT 2017 - 8th International Conference on Information Technology, Proceedings, pp. 685–690, Oct. 2017, doi: 10.1109/ICITECH.2017.8079928.

[40] Mehmood, Y., Ahmad, F., Yaqoob, I., Adnane, A., Imran, M. et al. (2017). Internet-of-Things-based smart cities: recent advances and challenges. IEEE Communications Magazine 55(9): 16–24, doi: 10.1109/MCOM.2017.1600514.

[41] Velasquez, W., Munoz-Arcentales, A., Yanez, W. and Salvachua, J. (2018). Resilient smart cities: An approach of damaged cities by natural risks. 2018 IEEE 8th Annual Computing and Communication Workshop and Conference, CCWC 2018, vol. 2018-January, pp. 591–597, Feb. 2018, doi: 10.1109/CCWC.2018.8301649.

[42] Dillon, T., Wu, C. and Chang, E. (2010). Cloud computing: Issues and challenges. Proceedings - International Conference on Advanced Information Networking and Applications, AINA, pp. 27–33, doi: 10.1109/AINA.2010.187.

[43] What is pay-as-you-go cloud computing (PAYG cloud computing)? - Definition from WhatIs.com. https://www.techtarget.com/searchstorage/definition/pay-as-you-go-cloud-computing-PAYG-cloud-computing (accessed May 08, 2022).

[44] Hossain, M.M., Fotouhi, M. and Hasan, R. (2015). Towards an analysis of security issues, challenges, and open problems in the Internet of Things. Proceedings - 2015 IEEE World Congress on Services, SERVICES 2015, pp. 21–28, Aug. 2015, doi: 10.1109/SERVICES.2015.12.

[45] Shi, W. and Dustdar, S. (2016). The promise of edge computing. Computer (Long Beach Calif) 49(5): 78–81, May 2016, doi: 10.1109/MC.2016.145.

[46] Chen, J. and Ran, X. (2019). Deep learning with edge computing: a review. Proceedings of the IEEE, doi: 10.1109/JPROC.2019.2921977.

[47] What Is Edge Computing? Everything You Need to Know. https://www.techtarget.com/searchdatacenter/definition/edge-computing (accessed Apr. 22, 2022).

[48] Shi, W., Cao, J., Zhang, Q., Li, Y. and Xu, L. (2016). Edge computing: vision and challenges. IEEE Internet of Things Journal 3(5): 637–646, Oct. 2016, doi: 10.1109/JIOT.2016.2579198.

[49] Nakkar, M., Altawy, R. and Youssef, A. (2020). Lightweight broadcast authentication protocol for edge-based applications. IEEE Internet of Things Journal 7(12): 11766–11777, Dec. 2020, doi: 10.1109/JIOT.2020.3002221.

[50] Prasad, A.S., Arumaithurai, M., Koll, D. and Fu, X. (2017). RAERA: A robust auctioning approach for edge resource allocation. Proceedings of the Workshop on Mobile Edge Communications, vol. 6, doi: 10.1145/3098208.

[51] Nandury, S.v. and Begum, B.A. (2016). Strategies to handle big data for traffic management in smart cities. 2016 International Conference on Advances in Computing, Communications and Informatics, ICACCI 2016, pp. 356–364, Nov. 2016, doi: 10.1109/ICACCI.2016.7732072.

[52] Jan, M.A., Zhang, W., Usman, M., Tan, Z., Khan, F. et al. (2019). SmartEdge: An end-to-end encryption framework for an edge-enabled smart city application. Journal of Network and Computer Applications 137: 1–10, Jul. 2019, doi: 10.1016/J.JNCA.2019.02.023.

[53] Yu, W. et al. (2017). A survey on the edge computing for the internet of things. IEEE Access 6: 6900–6919, Nov. 2017, doi: 10.1109/ACCESS.2017.2778504.

[54] Ni, J., Zhang, K., Lin, X. and Shen, X.S. (2018). Securing fog computing for Internet of Things applications: challenges and solutions. IEEE Communications Surveys and Tutorials 20(1): 601–628, Jan. 2018, doi: 10.1109/COMST.2017.2762345.

[55] Zhang, T., Li, Y. and Philip Chen, C.L. (2021). Edge computing and its role in Industrial Internet: Methodologies, applications, and future directions. Information Sciences 557: 34–65, May 2021, doi: 10.1016/J.INS.2020.12.021.

[56] Sagiroglu, S. and Sinanc, D. (2013). Big data: A review: Proceedings of the 2013 International Conference on Collaboration Technologies and Systems, CTS 2013, pp. 42–47, doi: 10.1109/CTS.2013.6567202.

[57] Meehan, J., Aslantas, C., Zdonik, S., Tatbul, N., Du, J. et al. Data ingestion for the connected World.

[58] Kalamkar, S. and Mary, G.A. (2020). Clinical data fusion and machine learning techniques for smart healthcare. 2020 International Conference on Industry 4.0 Technology, I4Tech 2020, pp. 211–216, Feb. 2020, doi: 10.1109/I4TECH48345.2020.9102706.

[59] Ji, C., Liu, S., Yang, C., Wu, L., Pan, L. et al. (2016). IBDP: An industrial big data ingestion and analysis platform and case studies. Proceedings - 2015 International Conference on Identification, Information, and Knowledge in the Internet of Things, IIKI 2015, pp. 223–228, Mar. 2016, doi: 10.1109/IIKI.2015.55.

[60] Elmaghraby, A.S. and Losavio, M.M. (2014). Cyber security challenges in smart cities: Safety, security and privacy. Journal of Advanced Research 5(4): 491–497, doi: 10.1016/J.JARE.2014.02.006.

[61] Ullah, Z., Al-Turjman, F., Mostarda, L. and Gagliardi, R. (2020). Applications of artificial intelligence and machine learning in smart cities. Computer Communications 154: 313–323, Mar. 2020, doi: 10.1016/J.COMCOM.2020.02.069.

[62] Talebkhah, M., Sali, A., Marjani, M., Gordan, M., Hashim, S.J. et al. (2021). IoT and big data applications in smart cities: recent advances, challenges, and critical issues. IEEE Access 9: 55465–55484, doi: 10.1109/ACCESS.2021.3070905.

[63] Li, W. et al. A comprehensive survey on machine learning-based big data analytics for IoT-enabled smart healthcare system. doi: 10.1007/s11036-020-01700-6/Published.

[64] Vilajosana, I., Llosa, J., Martinez, B., Domingo-Prieto, M., Angles, A. et al. (2013). Bootstrapping smart cities through a self-sustainable model based on big data flows. IEEE Communications Magazine 51(6): 128–134, doi: 10.1109/MCOM.2013.6525605.

[65] Huang, X.-L. et al. (2017). Editorial: machine learning and intelligent communications. Mobile Networks and Applications 23(1): 68–70, Oct. 2017, doi: 10.1007/S11036-017-0962-2.

[66] Muthu Kumaran, E., Velmurugan, K., Venkumar, P., Amutha Guka, D. and Divya, V. et al. (2022). Artificial intelligence-enabled IoT-based smart blood banking system. pp. 119–130, doi: 10.1007/978-981-16-6332-1_12.

[67] Ramu, S.P. et al. (2022). Federated learning enabled digital twins for smart cities: Concepts, recent advances, and future directions. Sustainable Cities and Society 79: 103663, Apr. 2022, doi: 10.1016/J.SCS.2021.103663.

[68] Samie, F., Bauer, L. and Henkel, J. (2019). From cloud down to things: An overview of machine learning in internet of things. IEEE Internet of Things Journal 6(3): 4921–4934, Jun. 2019, doi: 10.1109/JIOT.2019.2893866.

[69] Zhou, Y., Han, M., Liu, L., He, J.S., Wang, Y. et al. (2018). Deep learning approach for cyberattack detection. INFOCOM 2018 - IEEE Conference on Computer Communications Workshops, pp. 262–267, Jul. 2018, doi: 10.1109/INFOCOMW.2018.8407032.

[70] Deep-learning pro.pdf - Introduction to Deep Learning MIT 6.S191 Alexander Amini January 28, 2019 Follow me of LinkedIn for more: Steve | Course Hero. https://www.coursehero.com/file/52574022/deep-learning-propdf/ (accessed May 08, 2022).

[71] Deng, L. (2014). A tutorial survey of architectures, algorithms, and applications for deep learning. APSIPA Trans Signal Inf Process, vol. 3, Dec. 2014, doi: 10.1017/ATSIP.2013.9.

[72] Kumar, P. et al. (2021). PPSF: A privacy-preserving and secure framework using blockchain-based machine-learning for IoT-driven smart cities. IEEE Transactions on Network Science and Engineering 8(3): 2326–2341, Jul. 2021, doi: 10.1109/TNSE.2021.3089435.

[73] Dai, H.N., Zheng, Z. and Zhang, Y. (2019). Blockchain for Internet of Things: A survey. IEEE Internet of Things Journal 6(5): 8076–8094, Oct. 2019, doi: 10.1109/JIOT.2019.2920987.

[74] Singh, S., Sharma, P.K., Yoon, B., Shojafar, M., Cho, G.H. et al. (2020). Convergence of blockchain and artificial intelligence in IoT network for the sustainable smart city. Sustainable Cities and Society, vol. 63, Dec. 2020, doi: 10.1016/J.SCS.2020.102364.

[75] Introduction to edge computing. doi: 10.1049/PBPC033E_ch1.

[76] Shamsuzzoha, A., Niemi, J., Piya, S. and Rutledge, K. (2021). Smart city for sustainable environment: A comparison of participatory strategies from Helsinki, Singapore and London. Cities, vol. 114, Jul. 2021, doi: 10.1016/J.CITIES.2021.103194.

[77] Chang, F. and Das, D. (2020). Smart nation singapore: developing policies for a citizen-oriented smart city initiative. Developing National Urban Policies, pp. 425–440, doi: 10.1007/978-981-15-3738-7_18.

[78] Veronica CRISTEA, C., Alexandru, D., Suleski, D. and Birsan, A. Management and innovation for competitive advantage.

[79] Mark, R. and Anya, G. (2019). Ethics of using smart city AI and big data: the case of four large European cities. The ORBIT Journal 2(2): 1–36, doi: 10.29297/ORBIT.V2I2.110.

[80] Bibri, S.E. and Krogstie, J. Alfred Getz vei 3, Sentralbygg 1, 5th floor. Technology (Singap World Sci), no. 7491, doi: 10.1186/s42162-020-00108-6.

[81] Menendez, M. and Ambühl, L. (2022). Implementing design and operational measures for sustainable mobility: lessons from Zurich. Sustainability 14(2): 625, Jan. 2022, doi: 10.3390/SU14020625.

[82] Okai, E., Feng, X. and Sant, P. (2019). Smart cities survey. Proceedings - 20th International Conference on High Performance Computing and Communications, 16th International Conference on Smart City and 4th International Conference on Data Science and Systems, HPCC/SmartCity/DSS 2018, pp. 1726–1730, Jan. 2019, doi: 10.1109/HPCC/SMARTCITY/DSS.2018.00282.

[83] Chakraborty, C., Lin, J.C.-W. and Alazab, M. (eds.). (2021). Data-driven mining, learning and analytics for secured smart cities. doi: 10.1007/978-3-030-72139-8.

[84] Bonino, D. et al. (2015). ALMANAC: Internet of things for smart cities. Proceedings - 2015 International Conference on Future Internet of Things and Cloud, FiCloud 2015 and 2015 International Conference on Open and Big Data, OBD 2015, pp. 309–316, Oct. 2015, doi: 10.1109/FICLOUD.2015.32.

[85] Ahmad, A.F., Sayeed, M.S., Tan, C.P., Tan, K.G., Bari, M.A. et al. (2021). A review on IoT with big data analytics. 2021 9th International Conference on Information and Communication Technology, ICoICT 2021, pp. 160–164, Aug. 2021, doi: 10.1109/ICOICT52021.2021.9527503.

[86] Dameri, R.P. (2017). Smart city implementation, doi: 10.1007/978-3-319-45766-6.

[87] Internet Applications Naming and Identifiers in IoT - Security Boulevard. https://securityboulevard.com/2021/12/internet-applications-naming-and-identifiers-in-iot/ (accessed Apr. 23, 2022).

[88] Fog-empowered anomaly detection in IoT using hyperellipsoidal clustering. ieeexplore.ieee.org, Accessed: May 08, 2022. [Online]. Available: https://ieeexplore.ieee.org/abstract/document/7936471/

[89] Kumar, P., Gupta, G.P. and Tripathi, R. (2021). TP2SF: A trustworthy privacy-preserving secured framework for sustainable smart cities by leveraging blockchain and machine learning. Journal of Systems Architecture 115: 101954, May 2021, doi: 10.1016/J.SYSARC.2020.101954.

[90] Algarni, M., Alkhelaiwi, M. and Karrar, A. (2021). Internet of Things security: a review of enabled application challenges and solutions. (IJACSA) International Journal of Advanced Computer Science and Applications 12(3): 2021, Accessed: May 08, 2022. [Online]. Available: www.ijacsa.thesai.org.

[91] Rizvi, S., Kurtz, A., Pfeffer, J. and Rizvi, M. (2018). Securing the Internet of Things (IoT): A security taxonomy for IoT. Proceedings - 17th IEEE International Conference on Trust, Security and Privacy in Computing and Communications and 12th IEEE International Conference on Big Data Science and Engineering, Trustcom/BigDataSE 2018, pp. 163–168, Sep. 2018, doi: 10.1109/TRUSTCOM/BIGDATASE.2018.00034.

[92] Zhang, Y.C. and Yu, J. (2013). A study on the fire IOT development strategy. Procedia Engineering 52: 314–319, Jan. 2013, doi: 10.1016/J.PROENG.2013.02.146.

[93] Peng, S.-L., Pal, S. and Huang, L. (eds.). (2020). Principles of Internet of Things (IoT) ecosystem: insight paradigm. vol. 174, doi: 10.1007/978-3-030-33596-0.

[94] Welch, D. and Lathrop, S. (2003). Wireless security threat taxonomy. IEEE Systems, Man and Cybernetics Society Information Assurance Workshop, pp. 76–83, doi: 10.1109/SMCSIA.2003.1232404.

[95] Maheswaran, M. and Badidi, E. (2018). Handbook of smart cities: Software services and cyber infrastructure. Handbook of Smart Cities: Software Services and Cyber Infrastructure, pp. 1–406, Nov. 2018, doi: 10.1007/978-3-319-97271-8.

[96] Dua, A., Kumar, N., Singh, M., Obaidat, M.S., Hsiao, K.F. et al. (2016). Secure message communication among vehicles using elliptic curve cryptography in smart cities. IEEE CITS 2016 - 2016 International Conference on Computer, Information and Telecommunication Systems, Aug. 2016, doi: 10.1109/CITS.2016.7546385.

[97] Cekerevac, Z., Dvorak, Z., Prigoda, L. and Cekerevac, P. (2017). MEST Journal Internet of Things and The Man-In-The-Middle Attacks-Security and Economic Risks. doi: 10.12709/mest.05.05.02.03.

[98] Gupta, B.B., Perez, G.M., Agrawal, D.P. and Gupta, D. (2019). Handbook of computer networks and cyber security: Principles and paradigms. Handbook of Computer Networks and Cyber Security: Principles and Paradigms, pp. 1–959, Jan. 2019, doi: 10.1007/978-3-030-22277-2.

[99] Whalen, S., Engle, S. and Romeo, D. (2001). An Introduction To ARP Spoofing. Accessed: Apr. 24, 2022. [Online]. Available: http://securityportal.com.

[100] Chen, K. et al. (2018). Internet-of-Things Security and Vulnerabilities: Taxonomy, Challenges, and Practice. Journal of Hardware and Systems Security 2(2): 97–110, Jun. 2018, doi: 10.1007/S41635-017-0029-7.

[101] Swamy, S.N. and Kota, S.R. (2020). An empirical study on system level aspects of Internet of Things (IoT). IEEE Access 8: 188082–188134, doi: 10.1109/ACCESS.2020.3029847.

[102] Badhib, A., Alshehri, S. and Cherif, A. (2021). A robust device-to-device continuous authentication protocol for the Internet of Things. IEEE Access 9: 124768–124792, doi: 10.1109/ACCESS.2021.3110707.

[103] Igure, V.M., Laughter, S.A. and Williams, R.D. (2006). Security issues in SCADA networks. Computers and Security 25(7): 498–506, Oct. 2006, doi: 10.1016/J. COSE.2006.03.001.

[104] Moin, S., Karim, A., Safdar, Z., Safdar, K., Ahmed, E. et al. (2019). Securing IoTs in distributed blockchain: Analysis, requirements and open issues. Future Generation Computer Systems 100: 325–343, Nov. 2019, doi: 10.1016/J.FUTURE.2019.05.023.

[105] Murtala Zungeru, A., Chuma, J.M., Lebekwe, C.K., Phalaagae, P., Gaboitaolelwe, J. et al. (2020). Green Internet of Things sensor networks. Green Internet of Things Sensor Networks, doi: 10.1007/978-3-030-54983-1.

[106] Ghosh, J., Chakrabarty, S.P. and Mukherjee, S. (2021). Data-driven mining, learning and analytics for secured smart cities. doi: 10.1007/978-3-030-72139-8_14.

[107] Caprolu, M., di Pietro, R., Lombardi, F. and Raponi, S. (2019). Edge computing perspectives: architectures, technologies, and open security issues. Proceedings - 2019 IEEE International Conference on Edge Computing, EDGE 2019 - Part of the 2019 IEEE World Congress on Services, pp. 116–123, Jul. 2019, doi: 10.1109/EDGE.2019.00035.

[108] Jr., S.O. (2006). How secure is RFID? Computer (Long Beach Calif) 39(07): 17–19, Jul. 2006, doi: 10.1109/MC.2006.232.

[109] Katagi, M. and Moriai, S. (2022). Lightweight Cryptography for the Internet of Things. Accessed: Apr. 27, 2022. [Online]. Available: http://www.ecrypt.eu.org/stream/.

[110] Azad, M.A., Bag, S., Hao, F. and Shalaginov, A. (2020). Decentralized self-enforcing trust management system for social Internet of Things. IEEE Internet of Things Journal 7(4): 2690–2703, Apr. 2020, doi: 10.1109/JIOT.2019.2962282.

[111] Dhanda, S.S., Singh, B. and Jindal, P. (2020). Lightweight cryptography: a solution to secure IoT. Wireless Personal Communications 112(3): 1947–1980, Jun. 2020, doi: 10.1007/S11277-020-07134-3.

[112] Su, J., Danilo Vasconcellos, V., Prasad, S., Daniele, S., Feng, Y. et al. (2018). Lightweight classification of IoT malware based on image recognition. Proceedings - International Computer Software and Applications Conference 2: 664–669, Jun. 2018, doi: 10.1109/ COMPSAC.2018.10315.

[113] Su, S., Chen, Y., Tsai, S., Y. L.-S. and Communication, and undefined. (2018). Detecting p2p botnet in software defined networks. hindawi.com, Accessed: May 08, 2022. [Online]. Available: https://www.hindawi.com/journals/scn/2018/4723862/.

[114] Chaudhari, N. and Srivastava, S. (2017). Big data security issues and challenges. Proceeding - IEEE International Conference on Computing, Communication and Automation, ICCCA 2016, pp. 60–64, Jan. 2017, doi: 10.1109/CCAA.2016.7813690.

[115] Hussain, F., Hussain, R., Hassan, S.A. and Hossain, E. (2020). Machine learning in IoT security: current solutions and future challenges. IEEE Communications Surveys and Tutorials, vol. 22, no. 3, pp. 1686–1721, Jul. 2020, doi: 10.1109/COMST.2020.2986444.

[116] Al-Garadi, M.A., Mohamed, A., Al-Ali, A.K., Du, X., Ali, I. et al. (2020). A survey of machine and deep learning methods for Internet of Things (IoT) security. IEEE Communications Surveys and Tutorials 22(3): 1646–1685, Jul. 2020, doi: 10.1109/COMST.2020.2988293.

[117] Yang, X., Shu, L., Liu, Y., Hancke, G.P., Ferrag, M.A. et al. (2022). Physical security and safety of IoT equipment: a survey of recent advances and opportunities. IEEE Transactions on Industrial Informatics, doi: 10.1109/TII.2022.3141408.

[118] Yadav, Anuj and Madan Lal Garg Ritika. (2019). Monitoring based security approach for cloud computing. Journal homepage: http://iieta.org/journals/isi, 24(6): 611–617.

[119] Khan, M.A. and Salah, K. (2018). IoT security: Review, blockchain solutions, and open challenges. Future Generation Computer Systems 82: 395–411, May 2018, doi: 10.1016/J.FUTURE.2017.11.022.

[120] Srivastava, R., Tomar, R., Gupta, M., Yadav, A.K., Park, J. et al. (2021). Image watermarking approach using a hybrid domain based on performance parameter analysis. Information 12(8): 31.

[121] Bhuyan, B.P., Tomar, R., Gupta, M. and Ramdane-Cherif, A. (2021). An ontological knowledge representation for smart agriculture. 2021 IEEE International Conference on Big Data (Big Data), pp. 3400–3406, doi: 10.1109/BigData52589.2021.9672020.

[122] Yadav, A.K. and Ritika, M.G. (2021). Cryptographic solution for security problem in cloud computing storage during global pandemics. International Journal of Safety and Security Engineering, pp. 193–199.

[123] Gupta, Maanak, James Benson, Farhan Patwa and Ravi Sandhu. (2019). Dynamic groups and attribute-based access control for next-generation smart cars. In Proceedings of the Ninth ACM Conference on Data and Application Security and Privacy, pp. 61–72.

[124] Gupta, Maanak and Ravi Sandhu. (2021). Towards activity-centric access control for smart collaborative ecosystems. In Proceedings of the 26th ACM Symposium on Access Control Models and Technologies, pp. 155–164.

Chapter 5

Knowledge Representation to Expound Deep Learning Black Box

Bikram Pratim Bhuyan,[1,*] *Ravi Tomar*[2] and *Vivudh Fore*[3]

◇◇◇

Deep Learning techniques are evolving and implemented in various fields of study. Traditionally, in classification, input data is subjected to the training model and performance measures like accuracy, precision and recall are obtained. Exploration on the reasoning behind the model performance falls under the domain of explainable artificial intelligence. Why can the model classify some items correctly and not the others? Questions like these are categorized under explainable-AI (XAI).

Objects and attributes construct the relational data and its structure validates the dependency between the attributes. In this paper we provide an exploratory context behind the performance measure on the outputs generated. Formal concept analysis, which belongs to the class of knowledge representation and reasoning is used for this purpose. The chapter tries to collect data as a relational model and then provides mathematical and formal definitions to construct tuples of objects and their corresponding attributes with a closure property to strengthen the bond. As an explosion of the number of tuples (concepts) can take place, a measure of stability index is introduced to collect concepts bearing a high

---

[1] Department of Informatics, School of Computer Science, University of Petroleum and Energy Studies, Dehradun.

[2] Senior Architect, Persistent Systems, India.

[3] Department of Informatics, School of Computer Science, Gurukul Kangri University, Haridwar.
Email: ravitomar7@gmail.com

* Corresponding author: bikram23bhuyan@gmail.com

importance measure. A meet semi-lattice is generated from the tuples and implication rules are spawned from it. The focus point of the formal study is to analyze the classification, based on the meet semi lattice formed. The outcome is thus elucidated with a sound theoretical base. Other exploratory approaches for model predictions like LIME and SHAP are also delineated in details. A data set on diabetics is implemented and formal lattice based explanations are forwarded for the sake of completeness.

1. Introduction

Increasingly, we are relying on AI-based systems for decision making and prediction, from image and facial recognition systems to machine learning-powered predictive analytics, conversational applications, and hyper-personalized systems. In a wide range of areas, such as education, construction, health care, manufacturing, law enforcement and finance, artificial intelligence is making inroads. Humans no longer comprehend the intricate mechanics through which AI systems function or how they make certain judgments, which is especially problematic when AI-based systems produce unexpected or unforeseen results.

Decisions and forecasts produced by AI-enabled systems are getting more complex and, in some circumstances, a matter of life-or-death. In particular, this is true for AI systems employed in healthcare, autonomous automobiles, and even war-fighting drones. Although AI and machine learning systems are used in a variety of industries, most of us have limited visibility into how AI systems make choices or how the outcomes of AI and machine learning are implemented. Several machine learning algorithms cannot be evaluated to determine exactly how and why a decision was reached. Particularly opaque decision-making systems, such as those based on deep neural networks (DNNs) called sophisticated black-box models, are at a risk of being exposed.

A lack of transparency, understandability, and explainability of AI products/outputs might impede AI acceptance (and potentially its further development) because humans are unable to look inside black boxes (such as predictions, decisions, actions, and recommendations). Humans must be able to comprehend and, therefore, trust AI-based systems [1] if they are to benefit from them. To trust AI systems, people must be able to completely comprehend how choices are made. Because AI systems are difficult to understand and trust, we cannot rely on them. It is important that computer systems perform as expected and that their judgments be transparently explained and justified. Explainable AI (XAI) is the term used to describe this type of technology. Why and how an AI system arrives at a given choice may be accurately explained by XAI methodologies and approaches, allowing humans to understand the AI solution's outcomes [2].

2. Importance of Explainability

Artificial Intelligence (AI) technology has made great strides from its start in the middle of the 20th century. As of today, companies throughout the world are adopting what was previously the domain of science fiction and academic discussion. Application areas for artificial intelligence (AI) include medication research and patient data analysis [3] as well as fraud detection [4] and consumer engagement [5]. The technology's potential is undeniable, and firms that want to stay competitive are using it more and more.

Explicable AI is the capability of algorithmic thinking and decision-making processes to be explained. XAI could even give a hint as to how algorithms will act in the future if it is implemented correctly. Discussing corporate governance and regulation brings to light this new potential, which has a number of legal, social and ethical ramifications for companies. To ensure accuracy, decision-makers should use predictive models so that the choice consequences can be monitored and regulated.

The AI's reasoning must also be sound, and its duties must be completed safely and in conformity with laws and regulations, in addition to being sound. The insurance, banking, and healthcare industries are among the most tightly regulated. It is important for people to be able to comprehend why and how an occurrence occurs.

Accounting and auditability, which will remain the responsibility of an organization's people rather than its technologies, will also benefit from AI that is easily explained. To detect incorrect outcomes caused by problems such as prejudiced or inadequately adjusted training data and other concerns, AI that can be explained is vital. If one realizes how an AI system got into trouble, we can go back and correct the problem and prevent it from happening again in the future. Explicable AI is ultimately about making AI more beneficial in commercial contexts and in our daily lives—while also preventing unwanted results. Regulatory industries like healthcare and finance will need to be able to demonstrate how an AI system arrived at a decision or conclusion. But even in businesses where AI auditing isn't required for regulatory compliance, the trust and openness that explainable AI fosters are well worth the effort. As a bonus, they're also a smart business move.

Enterprise executives want to explore alternate options and examine the economic effects of their technology investments, but harnessing AI models to accomplish this objective is fraught with uncertainty. XAI is the next critical step in the growth of increasingly complex applications. AI models may be incorporated into current business processes to improve outcomes. AI models will eventually replace traditional advanced analytics processes and become adaptive as corporations continue to grow, provided that they can be managed and directed by human involvement. This shift will be facilitated by XAI's services.

3. Explainability in Machine Learning

An obvious trade-off exists between an algorithm's efficiency as well as its capacity to provide explainable, comprehensible forecasts. Black-box models incorporate assemblage with higher level modelling on deep learning methodology on the one hand. However, white-box or "glass box" models, which give readily excusable outcomes (such as linear and decision tree-based models), are also widely used in the industry. Whilst the later models are more explainable and understandable, they are not as robust as the former, and thus do not perform as well as the former. Because of their economic design, efficiency and performance deficiency and their capacity interpretation and explainability are to be projected reliably. Especially in fields such as healthcare or self-driving vehicles, where moral and justice concerns have inevitably emerged, it is difficult to trust systems whose choices cannot be well-interpreted. Because of this, the area of explainable Artificial Intelligence has seen a resurgence.

For years, the scientific community has ignored the area of XAI, which focuses on the behavior mechanism of interpretation and understandability. Despite their close relationship, academics often use the words interpretability and explainability interchangeably. Interpretability and explainability do not have a specific mathematical definition, nor have they been quantified by some metric. A commendable work is put forward in [6] which concentrates on that fact that when it pertains to interpretability, the work offered the following ground classification: functionality, biological and application oriented. Next, he evaluates the various trade-offs between them. Miller in his work [7] defines interpretability as "The degree to which a person can grasp the reason for a choice," he says. These concepts are obvious, yet they require mathematical clarity and consistency. Basically, the causal effect to compute the correlation between input and output is far comprehensible when the interpretability of a machine learning system is increased [8]. Machine learning systems have underlying logic and dynamics that make them explainable, on the other hand. As a result, people get a greater grasp of the underlying processes that occur while the peculiar concept of model training and choice selection is involved. Having an interpretable model doesn't always mean that people can decipher its inherent logic or process. The converse is also true when it comes to machine learning.

As the name implies, application-based assessment is concerned with how a particular task or application is affected by the outcomes of the interpretation process. Interpretability methods may be evaluated to see whether they improve error detection or reduce discrimination, for example. There are two main differences between human-centered evaluation and application-centered evaluation. The first is that the tester does not have the hard requirement to be an expert in her/his own domain while remaining to be a simple guy with regular knowledge. Classification of models based on the requirement interpretability via human-centered or application-centered trials and formal parameters may be used to rate the quality of the self-adaptive models. Evaluating the technique in terms of its usefulness is also suitable when human trials cannot be conducted for ethical reasons, or when the suggested method has not yet matured sufficiently to be assessed by human users. While this may be true, it is still difficult to choose the proper measuring criteria and metrics for each situation.

Today's AI algorithms are developed with trillions of instances, which allow them to see patterns and relationships that humans, who can only learn with a limited number of examples, may not be able to see. To get fresh insights from explainable AI systems, we can try to extract the system's condensed wisdom.

In [9], it is suggested that random forests (RF) be approximated with simpler models. In order to distil a model's intrinsic logic, users are just required to indicate how many rules the new mix of models should have. It then approximates the original model by employing just the number of rules that the user has chosen to include in the mixture. In [10], the article cites information gain-based heuristics to build a tree that is compact enough to be interpretable. In [11], the authors developed a mechanism for extracting the more representative rules that an RF has gained. That's the major contribution of the study. Since a result of this, the number of rules in RFs is substantially decreased, as only the most important ones are selected. It's the same in this instance, except that rules are retrieved straight from the RF instead of learning them via a new model. It is also possible to mix the acquired rules and construct a new rule based classifier. When analyzing a training data set, the authors in [12] look for items based on the class specification. Because of its adaptive nature, this approach offers some assurances as to how well-chosen examples will be. The user chooses the algorithm (Deep learning) to focus on the input data items or instances to formulate from the collective cluster examples in totality.

4. Explainability in Deep Learning

According to explainable machine learning principles, a system must create knowledge that enables a user to correlate input qualities with its output, and vice versa. It's important to remember that deep learning approaches aren't "explainable." DNN parameters connected with input features are entangled and compressed via a non-linear transformation of a weighted sum of feature values. Relative to the amount of activations in the first hidden layer, this compression occurs numerous times with varying weight vectors. In the following layers, non-linear transforms of weighted sums of these compressions are produced. As a result, it is extremely difficult to determine which stimulus qualities are responsible for this decision-making process. Neural networks (NN) are cognitive processes that are extremely expressive and achieve state of the art performance in a wide variety of applications Due to a computationally demanding architecture, their design and learning regimes do not fulfil any degree of transparency at least when we move beyond basic models, including such single layer perceptrons, as previously noted. Thus, NN-specific XAI techniques have been developed, which make use of the NN's unique topology. Almost all these approaches come under either model streamlining or feature relevancy.

Rule generation and exploration projects on simplification of models, project themselves as one of the most used techniques. Decompositional rule extraction [13] approaches are those that extract rules at the neuronal level rather than the entire model. To portray the derived rules, CRED [14] makes use of decision trees. Extending CRED [15], is one of the most prominent approaches of this type. There are more decision trees and intermediary rules in the algorithm. This way, each layer is described based on the preceding one, and the findings are then summed up to explain the entire network [16].

Whereas techniques that do not take into consideration a NN's internal structure are considered "pedagogical." To put it another way, methods that consider the entire network as a black-box function and do not analyze it at a neuron-level to explain it. In [17] the authors discuss an algorithm which is a decision tree-based technique that also includes a query-and-sample technique.

As the size in terms of layers in a NN increases, it becomes increasingly challenging to create methods for model simplification. In recent years, feature relevance methods have become increasingly prominent. NNs can be used to estimate neuron-wise signals, according to the authors' study in [18]. Researchers have developed a method for superimposing neuron-specific explanations in order to create more broad ones.

There is also a common technique called Integrated Gradients [19]. When travelling along a line that connects an instance to another instance connectivity is exploited with (acting as a "neutral" instance), the examined model's behavior. Aside from that, this technique has several excellent theoretical features, such as completeness and symmetry preservation, which give guarantees regarding the provided explanations.

4.1 LIME

Lime helps shine light on a learning model and makes your forecasts personally understandable. Lime (Local Interpretable Model-Agnostic Explanations) [20]. The approach describes the classifier for a single instance and is hence confined to investigate. LIME handles the incoming data to simplify the task and produces fake data that only includes a portion of the actual properties. For example, in the case of text data multiple text versions are generated which delete a specified amount of distinct, randomly picked words. These new fake datasets are subsequently allocated to several groups (classified). Therefore, we can detect their impact on the classification of the selected text by the presence or absence of particular keywords.

For example, the interpretable models at LIME can be linear regression or decision trees that are trained to produce a proper local approach to tiny disturbances (e.g., adding noise, deleting words, concealing picture portions).

The assumption behind the operation of LIME is that each complicated model is locally linear. LIME seeks to fit a basic model around a single observation that reflects the behavior of the global model there. The basic model can then be used to explain locally the forecasts of the more sophisticated model.

To put it in steps, LIME does the following:

a) To explain the finding, disrupt 'n' times to produce duplicated functional data with small value changes. This disturbed data is a false dataset produced to develop the local linear model using LIME around the observation.

b) The result of the disturbed data is predicted.

c) Distance to the original observation from each disturbed data point is computed.

d) A similarity metric is generated for the inverse of the distance found.

e) 'k' dimensions representing the data in a perfect form are selected.

f) For the 'k' dimensions selected, a simpler model is fitted to the disturbed data.

g) The simpler model is now used for explanations of different findings observing the weights of the dimensions.

For a deeper understanding of the model, let us try to analyze the diabetic dataset imported from https://www.kaggle.com/uciml/pima-indians-diabetes-database. Figure 1 depicts the dimensions (properties) of the dataset bearing 9 classes. The 'Outcome' variable is taken as the target class for classification.

	Pregnancies	Glucose	BloodPressure	SkinThickness	Insulin	BMI	DiabetesPedigreeFunction	Age	Outcome
0	6	148	72	35	0	33.6	0.627	50	1
1	1	85	66	29	0	26.6	0.351	31	0
2	8	183	64	0	0	23.3	0.672	32	1
3	1	89	66	23	94	28.1	0.167	21	0
4	0	137	40	35	168	43.1	2.288	33	1

Fig. 1. A look on the diabetes data-set.

Table 1. Accuracy results.

Model	Accuracy
Random Forest Classifier	76%
Multi-Layered Perceptron	70%

Two of the most popular black box models-Random Forest Classifier and Multi-Layered Perceptron models are selected for analysis.

The results are shown in Table 1. Adam solver is used for the Multilayer perceptron model with 10 hidden layers to produce the result.

Now, we analyze the inputs using the LIME algorithm. The training data is feed to the LIME algorithm.

Figure 2 shows the outcome of a candidate with the Feature-value set shown on its right side and the probability dimension to its left. The data is most likely (with a probability of 0.79) to be predicted as having no diabetes against the probability of 0.21 supporting it; because of the feature (dimension) properties that LIME was able to decode as: Blood Pressure > 72 with a weight of and Glucose > 100 with a weight of 0.04. Because of these prime properties (shown in blue in the left portion of the figure) it has such a high probability of being classified as 0 instead of 1 which is supported by Insulin <= 0.00 and Skin Thickness > 23.00 (denoted in yellow).

Let us also analyze the properties for a sample with a high probability of Outcome = 1 as shown in Figure 3.

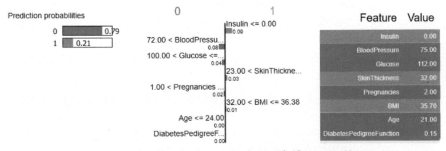

Fig. 2. LIME results for a train data with 'Outcome: 0'.

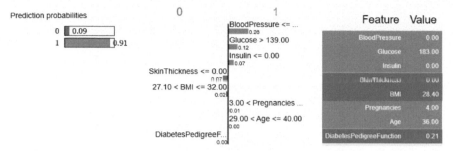

Fig. 3. LIME results for a train data with 'Outcome: 1'.

It is seen that with a high probability (0.91) the data is to be predicted as '1' because of some unique characteristics shown in the right hand side of the figure with the weights shown in the middle part. Hence a proper analysis of the input data will play a role in the generated black box. We now take a look on the SHAP algorithm for the same.

4.2 SHAP

SHAP is a theoretical way to describe the output of any machine learning model, or SHapley Additive exPlanations. The optimum credit distribution is connected to local explanations utilizing the classical Shapley game theory values and associated expansions. The value of Shapley [21] is the average marginal feature value contribution over all feasible coalitions. When 'K' dimensions or features are available, different order combinations of Shapley values [22] from K! are calculated, thereby making it a NP-hard model issue [23]. The Shap library saves us all the details and completes the calculation quite quickly. It is convenient and trustworthy since results based on a sound theory are computed in comparison with other approaches.

Figure 4 depicts the feature importance depicted from the model generated from the Random Forest classifier which will be used for understanding the role of the features again when we analyze the data using SHAP.

The impact fullness of a dimension is analyzed in Figure 5 on the binary detection of diabetes denoted by '0' and '1'. So we can view the plot when you have generated characteristics that distinguish a certain class from the rest. In other words, the binary classification synopsis may show you how the computer has learned from its characteristics.

In order to understand the dimensions in higher detail, the SHAP value was plotted as a summary as shown in Figure 6. Each point as a value depicts the Shapley value for a dimension corresponding to a data instance. The y-axis location is controlled by the characteristic and the Shapley value on the x-axis. Analyzing the figure, we notice that 'Blood

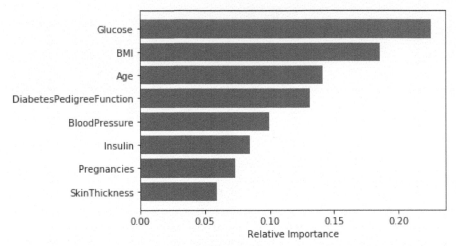

Fig. 4. Feature importance.

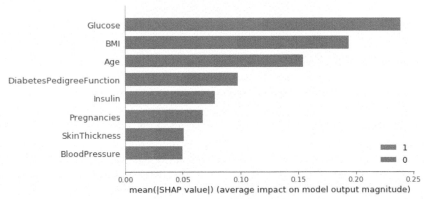

Fig. 5. Feature importance by SHAP.

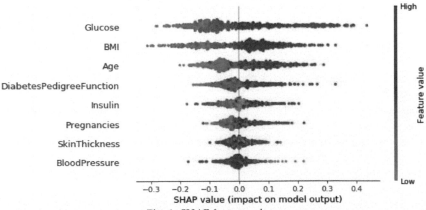

Fig. 6. SHAP feature values.

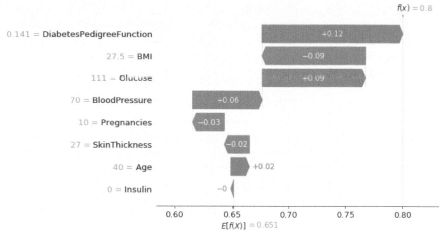

Fig. 7. Waterfall plot.

Pressure' is the least important feature comprising of the minimum Shapley value as the color changes from blue to red with increasing Shapley values. The coinciding points are moved in the direction of the y-axis, such that the Shapley values are distributed according to the feature. The characteristics are sorted by their significance. In the short plot, the link between a feature's value and its forecast is indicated first.

Figure 7 represents a waterfall plot for the prediction of a single data item. For the data item the prediction value is given by the function $f(x)$ and the expected value which denoted by $E[f(x)]$ represents the base value. $f(x) = 0.8$ and $E[f(x)] = 0.651$. The value of the characteristics and the contribution to the forecast are on the arrows to the left. Each line indicates how the positive (red) or negative (blue) contribution of each feature transfers the value from the predicted model output to the model output for this prediction across the background dataset.

Now, after a preview of the results based upon the traditional algorithms, we now propose a knowledge representation technique for the requirement.

5. Knowledge Based Explainable AI

We begin off the knowledge based explainable AI technique by preprocessing the input data as a binary context with 'i' representing the presence of an attribute for the data item and 'n' depicting otherwise. The context (input data) so collected is then subjected to some mathematical subjugation in order to form some closed set relations. The tuples are then collected in turn form the basis of the lattice creation which is in fact a meet semi-lattice. The lattice formed can be used for various analyses subjectable to attribute relationships, clustering and classification which are some examples of various machine learning methodologies. The matter in which the lattice creates such information and the way it is represented in an easy to use way makes it suitable for knowledge representation and reasoning. The terminology put forward to such an ontology is Formal Concept Analysis [24, 28, 29].

In order to formally define a concept, we first define a context as (X, Y, Z) where X represents the set of items or objects; Y denotes the set of attributes or dimensions or variables and $Z \subseteq X \times Y$; which means that the Z is the subset of the $X \times Y$ relation with the presence of 'i'. In yet another notation, we can use $(x, y) \in Z$ stating the possessing property of 'y' by the data item 'x'. Also Galois operations which form a perfect closed set defined under the $(.)^\Omega$ operator is defined such that:

$$K^\Omega = \{y \in Y \mid \forall x \in L \text{ such that } i \subseteq X \times Y\} \quad (1)$$

which states the set $K \subseteq X$ has some common properties $y \subseteq Y$.

Also,

$$L^\Omega = \{x \in X \mid \forall y \in K \text{ such that } i \subseteq X \times Y\} \quad (2)$$

which states the set $L \subseteq Y$ has some common data items $x \subseteq X$.

Now for a properly closed set we should have:

$$K^{\Omega\Omega} = K \quad (3)$$

$$L^{\Omega\Omega} = L \quad (4)$$

The equations set a closure operation as the common data items with the corresponding properties or attributes are grouped together to form a tuple (K, L) where $K \subseteq X$, $L \subseteq Y$, $K^\Omega = L$ and $L^\Omega = K$.

The tuple (K, L) is defined as a one formed from the input data context (X, Y, Z). Now there could be exponential count of the number of tuples (K_n, L_n) [26, 30, 31]. Hence the need of the most important concept structures defined in [25]. Now, the concepts form a meet semi lattice with a partial ordered relation $\models$; this type of ordering creates a super and sub-concept hierarchy in accordance to the lattice. Let us explain the definitions with the help of an example.

Table 2 is an example of a context taken as an example for analysis. Using Equations 1–4, we form a set of concepts defined in Table 3.

As seen in Table 3, we have computed a set of 9 tuples which are closely operated using the Galois operator defined. Now, using the poset (partial ordered relation) $\models$, we further develop a meet semi lattice as shown in Figure 8.

Trending into further analysis, implication rules are generated from the lattice such as C -> B where C, $B \subseteq Y$ and $C^\Omega \subseteq B^\Omega$. In order to reflect

Table 2. Toy context.

	K_1	K_2	K_3	K_4	K_5
L_1	i	n	i	n	i
L_2	n	i	n	n	n
L_3	i	n	n	i	n
L_4	n	i	n	n	n
L_5	n	n	i	n	i
L_6	i	n	n	n	n
L_7	n	i	n	n	i

Table 3. Concept table.

# Tuple (K$_n$, L$_n$)	Data item	Property or attribute
(K$_1$, L$_1$)	Φ	{ K_1, K_2, K_3, K_4, K_5 }
(K$_2$, L$_2$)	{ L_1 }	{ K_1, K_3, K_5 }
(K$_3$, L$_3$)	{ L_7 }	{ K_2, K_5 }
(K$_4$, L$_4$)	{ L_1, L_3, L_6 }	{ K_1 }
(K$_5$, L$_5$)	{ L_2, L_4, L_7 }	{ K_2 }
(K$_6$, L$_6$)	{ L_1, L_5, L_7 }	{ K_5 }
(K$_7$, L$_7$)	{ L_1, L_5 }	{ K_3, K_5 }
(K$_8$, L$_8$)	{ L_3 }	{ K_1, K_4 }
(K$_9$, L$_9$)	{ L_1, L_2, L_3, L_4, L_5, L_6, L_7 }	Φ

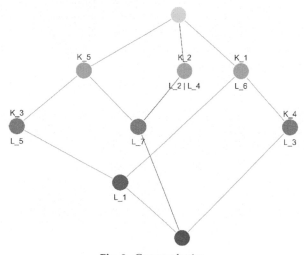

Fig. 8. Concept lattice.

the underlying knowledge of the relationship, such implications play a vital role between characteristics and contain support and confidence like easily computed statistical values.

6. Implementation and Results

We then implemented the above definitions using the diabetic dataset. For classification, the binary target class 'Outcome', i.e., Outcome = 0 and Outcome = 1 are segregated for the training data and concepts are created for each of them individually. After the concept creation process, a unique lattice is generated for both the classes.

Now, for each data item present in the test data, concepts are generated. The tuple thus formed with the property set is compared with that of the already generated lattices. The similarity index [25] thus formed is computed using a simple tree pattern based subset matching in linear time [27] with the highest similarity index classified under the lattice with the required 'Outcome'.

This methodology has resulted in 79% accuracy which is far better than that found in Table 1. The rules generated can be used for further analysis.

7. Conclusion

The general black box techniques of machine learning for data analysis are being studied along with the importance of Explainable AI. Two major algorithms LIME and SHAP were implemented along the lines of Random Forest classifier and Multi-Layered Perceptron. Finally, a knowledge based representation using ontology was defined and implemented which generated rules for analysis of the algorithm. The results of the comparative analysis look promising. For future studies, multi class classification can be taken into account and rules could be further studied along with the support and confidence to generate rare association mining and a better understanding of the black box model usually used.

References

[1] Mujumdar, A., Cyras K., Singh S. and Vulgarakis, A. (2020). Trustworthy AI: explainability, safety and verifiability.

[2] Barredo Arrieta, A., Diaz Rodriguez, N., Del Ser, J., Bennetot, A., Tabik, S. et al. (2020). Explainable Artificial Intelligence (XAI): Concepts, taxonomies, opportunities and challenges toward responsible AI. Information Fusion 58: 82–115.

[3] Hamet, P. and Tremblay, J. (2017). Artificial intelligence in medicine. Metabolism 2017 Apr 1; 69: S36–40.

[4] Bolton, R.J. and Hand, D.J. (2002). Statistical fraud detection: A review. Statistical Science 2002 Aug; 17(3): 235–55.

[5] Moriuchi, E. (2019). Okay, Google!: An empirical study on voice assistants on consumer engagement and loyalty. Psychology & Marketing 2019 May; 36(5): 489–501.

[6] Doshi-Velez, F. and Kim, B. (2017). Towards a rigorous science of interpretable machine learning. arXiv preprint arXiv:1702.08608. 2017 Feb 28.

[7] Miller, T. (2019). Explanation in artificial intelligence: Insights from the social sciences. Artif. Intell. 267: 1–38.

[8] Adadi, A. and Berrada, M. (2018). Peeking inside the black-box: A survey on Explainable Artificial Intelligence (XAI). IEEE Access 6: 52138–52160.

[9] Hara, S. and Hayashi, K. (2016). Making tree ensembles interpretable. arXiv preprint arXiv:1606.05390.

[10] Van Assche, A. and Blockeel, H. (2007). Seeing the forest through the trees: learning a comprehensible model from an ensemble. pp. 418–429. In: Kok, J.N., Koronacki, J., Mantaras, R.L.d., Matwin, S., Mladenič, D. and Skowron, A. (eds.). Machine Learning: ECML 2007 (Berlin, Heidelberg: Springer Berlin Heidelberg), doi:10.1007/978-3-540-74958-5_39.

[11] Deng, H. (2014). Interpreting Tree Ensembles with Intrees. arXiv:1408.5456.

[12] Tan, H.F., Hooker, G. and Wells, M.T. (2016). Tree Space Prototypes: Another Look at Making Tree Ensembles Interpretable. New Orleans, LA: ArXiv, abs/1611.07115.

[13] Özbakundefinedr, L., Baykasoundefinedlu, A. and Kulluk, S. (2010). A soft computing-based approach for integrated training and rule extraction from artificial neural networks: Difaconn-Miner. Appl. Soft Comput. 10(1): 304–317. doi:10.1016/j.asoc.2009.08.008.

[14] Sato, M. and Tsukimoto, H. (2001). Rule extraction from neural networks via decision tree induction. IJCNN'01. International Joint Conference On Neural Networks. Proceedings (Cat. No.01CH37222), Washington, DC, July 2001. 3: 1870–1875.

[15] Zilke, J.R., Loza Mencía, E. and Janssen, F. (2016). DeepRED - Rule Extraction from Deep Neural Networks. Discovery Science. Manhattan, NY: Springer International Publishing, 457–473. doi:10.1007/978-3-319-46307-0_29.

[16] Sato, M. and Tsukimoto, H. (2001). Rule extraction from neural networks via decision tree induction. IJCNN'01. International Joint Conference On Neural Networks. Proceedings (Cat. No.01CH37222), Washington, DC, July 2001. 3: 1870–1875.

[17] Craven, M.W. and Shavlik, J.W. (1994). Using sampling and queries to extract rules from trained neural networks. pp. 37–45. In: Cohen, W.W. and Hirsh, H. (eds.). Machine Learning Proceedings. (San Francisco (CA): Morgan Kaufmann), doi:10.1016/b978-1-55860-335-6.50013-1.

[18] Kindermans, P.-J., Schütt, K.T., Alber, M., Müller, K.-R., Erhan et al. (2017). Learning How to explain neural networks: Patternnet and Patternattribution. Vancouver, Canada: International Society of the Learning Sciences.

[19] Sundararajan, M., Taly, A. and Yan, Q. (2017). Axiomatic attribution for deep networks. pp. 3319–3328. In: Proceedings of the 34th International Conference on Machine Learning-, Sydney, NSW, August 2017. Volume 70, JMLR.org.ICML'17.

[20] Ribeiro, M.T., Singh, S. and Guestrin, C. (2016). Why should i trust you? Explaining the predictions of any classifier. pp. 1135–1144. In: Proceedings of the 22nd ACM SIGKDD International Conference on Knowledge Discovery and Data Mining 2016 Aug 13.

[21] Lundberg, S.M., Erion, G., Chen, H., DeGrave, A., Prutkin, J.M., Nair, B., Katz, R., Himmelfarb, J., Bansal, N. and Lee, S.I. (2020). From local explanations to global understanding with explainable AI for trees. Nature Machine Intelligence. 2020 Jan; 2(1): 56–67.

[22] Winter, E. (2002). The shapley value. Handbook of game theory with economic applications. 2002 Jan 1; 3: 2025–54.

[23] Deng, X. and Papadimitriou, C.H. (1994). On the complexity of cooperative solution concepts. Mathematics of Operations Research 1994 May; 19(2): 257–66.

[24] Ganter, B. and Wille, R. (2012). Formal Concept Analysis: Mathematical Foundations. Springer Science & Business Media; 2012 Dec 6.

[25] Bhuyan, B.P. (2017). Relative similarity and stability in FCA pattern structures using game theory. pp. 207–212. *In*: 2017 2nd International Conference on Communication Systems, Computing and IT Applications (CSCITA) 2017 Apr 7. IEEE.

[26] Bhuyan, B.P., Karmakar, A. and Hazarika, S.M. (2018). Bounding stability in formal concept analysis. pp. 545–552. *In*: Advanced Computational and Communication Paradigms 2018. Springer, Singapore.

[27] Cole, R. and Hariharan, R. (2003). Tree pattern matching to subset matching in linear time. SIAM Journal on Computing 32(4): 1056–66.

[28] Bhuyan, B.P., Tomar, R., Gupta, M. and Ramdane-Cherif, A. (2021). An ontological knowledge representation for smart agriculture. pp. 3400–3406. *In*: 2021 IEEE International Conference on Big Data (Big Data) 2021 Dec 15. IEEE.

[29] Bhuyan, B.P., Um, J.S., Singh, T.P. and Choudhury, T. (2022). Decision intelligence analytics: making decisions through data pattern and segmented analytics. pp. 99–107. *In*: Decision Intelligence Analytics and the Implementation of Strategic Business Management 2022. Springer, Cham.

[30] Kimmell, Jeffrey C., Mahmoud Abdelsalam and Maanak Gupta. (2021). Analyzing machine learning approaches for online malware detection in cloud. pp. 189–196. *In*: 2021 IEEE International Conference on Smart Computing (SMARTCOMP), IEEE, 2021.

[31] McDole, Andrew, Maanak Gupta, Mahmoud Abdelsalam, Sudip Mittal and Mamoun Alazab. (2021). Deep learning techniques for behavioral malware analysis in cloud iaas. pp. 269–285. *In*: Malware Analysis Using Artificial Intelligence and Deep Learning, Springer, Cham, 2021.

Chapter 6
Heart Disease Prediction Based on Various Machine Learning Techniques

Bharti Mahara, Chayal, Bhawnesh Kumar* and
Harendra Singh Negi

∞∞

Heart related diseases affect a great many individuals and, in this day, and age they are leading causes of death. It is vital to research the matter; Artificial Intelligence and Machine Learning are very close to playing a very fundamental part for the prediction of such diseases. Extracting the data and handling it wisely is one of them. This paper attempts to anticipate coronary illnesses investigating the different characteristics identified with them. This paper utilizes different techniques such as Logistic Regression Models, Support Vector Machines, KNN nearest neighbor classifications and many more that foresee the disease in an effective manner. The dataset contains 1025 instances and 14 attributes. This research paper gives the probability of patients developing a heart disease as per the attributes. The aim of this research paper is to find out the accuracy and the absolute and squared errors of different machine learning models. The outcome of the paper enhances the medical care system and minimizes the cost as well.

Graphic Era University, Dehradun, UK, India.
Emails: bhartivmahara@gmail.com; chayalnegi9211@gmail.com; mail.harendrasinghnegi@
  gmail.com
* Corresponding author: bhawneshmca@gmail.com

1. Introduction

In today's realm, heart related sicknesses have turned into issues of extreme importance. As indicated by a review, cardiovascular diseases (CVDs) are the main source of death universally. An expected 17.9 million individuals kicked the bucket from CVDs in 2019, causing 32% of demises worldwide [1]. Off those passing away, 85% did because of a coronary episode and stroke. More than 3/4 of patients passing away due to CVDs occurs in low and middle income countries. Hypertension, high blood cholesterol, and smoking are key causes of coronary illnesses [2]. A few other ailments and life style decisions can likewise put individuals at a higher risk of coronary illnesses, diabetes, obesity and corpulence. Machine learning (ML) assumes an extremely fundamental part in foreseeing such sicknesses from past datasets utilizing the properties identified with coronary illnesses. Information mining is the extraction of subject oriented data from enormous datasets which are related to different areas such as medical science, business related and instructive domains [3]. Machine learning plays an important role in analyzing medical science datasets. ML techniques can conduct a positive analysis of clinical data. Implementing computer-based prediction approach models on datasets has a positive impact and reduces the complexity. It is possible to make future forecasts with the help of past data repositories. Investigations are conducted by medical experts on this information to come up with viable demonstrative choices [4]. Clinical based information mining utilizes sequenced monitoring that guides clinical domains through investigation. Through order monitoring it tests for coronary illnesses in patients [5]. This paper presents the performance analysis parameters of various learning techniques such as Logistics Regression, K-nearest Neighbors, Support Vector Machines, Linear and Naïve Bayes. These techniques are helpful in the early stages of a heart disease as per the attributes of the considered dataset.

2. Background

Heart diseases affect people (in millions) and still remains the main cause of death. Medical science analysis must be efficient and also reliable with the help of computer equipments for minimizing the cost of medical testing. As per the test cases, data should be designed in a way such that it can build future classifications. To predict heart diseases the usage of learning techniques along with different performance parameters is needed [6]. Here in this background section authors give their views about the machine learning techniques helpful for heart disease prediction. Aditya Methaila et al. [7] proposed a data mining based approach for early prediction of heart disease. In this paper decision tree performed well with a 99.62% accuracy rate. Animesh Hazra et al. [8] investigated the reviews on data mining and machine learning techniques and the combination also helped to find out the prediction level of heart diseases which is helpful for medical science. V.V. Ramalingam et al. [9] presented a survey which shows that the Random Forest and Ensemble models performed better than other methods for heart decision prediction. They also applied multiple algorithms in place of random forest which uses multiple decision trees for the over-fitting problem. R. Katarya and Sunit Kumar Meena [10] give a comparative analysis and system literature review on using ML techniques to make predictions of heart related diseases which enhances the medical care system. Apurb Rajdhan et al. [11] suggested a prediction level of heart disease using multiple ML techniques on the UCI repository datasets. These mining algorithms are: Naïve Bayes, Decision Trees, Logistics regression and Random Forest. In this paper, various ML techniques have been implemented to predict the heart disease and random forest gives the highest accuracy among them, i.e., 90.16%. Various authors give their systematic literature reviews, comparative studies and some novel approaches too. ML techniques are implemented on various datasets to predict heart diseases.

3. Machine Learning Models

Machine learning models give direction to computers to improve their learning capability. In computer science ML is the branch that can make the model automatically through algorithms by learning the existing data and is also a part of Artificial Intelligence (AI). Machine learning is a part of software engineering that gets the computer system to learn itself giving a way to examine information to arrive at critical outcomes from it. Basically there are three Machine Learning techniques [12, 13]. Supervised Learning [14], is the type that works with labeled data from datasets along with input information and results as well. Ordered and parted information are converted into prepared and test datasets as well. It trains the model with prepared datasets and tests its capability with test datasets. Unsupervised Learning [15], in case of this type of learning unlabeled data used to prepare in the dataset. The point is to track down secret examples in the information. The model is prepared for the unarranged or unlabeled data. It can undoubtedly foresee stowed away information such new datasets. In this procedure no reactions in the dataset can be seen. Reinforcement Learning basically not related to the marked-dataset does not depend on the outcomes of the information. In this way, gains are collected from the experience. Through this strategy, the model further develops to show dependence on its relationship with climate and sorts out some way to point out its shortcomings and to get the right result through appraisals

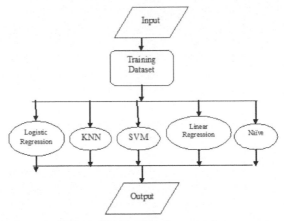

Fig. 1. Machine learning models.

and testing different possibilities [16]. Different machine learning models which are considered and implemented on datasets are shown in Figure 1.

3.1 *Logistic Regression Model*

A logistic regression version developed by Joseph Berkson [17] is a binomial based regression model. It is used to model the probability of occurrence of a certain magnificence or current occasion including, bypass/fails, wins/losses, alive/dead, or healthy/ill [18]. This version is likewise referred to as the logit version.

The formula used in the logistic model is,

Logit p = log (p/1 – p) (for zero less than p less than one)
log (p/1–p) is an ordinary ratio.

3.2 *Support Vector Machine*

This approach was created by Vladimir Vapnik along with his partners at AT&T labs. SVM [19] is the most popular supervised mastering algorithm, that is used for class as well as regression problems.

The equation of the hyper line is,

w. x + b = 0

where, w = vector normal to the hyper plane
b is an offset
If w. x + b is greater than zero
then it is a positive point.
else
0

3.3 KNN Classification Model

The KNN algorithm [20] is a simple set of rules, easy to implement and can be used to resolve both classification and regression issues. This is likewise known as a lazy learner set of rules.

3.4 Naive Bayes Theorem

The Naïve Bayes algorithm [21] is a supervised learning set of rules that are used to clear up class troubles. It is best for fast predictions when the independence assumption holds.

$$P (A \mid B) = P (B \mid A) * P (A)/P(B)$$

3.5 Linear Regression Model

Linear regression is a linear method that establishes a relationship between one explanatory variable and a dependent variable [22]. The equation used in this model is $Y = a + b X$.

Where, Y is the dependent variable, X is the explanatory variable, a represents the intercept and b is the slope of the line.

4. Performance Parameters

Accuracy is the measure which is used to find out which model is suitable for identifying the relationships and the patterns between variables in a dataset [23]. That is completely based on the input and training datasets. Precision refers to the number of true positives divided by the total number of positive predictions [24]. The F1 Score is calculated by using two more parameters, precision and recall, as 2 * ((precision * recall) divided by (precision + recall)). Mean Square Error (MSE) is defined as the average or mean of the square of the differences between estimated and actual values. Mean Absolute Error (MAE) is represented by the magnitude of difference between the predicted and the true value of an observation [25, 26, 27]. MAE is the average (AVG) of the absolute errors for a prediction group and the taken observations work as measurements of the magnitudes of errors for the complete group [28]. The Root Mean Squared Error (RMSE) value is represented as the standard deviation (SD) of the errors which is a measure of the square of the error in the prediction made on a dataset. RMSE is related to the MSE but the RMSE value depends on the accuracy of the model [29, 30, 31]. Figure 2 shows the generic structure or model used for predicting heart disease.

5. Result Analysis and Performance Evaluation

The output of this research work is used to forecast whether a patient will develop heart disease or not. This work has been implemented

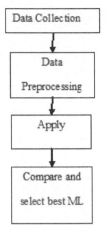

Fig. 2. Generic structure or model for predicting heart disease.

using different machine learning techniques on datasets. The dataset is divided into a training and test dataset. This is an experiment based work where the results have been predicted using Python on an Asus Laptop with processor configuration Advance Micro Devices Ryzen-5 3550H (Radeon Vega Mobile Gfx 2.10 GHz) and 8GB RAM. This work has been performed using various ML techniques such as Logistic Regression, SVM, KNN, Naive Bayes and Linear regression on the given dataset. Various performance parameters such as accuracy, precision, recall and F1-score have been calculated; error values such as MAE, MSE and RMSE are also found to distinguish ML techniques. Figure 3 shows the accuracy measures of KNN, Linear regression and SVM. KNN and Linear regression both have the highest accuracy of 81.95% and SVM has an accuracy of 81.46%.

Precision, recall and F1-score are represented in Figure 4 for the respective models. As different ML techniques works differently, output values also vary. Here performance parameter precision values for liner regression and SVM are higher than those of other ML techniques. With regard to recall value the KNN shows an improved performance is in comparison to the remaining techniques. The F1-score for KNN again indicates the best outcome compared to the other techniques. Figure 5 depicts the calculated error parameter values like MAE, MSE and RMSE error. Linear regression shows a high MAE compared to others whereas both Naïve Bayes and Logistic regression are close. The MSE for the linear regression is at a lower level in comparison whereas both Naïve Bayes and Logistic Regression have the same value. MAE and MSE values are the same for both SVM and KNN.

Accuracy score of different authors given in Table 1 to predict heart disease using different learning models.

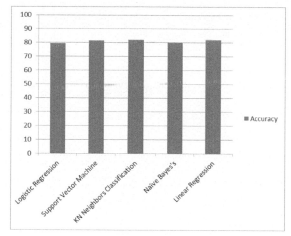

Fig. 3. Accuracy.

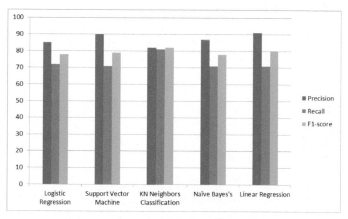

Fig. 4. Precision, Recall and F1-Score.

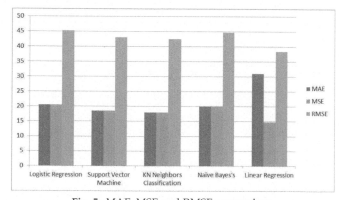

Fig. 5. MAE, MSE and RMSE error values.

Table 1. Summary of machine learning techniques-based solutions for prediction of heart disease by authors.

Sr. no.	Year	Author	Purpose	Technique Used	Accuracy
1	2015	Rucha Shinde [32]	To predict heart disease	Naïve byes KN Algorithm	88.7%
2	2015	Sairabi H Mujawar et al. [33]	Demonstrate Heart Disease prediction model	Modified k-means algorithm Naïve Bayes as well	k-means accuracy is 93% and Naïve Bayes is 89% accurated
3	2016	Sharma Purushottam et al. [34]	Evaluate the Heart Disease prediction system using rules and partial tree of C - 4.5	Rules of C - 4.5 rules and also usage of Naïve Bayes	C - 4.5 is better than Naïve Bayes technique.
4	2016	Ashok Kumar Dwivedi [35]	Heart Disease prediction	Naïve Bayes, KNN Logistic Regression Classification Tree	83% 80% 85% 77%
5	2016	Jaymin Patel et al. [36]	To predict the presence of heart disease	J48 with Reduced Error pruning Algorithm, Logistic Model Tree Algorithm, Random Forest algorithm	J48 gives better accuracy than the other two techniques
6	2017	T. Karaylan et al. [37]	Proposed a artificial neural network (ANN) based prediction of heart disease	Use of back-propagation algorithm	95%
7	2018	Aditi Gavhane et al. [38]	To develop an application that can predict the vulnerability of a heart disease	Neural network algorithm multi-layer perceptron	Precision is 0.91 Recall is 0.89
8	2018	R. Sharmila et al. [39]	Gives a method to increase the chances of prediction of heart disease.	SVM (parallel fashion)	Parallel SVM is having accuracy level of 85% and for SVM is 82.35%.

#	Year	Author	Objective	Techniques	Accuracy	Remarks
9	2019	Senthil Kumar Mohan [40]	To predict the cardiovascular disease	Naïve byes, Generalized linear-model Logistic Regression Deep Learning Decision Tree Random Forest Gradient boosted SVM VOTE HRFLM	75.8% 85.1% 82.9% 87.4% 85% 86.1% 78.3% 86.1% 87.41% 88.4%	
10	2019	A. Lakshmanarao et al. [41]	Detection of heart disease	Logistic Regression KNN AdaBoost Decision Tree Naïve Bayes Random Forest SVM Extra Tree Gradient Boosting	65.7% 80.5% 78% 81.8% 61% 90.3% 82.3% 90.3% 87.4%	
11	2020	Harshit Jindal [42]	To predict whether a patient is likely to be diagnosed with heart disease.	KNN Algorithm, Logistic Regression, Random Forest Classifier		Logistic and KNN has an efficiency of 88.5%
12	2020	Devansh Shah et al. [43]	Suggested a probability model for heart disease in the patients	Naïve Bayes, decision tree, KNN, Random forest		The highest accuracy score is achieved with KNN
13	2021	Rohit Bharti [44]	To predict heart disease	Machine learning and deep learning		Accuracy is 94.2%

6. Conclusion

To enhance the performance of the medical care system machine learning gives the direction to predict heart diseases. Various machine learning models are available which can be implemented on datasets. In this work the dataset consists of 1025 instances and 14 essential attributes. This paper has been implemented to distinguish machine learning models on datasets to find out the prediction level of heart disease. KNN, Linear regression and SVM have a high accuracy rate in comparison to the logistics and naïve bayes approaches. In the future to improve this research other data mining techniques such as time series, clustering along with association rules and some genetic algorithm can also implemented. This work was implemented on small data sets; for large datasets more Deep Learning and ML may be used to improve the accuracy and prediction levels.

References

[1] Raj, P., Chatterjee, J.M., Kumar, A. and Balamurugan, B. (2020). Internet of Things Use Cases for the Healthcare Industry, 1st ed. Springer, Cham.

[2] Wilson, P.W.F., D'Agostino, R.B., Levy, D., Belanger, A.M., Silbershatz, H. et al. (1998). Prediction of coronary heart disease using risk factor categories. Am. Hear. Assoc. 97(18): 1837–1847, doi: https://doi.org/10.1161/01.CIR.97.18.1837.

[3] Sarker, I.H. (2021). Machine learning: algorithms, real-world applications and research directions. SN Comput. Sci.

[4] Titler, M.G. (2008). The evidence for evidence-based practice implementation. *In*: Patient Safety and Quality: An Evidence-Based Handbook for Nurses.

[5] Ayatollahi, H., Gholamhosseini, L. and Salehi, M. (2019). Predicting coronary artery disease: A comparison between two data mining algorithms. BMC Public Health 19(1): 1–9, doi: 10.1186/s12889-019-6721-5.

[6] Khourdifi, Y. and Bahaj, M. (2019). Heart disease prediction and classification using machine learning algorithms optimized by particle swarm optimization and ant colony optimization. Int. J. Intell. Eng. Syst. 12(1): 242–252, doi: 10.22266/ijies2019.0228.24.

[7] Methaila, A., Kansal, P., Arya, H. and Pankaj Kumar. (2014). Early heart disease prediction using data mining techniques. Comput. Sci. Inf. Technol. (CS IT), pp. 53–59, doi: 10.5121/csit.2014.4807.

[8] Animesh, H., Subrata, K.M., Amit, G., Arkomita, M., Mukherje, A. et al. (2017). Heart disease diagnosis and prediction using machine learning. Adv. Comput. Sci. Technol. 10(7): 2137–2159, [Online]. Available: http://www.ripublication.com.

[9] Ramalingam, V.V., Dandapath, A. and Karthik Raja, M. (2018). Heart disease prediction using machine learning techniques: A survey. Int. J. Eng. Technol. 7(2.8 Special Issue 8): 684–687, doi: 10.14419/ijet.v7i2.8.10557.

[10] Katarya, R. and Meena, S.K. (2020). Machine Learning Techniques for Heart Disease Prediction: A Comparative Study and Analysis. doi: 10.1007/s12553-020-00505-7.

[11] Rajdhan, A., Sai, M., Agarwal, A. and Ravi, D. (2020). Heart disease prediction using machine learning. Int. J. Eng. Res. Technol. 9(4): 659–662.

[12] Bharathi, K., Bhagyasri, M.U.N., Lakshmi, G.M. and Javvaji, H.S. (2021). Heart disease prediction using machine learning. Rev. GEINTEC-GESTAO Inov. E Tecnol. 11(4): 3694–3702.

[13] Davarzani, S., Jafari, R. and Smith, B.K. (2019). Supervised and unsupervised machine learning techniques in heart disease prediction. October 2020, pp. 2–3, doi: 10.13140/RG.2.2.20961.94564.

[14] Krishnani, D., Kumari, A., Dewangan, A., Singh, A., Naik, N.S. et al. (2019). Prediction of coronary heart disease using supervised machine learning algorithms. doi: 10.1109/TENCON.2019.8929434

[15] Ali, M.M., Paul, B.K., Ahmed, K., Bui, F.M., Quinn, J.M.W. et al. (2021). Heart disease prediction using supervised machine learning algorithms: Performance analysis and comparison. Comput. Biol. Med. doi: 10.1016/j.compbiomed.2021.104672.

[16] Singh, R. (2020). A review on heart disease prediction using unsupervised and supervised learning. Neural Networks 99(August): 430–434, doi: 10.13140/RG.2.2.20425.57443.

[17] Maalouf, M. (2011). Logistic regression in data analysis: An overview. Int. J. Data Anal. Tech. Strateg. 3(3): 281–299, doi: 10.1504/IJDATS.2011.041335.

[18] Field, A. (2012). Logistic regression. Discov. Stat. Using SPSS, pp. 731–735.

[19] Evgeniou, T. and Pontil, M. (2001). Support vector machines: Theory and applications. Lect. Notes Comput. Sci. (including Subser. Lect. Notes Artif. Intell. Lect. Notes Bioinformatics), vol. 2049 LNAI, no. May, pp. 249–257, doi: 10.1007/3-540-44673-7_12.

[20] Guo, G., Wang, H., Bell, D., Bi, Y., Greer, K. et al. (2003). KNN model-based approach in classification. Lect. Notes Comput. Sci. (including Subser. Lect. Notes Artif. Intell. Lect. Notes Bioinformatics), vol. 2888, no. November 2012, pp. 986–996, doi: 10.1007/978-3-540-39964-3_62.

[21] Rish, I. (2014). An Empirical Study of the Naïve Bayes Classifier An empirical study of the naive Bayes classifier. Cc.Gatech.Edu, no. January 2001, pp. 41–46, [Online]. Available: https://www.cc.gatech.edu/~isbell/reading/papers/Rish.pdf.

[22] Rong, S. and Bao-Wen, Z. (2018). The research of regression model in machine learning field. MATEC Web Conf. 176: 8–11, doi: 10.1051/matecconf/201817601033.

[23] Hasan, S.M.M., Mamun, M.A., Uddin, M.P. and Hossain, M.A. (2018). Comparative analysis of classification approaches for heart disease prediction. doi: 10.1109/IC4ME2.2018.8465594.

[24] Rashme, T.Y., Islam, L., Jahan, S. and Prova, A.A. (2021). Early prediction of cardiovascular diseases using feature selection and machine learning techniques. doi: 10.1109/ICCES51350.2021.9489057.

[25] Bouali, H. and Akaichi, J. (2014). Comparative study of different classification techniques: heart disease use case. doi: 10.1109/ICMLA.2014.84.

[26] Bethel, G.N.B., Rajinikanth, T.V. and Raju, S.V. (2017). An improved analysis of heart MRI images using the morphological operations. doi: 10.1109/CTCEEC.2017.8455050.

[27] Kimmel, J.C., Mcdole, A.D., Abdelsalam, M., Gupta, M., Sandhu, R. et al. (2021). Recurrent neural networks based online behavioural malware detection techniques for cloud infrastructure. IEEE Access 9: 68066–68080.

[28] Gupta, Maanak, Farhan Patwa and Ravi Sandhu. (2018). An attribute-based access control model for secure big data processing in hadoop ecosystem. pp. 13–24. *In*: Proceedings of the Third ACM Workshop on Attribute-Based Access Control.

[29] Sarishma, Dangi, Sumitra Sangwan, Ravi Tomar, Rohit Srivastava et al. (2021). A review on cognitive computational neuroscience: overview, models, and applications. Innovative Trends in Computational Intelligence, pp. 217–234.

[30] Asthana, Rashi, Shubham Dhanetwal, Tanupriya Choudhury, Ravi Tomar et al. (2020). Study of sentiment analysis in mental health using speech recognition and image to text conversion. pp. 113–122. *In*: Computational Intelligence in Pattern Recognition. Springer, Singapore.

[31] Yadav, Anuj Kumar and Madan Garg Ritika. (2021). Cryptographic solution for security problem in cloud computing storage during global pandemics. International Journal of Safety and Security Engineering, pp. 193–199.

[32] Shinde, R., Arjun, S., Patil, P. and Waghmare, P.J. (2015). An intelligent heart disease prediction system using k-means clustering and Naïve Bayes algorithm. Int. J. Comput. Sci. Inf. Technol. 6(1): 637–639.

[33] Mujawar, S.H. and Devale, P.R. (2015). Prediction of heart disease using modified k-means and by using Naïve Bayes. Int. J. Innov. Res. Comput. Commun. Eng. 3: 10265–10273.

[34] Purushottam, Saxena, K. and Sharma, R. (2016). Efficient heart disease prediction system. Procedia Comput. Sci. 85: 962–969, doi: 10.1016/j.procs.2016.05.288.

[35] Dwivedi, A.K. (2016). Performance evaluation of different machine learning techniques for prediction of heart disease. Neural Comput. Appl. doi: 10.1007/s00521-016-2604-1.

[36] Patel, J., Upadhyay, T. and Patel, S. (2016). Heart disease prediction using machine learning and data mining technique. Int. J. Comput. Sci. Commun., pp. 129–137.

[37] Karayılan, T. and Kılıç, Ö. (2017). Prediction of heart disease using neural network. doi: 10.1109/UBMK.2017.8093512.

[38] Gavhane, A., Kokkula, G., Pandya, I. and Devadkar, P.K. (2018). Prediction of heart disease using machine learning. Int. Conf. Electron. Commun. Aerosp. Technol., pp. 1275–1278, doi: 10.1088/1742-6596/1916/1/012022.

[39] Sharmila, R. and Chellammal, S. (2018). A conceptual method to enhance the prediction of heart diseases using the data techniques. Int. J. Comput. Sci. Eng.

[40] Mohan, S., Thirumalai, C. and Srivastava, G. (2019). Effective heart disease prediction using hybrid machine learning techniques. IEEE Access 7: 81542–81554, doi: 10.1109/ACCESS.2019.2923707.

[41] Lakshmanarao, A., Swathi, Y. and Sundareswar, P.S.S. (2019). Machine learning techniques for heart disease prediction. Int. J. Sci. Technol. Res. 8(11): 374–377, doi: 10.31838/jcdr.2021.12.01.05.

[42] Jindal, H., Agrawal, S., Khera, R., Jain, R., Nagrath, P. et al. (2021). Heart disease prediction using machine learning algorithms. IOP Conf. Ser. Mater. Sci. Eng. 1022(1), doi: 10.1088/1757-899X/1022/1/012072.

[43] Shah, D., Patel, S. and Bharti, S.K. (2020). Heart disease prediction using machine learning techniques. SN Comput. Sci. 1(6): 177–181, doi: https://doi.org/10.1007/s42979-020-00365-y.

[44] Bharti, R., Khamparia, A., Shabaz, M., Dhiman, G., Pande, S. et al. (2021). Prediction of heart disease using a combination of machine learning and deep learning. Comput. Intell. Neurosci., vol. 2021, doi: 10.1155/2021/8387680.

Chapter 7

Cloud and Edge Computing
Architectures for Future Cloud Computing

Vitesh Sethi, Avita Katal* and Shubham Dabas

Cloud technology is progressing towards increased dispersion over multi-clouds and the integration of diverse devices, as indicated by the Internet of Things (IoT) in the context of edge, cloud, and fog computing. Lightweight virtualization techniques are advantageous in this architectural configuration, with smaller but still virtualized machines hosting program and infrastructure capabilities, as well as the logistics necessary to manage them. Edge computing refers to all the activities of IoT nodes linked to a remote cloud at the network's edge or limit. After a decade characterized by a rising dependence on centralized third-party public cloud services, the adoption of edge computing platforms and IoT devices indicates a complete lateral swing back to decentralized data management. On the other hand, large cloud providers are keen to extend cloud storage to the edge. As a result, companies must determine how closely they want to bind their developing infrastructure to a single provider. This chapter covers the introduction and background of edge computing architectures, as well as the integration of both technologies. The chapter includes information on edge and cloud computing

School of Computer Science, University of Petroleum and Energy Studies, Dehradun, Uttarakhand, India.
Emails: viteshsethi37@gmail.com; shubhamdabas2000@gmail.com
* Corresponding author: avita207@gmail.com

architectures, as well as their application, challenges and concludes with a case study.

1. Introduction

Edge computing's horizon is expanding due to the growth of Internet of Things (IoTs) and the advent of numerous cloud services. By putting cloud capabilities closer to mobile devices, edge computing is a viable model for solving numerous major difficulties in IoTs, such as bandwidth overload, energy limits, low latency communication, and privacy protection. In terms of boosting processing speed, cutting cloud hosting costs, and minimizing communication latency, the hybrid edge-cloud design delivered the best tradeoffs.

Around 2005, cloud computing became very popular [1]. The idea of keeping, analyzing, and controlling information in the cloud has shifted both living and working routines significantly. The Internet of Things (IoT) was founded in 1999, since then, the idea of "trying to make it all as smart as it can produce its own computer perception data, so that it can be monitored and maintained without human involvement" has been integrated into a variety of other fields, including home, surroundings, public transit, medical services, and so on [2].

However, since IoT has gained in popularity in recent years, the Cisco Global Cloud Index estimates that data generated by people, machines, and things will surpass 500 zettabytes by 2019 [3]. Thus, today it can be imagined where it might have reached. According to the GSMA, there will be 25 billion IoT links by 2025 [4]. Cloud computing is not capable of processing such a massive volume of data since it increases network traffic, as well as the calculation time of the process of cloud-based applications. As a result of the IoT's gaining popularity, it's critical to overcome the limits of cloud computing. The concept of edge computing is proposed to improve the efficacy of cloud computing. Figure 1 depicts the distinction between edge computing and cloud computing. The processing in cloud computing takes place on the remote server, while the processing in edge computing takes place on the endpoints.

Despite the fact that most energy saving systems still depend on cloud computing for data collection, pre-processing, and analysis, edge computing is gaining traction. Edge computing, on the other hand, still needs additional power to meet the heavy computational requirement of artificial intelligence-based energy-saving solutions. Meanwhile, the most successful current technique for implementing energy efficiency systems may be a hybrid edge-cloud design. It allows end users and utilities to have more control over their energy footprints, lowers cloud hosting costs, and increases online privacy. The IoT phenomena necessitates this

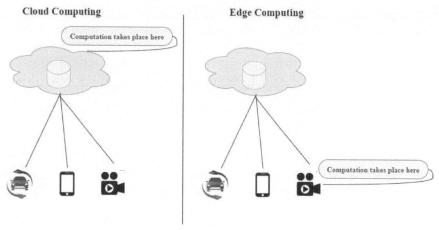

Fig. 1. Comparison between cloud and edge computing.

transformation in order for the cloud computing paradigm to adapt. The increased need for IoT and cloud interoperability has resulted in the development of the edge computing concept, which aims to offer storage and distribution capabilities as an expansion of accessible IoT devices without requiring data/processing to be transported to a centralized cloud datacenter. This reduces transmission latency as well as the quantity of data that must be moved across the Internet and between public and private data centers.

2. Background

The origins of edge computing may be established in the late 1990s, when Akamai created content delivery networks (CDNs) to improve internet speed [5]. A CDN uses edge nodes near users to prefetch and cache web content. These edge nodes may also customize content, for example, by displaying location-based branding. CDNs are especially beneficial for video content since caching may result in significant bandwidth savings.

By utilizing cloud computing infrastructure, edge computing generalizes and expands the CDN notion. Cloudlets, like CDNs, rely on their proximity to end users. A cloudlet, like cloud computing, may run any code and is not confined to storing online content. This code is typically wrapped in a Virtual Machine (VM) or a lightweight container for segregation, safety, strategic planning, and metering. Brian Noble and colleagues were the first to illustrate the usefulness of edge computing for mobile computing in 1997 [6]. By offloading computing to a nearby server, they demonstrated how voice recognition might be done on a resource-constrained mobile device with acceptable performance. The author in [7] improved battery life two years later by extending this strategy. The term "cyber foraging" was used by the author Satyanarayanan [8] in order to describe the process of enhancing a mobile device's processing skills by utilizing local infrastructure. Cloud computing has been the most apparent infrastructure to utilize a mobile device since the mid-2000s, when it first became popular.

The average round-trip time from 260 worldwide standpoints to their ideal Amazon Elastic Compute Cloud (EC2) machines, as per Ang Li and his colleagues, is 74 milliseconds [9]. To this, one must add the delay of a WLAN first hop. In considerations of jitter, a multi-hop network's intrinsic unpredictability must be considered. Using a cloud datacenter for initiatives in order to achieve end-to-end latency in the tens of milliseconds or less is definitely not a good idea. End-to-end delays and cloud computing were originally discovered in a 2009 study that established the groundwork for edge computing [10]. The system is two-tiered, with the first level consisting of history's unaltered public cloud and the second level consisting of cloudlets with the first state stored. Using permanent caching rather than hard state facilitates cloudlet management, regardless of their physical dispersal at the Internet edge. Fog computing was coined by Flavio Bonomi and colleagues in 2012 to characterize this scattered cloud infrastructure [11]. However, rather than the active efficiency of mobile applications, their motivation for decentralization was the flexibility of IoT infrastructure.

3. Integration of Edge and Cloud Computing

Since the cloud has greater processing capability than network edge devices, offloading all computing chores to the cloud has shown to be an effective approach to analyze information. However, although information processing rates have surged, the capacity of networks that transmit data to and from the cloud has not. As a result, the network is becoming a constraint for cloud computing as edge devices create more data. Devices at the network edge, such as mobile phones, have traditionally solely consumed data in cloud computing, such as allowing a user to watch a movie. Users' mobile gadgets are now producing data. More network edge functionality is required with this update. Many individuals, for example, submit images or videos to cloud-based social networking services such as Facebook, Twitter, or Instagram. On the other hand, uploading a huge image or video clip may take a substantial amount of bandwidth. A device at the network edge might lower the resolution and hence the size of the video clip gets reduced before uploading it to the cloud. In another scenario, properly configured edge devices may help shield anonymity by analyzing sensitive information acquired by wearing individual health devices rather than sending it across an insecure connection to the cloud.

The following are some of the reasons why edge computing is required in cloud computing and how it enhances cloud system throughput:

- *Edge Data Processing*: As mentioned in Section 3, the daily development of vast volumes of data known as big data from different platforms and social networks is expanding, and all of the data is calculated, analyzed, and kept in the cloud. As a consequence, the response time of the user has increased. It is preferable to have data processing capability at the network's edges to avoid this issue. Response time is lowered, process effectiveness is raised, and networking strain is reduced when information recorded by the origin is handled at the edge, i.e., close to the source.

- *IoT is becoming more popular*: As previously said, billions of gadgets will be connected to the Internet over the next several years, and nearly all electronic and electrical things will be connected to IoT. As a consequence, only cloud computing will be useless in dealing with such a massive volume of data generated by IoT devices for the following reasons:

  o There is a huge amount of information created at the edge, and getting it to the cloud requires a lot of excess bandwidth.

  o Data protection is a serious worry in cloud computing.

  o Trying to send a lot of raw materials' information to the cloud wastes system resources and increases energy usage.

As a result, shifting some computer processes to the edge could save energy. Edge computing can assist in overcoming the aforementioned cloud computing issues.

- *Changing from an extraction of knowledge to an information consumer and data producer mode of thinking*: Figure 2 depicts the typical approach utilized in the cloud computing concept. Edge devices are often merely data users, according to the traditional concept, like when a person views a video online on his smartphone. For IoT deployment,

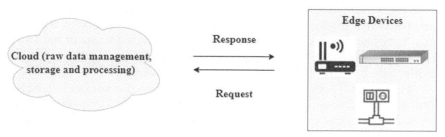

Fig. 2. Traditional cloud computing model.

this approach is inadequate. End devices, on the other hand, act as both data consumers and producers, according to the current model paradigm. Information is produced by people's mobile phones, for example. Smart edge capability is needed to make the transition from data user to manufacturer.

4. Edge Cloud Architecture

In the world of computing, edge computing is a comparatively recent notion. It brings cloud computing and utilities closer to the end consumers, with rapid computing and applications response time. Monitoring, virtual reality, and real-time traffic surveillance are just a few instances of internet-enabled applications that require quick processor and response times [12]. These applications are often run on the resource-constrained mobile devices of end users, with the main service and processing handled by cloud servers. When mobile devices employ cloud services, they encounter significant latency and mobility issues [13, 14]. Edge computing addresses the above program needs by relocating computation to the network's edge.

Various designs have been suggested to create edge computing systems. In these topologies, the network edge is not properly delineated, and the nodes willing to operate at the edge can vary. Moreover, the nomenclature for the edge is extremely diverse, with the same phrase being used to denote a variety of designs and functions [15, 16].

The authors in [10] present cloudlets that are built on virtual machines (VMs) that are installed on Wi-Fi access stations and are only a single hop away from end-devices.

Cloudlets, as depicted in Figure 3, are decentralized and widely spread Internet architectures that adjacent mobile computers can use to access computation cycles and storage capabilities. A cloudlet is a small data center. It's completely self-contained, needing only Electricity, Internet connectivity, and Security systems to get going. This ease of maintenance correlates to a computer resources appliance paradigm, which makes implementation in a business setting such as a coffee shop or a doctor's office a breeze. A cloudlet is a cluster of multi-core processors on the inside with a gigabit connection and a high-bandwidth wireless local area network. For secure installation in unsupervised areas of hardware integrity, the cloudlet can be packed in a tamper- resistant or tamper-evident shell with a third-party monitoring system.

Ha et al. [17] presented a multi-tiered system that uses cloudlets to just provide cognitive support to users. In order to obtain real help, the cloudlet analyses video and sensor information recorded from Google Glass users. Simoens et al. [18] presents cloudlets that are used to create a robust three-

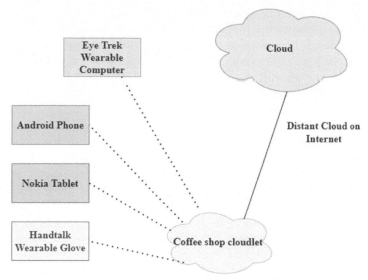

Fig. 3. Cloudlet concept.

tier system for analysis and automated labeling of audience video from consumer devices. Cloudlets could be integrated with femtocells, LTE base stations, or even automobiles, according to further research [19] since their introduction.

Greenberg et al. [20] proposed the development of micro data centers containing web servers capable of hosting apps that run for end customers These data centers were previously used to host CDNs and email application forms, and they can now multitude cloudlets as well. Wang et al. [21] proposed launching a limited handful of data centers on wireless access points or a central node in a radio access network. The scholars refer to this implementation as a micro cloud.

The integration of computer resources at the edge and centralized data centers is another technique for constructing edge platforms. Chang et al. [22] referred to this as an edge cloud. Edge applications are employed in their system to provide at both the edge and in faraway cloud data centers. The article describes using edge apps to implement indoor 3D translators and surveillance cameras requests. The edge cloud architecture, which has a global footprint, is intended to provide low-latency, throughput, and adaptable end user assistance. By employing user and vehicle aided large processing nodes at the edge, the edge cloud is intended to transport the data cloud all the way through to the end user's home or office. The edge service brings latency-sensitive simulations and usability testing aspects closer to end users at edge nodes, while also planning to host escalating point load processing and data system components in data center nodes by seamlessly interconnecting edge devices with data center networks. The edge cloud is made up of a federal state of data center endpoints and all edge zones. It is presumed that the edge cloud operator already has a conventional IaaS data center cloud in place. The edge cloud controller may extend the cloud's functionality to deploy application forms at the edge networks by adding edge cloud capabilities. Figure 4 depicts the existence of distinct edge zones in the edge cloud.

To enable integrated IoT applications, Farris et al. [23] propose federating private and public clouds. In this design, the edge node dynamically instigates the confederation to maximize job completion. In contrast to the fog computing idea, the network edge simply provides solutions for businesses and monitoring. The authors' proposed Mobile-IoT-Federation-as-a-Service (MIFaaS), minimizing the cost of peripheral micro data centers. Figure 5 depicts various private/public IoT Cloud Providers (ICPs). Users can, for example, benefit from the capabilities provided by their own clouds, that are made up of their own data and the resources made accessible to them by their local devices. Moreover, in a smart city, authorities use their cloud of things to deliver public services such as mobile terminals, security cameras, and so on.

Elias et al. [24] presented a classification technique with very minimal time and bandwidth needs using a confederal cloud with an edge cloud (that mimics public cloud services). Because of decentralized designers and public cloud mirroring, existing free software archives might be exploited for machine learning and classification methods at the edge. They identified the edge cloud as a modern computing entity for the edge tier that reflects on a lower level the properties of popular public cloud systems in order to give advanced analysis fusion and multiple layers to the sensing tier via a cloud service distribution system. The private

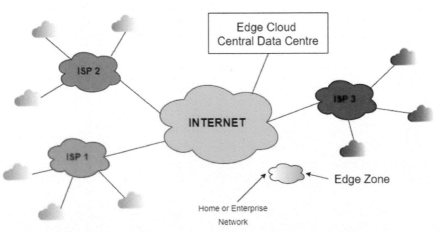

Fig. 4. Presence of edge zones in distributed edge cloud architecture.

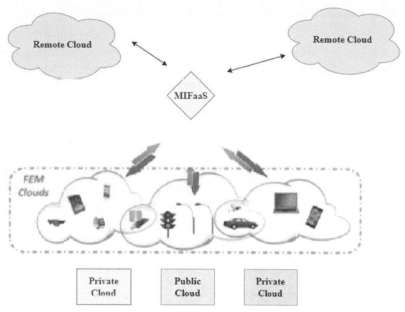

Fig. 5. Cloud scenario based on Federated Edge Assisted Mobile clouds.

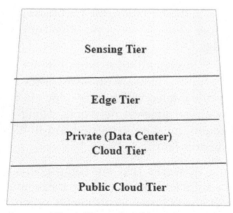

Fig. 6. Layered architecture.

data center tier offers information and calculate (software) functionality comparable to public clouds, but with greater confidentiality, safety, and controlling costs. When long-term data backup and latency-tolerant batch systems are required, the high latency, changeable, unreliable, and costly link to the public cloud layer is used (on-demand). The layered structure is as shown in Figure 6.

5. Requirements for Edge Cloud Technology

The network nodes that connect cloud Data Centers (DCs), edge DCs, and user devices are another component of edge computing facilities. Edge networks are divided into two layers: those that link user devices to edge DCs and those that connect edge DCs to cloud DCs.

- *Access network*: End users may be connected to edge DCs by one of three access methods, depending on their location: cellular wireless channels, optical communication system networks, or fiber-wireless access systems. Members can observe the edge DCs directly via the radio channels if they are placed at the wi-fi access point. In this situation, wireless channels' cooperative communications capacity can help in workload offloading by relaying via a nearby mobile device [25]. The fronthaul connects the radio head and baseband processing unit (BBU) in a Cloud Radio Access Network (C-RAN), and passive optical networks (PON) are a viable technology for fronthaul transmission. When an edge DC is implemented in the central office that contains the baseband processing unit, users' communication is consolidated to the edge DC through cellular lines and PON (Wang et al., 2018). In addition, in the case of C-RAN edge computing, the wireless access party might be standard RAN methods (such as WLAN) rather than cellular channels. In this situation, the traditional RAN and PON, also known as the fiber-wireless network, offer communication between users and the edge DC.

- *Transport Network*: In general, transportation networks are similar to cloud computing in that they are unaware of traffic flows for specific services. To provide interconnection for edge-cloud sharing resources and synchronization, transport networks, along with the link layer and optical domains, must be connected end-to-end with cloud/edge DCs and user devices [26].

Edge computing networks that are comprehensive require a long-term strategy with sufficient resources, partners, and implementation. Organizations can evaluate target locations for potential edge networks, find the appropriate hardware and software requirements, and continuously develop their newest network segment with a proper inventory of distributed network infrastructure.

Developing new edge networks necessitates taking inventory of existing data centers and distributed network infrastructure, including IoT devices and sensors. The next step is to look for edge computing solutions that are adaptable enough to work with both legacy systems and cutting- edge technology. Edge computing vendors provide organizations with the hardware, networking machinery, processors, connected data center contracts, and cutting-edge edge technologies they need to set up an edge network.

Edge devices and transforming legacy networks to serve physically close end users will be far easier for enterprise organizations with existing global infrastructure and networks. Startups and small businesses, on the other hand, will need to obtain the necessary infrastructure and solutions from edge computing providers in order to build edge networks. Organizations must choose appropriate solutions with caution due to the sensitive nature of uptime and reliable service. Edge computing networks, like any other IT network, require ongoing maintenance and performance tuning. Administrators can examine edge-specific traffic, assess potential issues, and take corrective action as needed to improve the distributed network's performance. Organizations that add more edge networks that are separated by long geographic distances must devise a strategy that accounts for and manages a slew of remote networks from a central location. To support edge clouds, for instance, one needs position and data processing, placing, propagation, and recovering. Consider a software that examines digital multimedia information hosted on the Internet. To handle the large amount of data, edge computing and storage capacities would be necessary. Edge assets could be distributed resources distributed across information distribution systems.

Edge clouds can be supported by a variety of virtualized resources, such as nodes and edges, which are all customizable but vary in size and kind (the latter being network nodes). As a consequence, a variety of resource limits emerge, requiring the deployment of a lightweight virtualization approach. Platform services and applications, as well as IoT devices linked to computing and storage resources, must be managed, i.e. bundled, distributed, and coordinated, in center and edge clouds.

- For managing cloud endpoints with rich (virtualized) services, location-based services, reduced latency, and mobility support are concrete requirements.

- Software Defined Networks (SDN)-virtualized nodes, as well as virtualized edges and connectors, need a lightweight virtualization approach to easily deploy portable services at the edges.

- This type of virtualized infrastructure might provide end-user access and IoT connections, possibly through private edge clouds.

The solution might include common topology designs, software lifecycle management, and an easy-to-use Application Programming Interface (API). At a typical PaaS layer, the correct abstractions for edge cloud focused management would be advantageous.

6. Edge as a Service (EaaS)

To solve future computing difficulties, the forthcoming IoT paradigm stimulates the development of distributed cloud architectures [27]. Distributed cloud architectures make use of spare computing resources at the network's edge, such as those found on mobile base stations, local routers, and switches [28]. This, however, is a tough and time-consuming job. To develop tiny clouds, low-cost, low-power computer nodes such as Raspberry Pi's might be positioned one step away from portable electronics. These nodes can house cloud servers, which are subsequently offloaded to serve a set of user devices, increasing overall Quality of Service (QoS) [29]. For a distributed cloud architecture to succeed, the network's edge must be incorporated into the computing ecosystem. For example, if a server is to be placed on a micro cloud, it must be available to applications and its owners. There are public resources, such as EC2, that help with cloud resource selection and deployment. There are no capabilities on edge nodes that allow application selection and deployment.

The architecture of the Edge as a Service (EaaS) platform is three-tiered. The cloud layer, which also contains cloud infrastructure, is the highest tier. A two-tier paradigm is common in a centralized cloud architecture style, with user devices connected to the application server. The device tier is the lowest layer, which contains consumer devices such as phones, wearable technology, and gadgets that link to cloud infrastructure. Devices link to relevant servers via traffic forwarding nodes in a centralized cloud architectural style. To take advantage of the computational power supplied by edge nodes, devices must interact with the cloud server. The edge node layer is an intermediary tier in which edge terminals are made available on demand to service a group of client systems that may be near to the node(s). When customers initiate an installation, for example, a link to the cloud application servers is initially created. On an edge node, an application server (whether it's a replica or a partitioned web application) can then be built. The EaaS platform is based on techniques for discovering edge nodes and procuring network edge services for workloads.

i) The Master Node Manager is the link between the web application's user input and the master controller. The monitor and the key generator communicate with this module. The user database on the master node keeps track of information that can be used to isolate people. The edge database keeps track of all edge nodes that have been detected and on which an edge manager has been deployed. .

ii) The monitor collects essential metrics from each edge node on a regular basis, such as CPU and memory usage. The administrator can control the frequency with which this information is obtained. However, because this module is centralized, it is expected to be less scalable. To make the EaaS work, different distribution automation systems must be developed.

iii) By establishing a public and private key for containers, the private key improves the security of the EaaS dashboard. Whenever a container is initiated for the first moment, consumers can use the Web App to install a private key.

iv) The user database manages the usernames and passwords of the EaaS system's users. This database keeps track of the current active users on the edge nodes as well as their activity times.

v) The edge database stores all recognized edge nodes' public IP, open port number, and coordinator metadata, as well as the name, status, and public IP of containers on the edge node.

vi) The master node communicator communicates with the edge node manager and acts as a liaison in between the console and the edge node. This program contains commands for beginning, halting, and aborting containers on edge nodes. The edge node manager is in charge of updating the dataset with the outcomes of the edge node's operations. Moreover, the monitor receives metric data from tracking via this module. The edge node administrator is placed on the edge node during identification and implements instructions received from the master node facilitation, providing the results to the communications.

The EaaS platform is accessed via a web application that serves as a user interface. Consumers who allow access to an edge node could be EaaS platform administrators or application owners. The supervisor screen offers global information on a variety of performance parameters, such as the CPU and memory use of containers utilized by edge node consumers. The management can launch, halt, or terminate containers. The software founder functionality gives information about the containers that the user has installed on an edge node. On the edge node, customers can execute a software container (such as Docker) or an operating system container (such as LXD). Figure 7 depicts the EaaS platform's component view.

7. Applications of Edge Computing

1. Image and Video Analysis

Edge computing, as stated previously, helps reduce the amount of data stored in clouds by having to process the vast bulk of information at the network's edge. This tool is highly useful in this day and age of smart

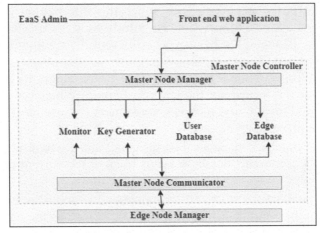

Fig. 7. Component view of EaaS platform.

devices and network cameras. The analysis of video and images has become very simple. For example, a system of cameras embedded in each vehicle and in city environments can click the picture of the child gone missing. However, transferring all of the camera's data to the cloud is extremely difficult. And, if this happens, it is best to avoid doing so due to privacy concerns. In this particular instance, the use of edge computing can help in resolving issues. The cloud would only start generating the application to search for the child, and this application will be sent to all edge devices in the targeted regions, such as cell devices, tablet devices, and so on, and the gadgets will search their local cameras and report the results back to the cloud.

2. Smart Home

Many gadgets used during our everyday lives, including TVs, lighting systems, smart fridges, and so on, are ingrained with various wireless sensors and devices that create a big quantity of information and are mostly used in homes. Thus, IoT plays a critical part in trying to make a home smart. Instead of having to send all data to the cloud, it is beneficial to handle and organize the information at the endpoint device, which has a specialized edgeOS and is connected to all home devices. EdgeOS should gather data from mobile and other devices via a range of communication methods, including Wi-Fi, Bluetooth, ZigBee, and cellular networks. As a result, each device's response time is reduced, and the strain on bandwidth is lowered. However, challenges like data protection, data separation, data reliability, and so on still exist.

3. Smart City

Cities are considered smart if they have smart transport services, smart healthcare, and smart utilities, among other things. The most viable option is edge computing for creating an urban development since all of the aforementioned fields or sectors are moving towards IoT, and the notion of edge computing is adaptable. The transition from a smart house to a smart city is simple. For the following reasons, edge computing would be the best platform:

- Reduced response time to users and low latency
- Data processing at the edge
- Location Awareness

4. Cloud Offloading

Almost all manipulations in cloud computing are performed in the cloud, i.e. data and demands are filtered in the cloud and then the outcome is produced. Since each small modification takes time, the user should accept the result. Numerous studies have discovered that clouds attempting to offload are determined by the energy-performance tradeoff in a dynamic context. The edge in edge computing contains data manipulating gadgets that reduce the volume of work of the cloud. Raw data was sent directly to the internet over the last few decades, resulting in an increase in response time. Information is produced and consumed at the edge in the case of IoT. In case of multiple edge nodes, synchronization issues arise, but edge computing has many applications, including lowering response time in real applications such as video gaming, virtual reality, and connected health, amongst many others, dramatically improving time-sensitive applications.

5. Healthcare Devices

Patients can track chronic disorders with health trackers and other wearable healthcare gadgets. It has the capability to survive by alerting caregivers promptly when aid is necessary. Robots aiding in surgery must be able to analyze data fast in order to assist safely, promptly, and precisely. If these gadgets rely on relaying data to the cloud without making decisions, the results might be disastrous.

6. Retail Advertising and Smart Speakers

For retail organizations, targeted marketing and information are dependent on essential factors specified on field devices, such as demographic data.

In this case, edge computing can assist safeguard user privacy. It may encrypt data and maintain the source rather than transferring unprotected data to the cloud. Smart speakers may be able to interpret voice commands locally in order to perform basic tasks. It would be possible to turn lights on and off, as well as adjust thermostat settings, even if internet connectivity was lost.

8. Challenges in Implementing Edge Computing

1. Data Privacy and Data Security

Because all information from end devices is sent to the edge OS for processing, the edge computing paradigm prioritizes privacy and security. In home automation, for example, different smart systems are placed with detectors and other IoT devices that share all of their data on the gateway, allowing one to quickly deduce if the home is vacant or not by simply analyzing readings of water or power usage. As a result, data security and privacy are two major challenges for edge computing design.

2. Cost

The cost of installing edge computing configurations is also a significant barrier. As the number of edge devices grows, the cost of handling the information by several end edge devices rises. As a consequence, a suitable payment model for implementing an edge computing device should be established.

3. Resource Management

Even though users send so many queries at the network's edge, including some that are critical assistance that necessitate real - time processing than ordinary services, one must prioritize tasks for various services, which would be a difficult task to handle. Another major issue at the network's edge is the separation of distinct requests; nevertheless, when data arrives at the edge at the same time, it's possible that data from separate requests is mixed together, resulting in the loss of accurate information. As a result, consumers continue being unable to receive the necessary output, resulting in a negative customer experience.

4. Offloading and Partitioning of Tasks

The emergence of distributed computing systems has led to the development of several approaches to permit division of jobs that may be completed at multiple geographic locations. Workflows, for example, are divided into sections for running in multiple locations. Task splitting is most often described directly in management or language tools. Using edge nodes for offloading computations, on the other hand, raises the difficulty of not only efficiently splitting computational activities, but also doing so in an automated way that does not need the explicit declaration of edge node capabilities or placement. A user of an edge node-supporting language could expect flexibility in building a computing cascade, either hierarchies or across several edge nodes in one go. It is intrinsically tied to the development of schedulers that deliver partitioned workloads to edge nodes.

9. Case Study

Purchase activity information for visitors to retail outlets could only be acquired from purchase records in POS data or from direct observation until recently [30]. As a result, retail-marketing managers are concerned with analyzing consumer behavior prior to purchase, as well as non-purchasers who leave the store without completing a purchase. These problems are solved by installing cameras in the store and using image analysis technologies to visualize visitors' in-store activities. These technologies detect people, monitor their movements, and extract their flow lines.

Pictures from the company's webcams are gathered first by a computer (edge) in the store. The smartphone's result and analysis recognize the motion area, compares pictures of face parts, derives folks from images taken, predicts and tracks their moves. The analysis component needs to perform these operations in the computer's RAM, and save only the derived persons' supporting information and throw away the seized images taken or data formed by the analysis generator during handling. One advantage of the model is that the data that leads to detecting the face is not saved. The produced information about the coordinate of each webcam is accumulated in the cloud and processed to gain the flow queue of people. The "heat map trying to represent a customer's in-store dwell time," the "number of individuals having to pass via in aisles per time zone," and the "transitions trying to represent the proportions of shelf-front passage time" are then gathered into numerous results obtained to be presented as the "heat map chosen to represent a customers in-store dwell time," the "number of individuals passing via in hallways per time zone," and the "conversions chosen to represent the ratios of racks. Even though all of this information is hosted in the cloud, the person in charge of in-store advertising can access it via the internet from any place, whether in or out of the store.

This system also integrates with the Field Analyst scheme, which instantly estimates sexual identity and age ranges, so that the outcomes of the "number of tourists and gender/age organizations per time zone" collected from store camera images are also saved in the cloud for later viewing.

The gathered data enables the marketing executive to continually and statistically monitor consumer sentiment, as well as plan activities based on the obtained data, such as shop preferences, and to validate the consequences of actions performed. Moreover, when the information is combined with the purchase record keeping in the independently collected POS data, visitors' quasi activity may be examined with their purchasing behavior. The architectural style of human behavioral science is depicted in Figure 8.

The demand to enhance work efficiency in factories and construction sites in order to boost production has never been stronger. If a survey is undertaken for work done by humans in the traditional manner, the time spent would have a negative influence on productivity, however IoT technology allows for efficient ways to increase it. The location might be determined by gathering movement data on sensing devices, charting it using location information, and eventually exhibiting and recording flow lines on a map. In order to acquire movement data, devices must be chosen based on the present environment. Outside, GPS is commonly used, but Quasi-Zenith Satellite System (QZSS) has recently been used as well. Indoors, technologies such as UWB (Ultra-Wide Band), Wi-Fi, and acoustic wave devices are available; although a beacon is appropriate in many circumstances due to its low cost (a few thousand yen per beacon).

Beacons' data may be received by mobile phones and tablets with BLE (Bluetooth Low Energy) capability. The IDs are sent by beacons at regular

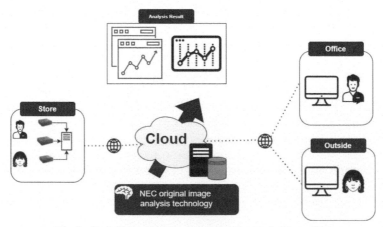

Fig. 8. Overall image of human behavior analysis service.

Beacon devices

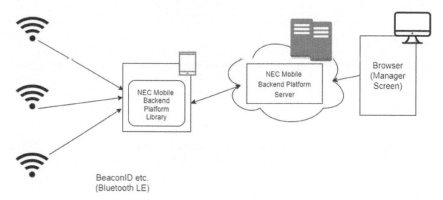

Fig. 9. An example of a beacon-based location application framework settings.

intervals and hence their positions are pre-mapped on the indoor maps. The information gathered by smartphones and terminals is maintained in the NEC Mobile Backend Platform, where it is displayed by converting it to precise location data and presenting it on a map. Figure 9 shows the configuration example.

10. Conclusion

Edge cloud structures are used to decentralize (processing) power to the edges of the network (clients/devices). Historically, server computer science power has been used to undertake services such as data minimization and the development of advanced distributed applications. Such 'intelligent' tasks are carried out by cloud servers so that they can be transmitted to systems with low or no computer resources. In contrast to a prototype, in which customers simply connect to servers, vast numbers of customers are all linked to each other to conduct smaller data processing. In ideal edge computing, millions of IoT devices can form an immense smart system capable of performing tasks normally only potential in very large data centers. The background and integration of cloud and edge computing, as well as the various requirements for edge cloud architectures were covered in detail in this chapter. It also discussed the various edge cloud architectures proposed by various researchers. In addition, it included case studies and brief information about the applications and challenges of edge cloud computing. The future of edge computing is very bright as it can be used in the process of manufacturing products that will revolutionize the industry sector.

References

[1] Oppitz, M. and Tomsu, P. (2018). Cloud computing. Inventing the Cloud Century, pp. 267–318. doi: 10.1007/978-3-319-61161-7_11.

[2] Perera, C., Zaslavsky, A., Christen, P. and Georgakopoulos, D. (2014). Sensing as a service model for smart cities supported by Internet of Things. Transactions on Emerging Telecommunications Technologies 25(1): 81–93. doi: 10.1002/ETT.2704.

[3] The fifth annual Cisco® Global Cloud Index (2014–2019), released today, forecasts that global cloud traffic will more than quadruple by the end of 2019, outpacing the growth of total global data center traffic, which is forecast to triple during the same time frame. | The Network. https://newsroom.cisco.com/press-release-content?articleId=1724918 (accessed Feb. 05, 2022).

[4] GSMA | IoT Connections Forecast: The Rise of Enterprise | Internet of Things. https://www.gsma.com/iot/resources/iot-connections-forecast-the-rise-of-enterprise/ (accessed Feb. 05, 2022).

[5] Dilley, J., Maggs, B.M., Parikh, J., Prokop, H., Sitaraman, R. and Weihl, B. (1998). Globally distributed content delivery. doi: 10.1184/R1/6605972.V1.

[6] Noble, B.D., Satyanarayanan, M., Narayanan, D., Tilton, J.E., Flinn, J. and Walker, K.R. (1997). Agile application-aware adaptation for mobility, pp. 276–287. doi: 10.1145/268998.266708.

[7] Flinn, J. and Satyanarayanan, M. (1999). Energy-aware adaptation for mobile applications. Proceedings of the 17th ACM Symposium on Operating Systems Principles, SOSP 1999: 48–63. doi: 10.1145/319151.319155.

[8] Satyanarayanan, M. (2001). Pervasive computing: Vision and challenges. IEEE Personal Communications 8(4): 10–17. doi: 10.1109/98.943998.

[9] Li, A., Yang, X., Kandula, S. and Zhang, M. (2010). CloudCmp: Comparing public cloud providers. Proceedings of the ACM SIGCOMM Internet Measurement Conference, IMC, pp. 1–14. doi: 10.1145/1879141.1879143.

[10] Satyanarayanan, M., Bahl, P., Cáceres, R. and Davies, N. (2009). The case for VM-based cloudlets in mobile computing. IEEE Pervasive Comput. 8(4): 14–23. doi: 10.1109/MPRV.2009.82.

[11] Bonomi, F., Milito, R., Zhu, J. and Addepalli, S. (2012). Fog computing and its role in the Internet of Things. Proceedings of the First Edition of the MCC Workshop on Mobile Cloud Computing - MCC 12. doi: 10.1145/2342509.

[12] Hassan, N., Gillani, S., Ahmed, E., Yaqoob, I. and Imran, M. (2018). The role of edge computing in Internet of Things. IEEE Communications Magazine 56(11): 110–115. doi: 10.1109/MCOM.2018.1700906.

[13] Ahmed, E., Akhunzada, A., Whaiduzzaman, M., Gani, A., Ab Hamid, S.H. and Buyya, R. (2015). Network-centric performance analysis of runtime application migration in mobile cloud computing. Simul. Model Pract. Theory 50: 42–56. doi: 10.1016/J.SIMPAT.2014.07.001.

[14] Pace, P., Aloi, G., Gravina, R., Caliciuri, G., Fortino, G. and Liotta, A. (2019). An edge-based architecture to support efficient applications for healthcare industry 4.0. IEEE Trans. Industr. Inform. 15(1): 481–489. doi: 10.1109/TII.2018.2843169.

[15] Mach, P. and Becvar, Z. (2017). Mobile edge computing: A survey on architecture and computation offloading. IEEE Communications Surveys and Tutorials 19(3): 1628–1656. doi: 10.1109/COMST.2017.2682318.

[16] Mao, Y., You, C., Zhang, J., Huang, K. and Letaief, K.B. (2017). A survey on mobile edge computing: The communication perspective. IEEE Communications Surveys and Tutorials 19(4): 2322–2358. doi: 10.1109/COMST.2017.2745201.

[17] Ha, K., Chen, Z., Hu, W., Richter, W., Pillai, P. and Satyanarayanan, M. (2014). Towards wearable cognitive assistance. MobiSys 2014 - Proceedings of the 12th Annual

International Conference on Mobile Systems, Applications, and Services, pp. 68–81. doi: 10.1145/2594368.2594383.

[18] Simoens, P., Xiao, Y., Pillai, P., Chen, Z., Ha, K. and Satyanarayanan, M. (2013). Scalable crowd-sourcing of video from mobile devices. MobiSys 2013 - Proceedings of the 11th Annual International Conference on Mobile Systems, Applications, and Services, pp. 139–152. doi: 10.1145/2462456.2464440.

[19] Satyanarayanan, M. et al. (2015). Edge analytics in the internet of things. IEEE Pervasive Comput. 14(2): 24–31. doi: 10.1109/MPRV.2015.32.

[20] Greenberg, A., Hamilton, J., Maltz, D.A. and Patel, P. (2008). The cost of a cloud. ACM SIGCOMM Computer Communication Review 39(1): 68–73. doi: 10.1145/1496091.1496103.

[21] Wang, S., Urgaonkar, R., He, T., Zafer, M., Chan, K. and Leung, K.K. (2014). Mobility-induced service migration in mobile micro-clouds. Proceedings - IEEE Military Communications Conference MILCOM, pp. 835–840.doi: 10.1109/MILCOM.2014.145.

[22] Chang, H., Hari, A., Mukherjee, S. and Lakshman, T.v. (2014). Bringing the cloud to the edge. Proceedings - IEEE INFOCOM, pp. 346–351. doi: 10.1109/INFCOMW.2014.6849256.

[23] Farris, I., Militano, L., Nitti, M., Atzori, L. and Iera, A. (2015). Federated edge-assisted mobile clouds for service provisioning in heterogeneous IoT environments. IEEE World Forum on Internet of Things, WF-IoT 2015 - Proceedings, pp. 591–596. doi: 10.1109/WF-IOT.2015.7389120.

[24] Elias, A.R., Golubovic, N., Krintz, C. and Wolski, R. (2017). Where's the bear?-Automating wildlife image processing using IoT and edge cloud systems. Proceedings - 2017 IEEE/ACM 2nd International Conference on Internet-of-Things Design and Implementation, IoTDI 2017 (part of CPS Week), pp. 247–258. doi: 10.1145/3054977.3054986.

[25] Hu, X., Wong, K.K. and Yang, K. (2018). Wireless powered cooperation-assisted mobile edge computing. IEEE Trans. Wirel. Commun., 17(4): 2375–2388. doi: 10.1109/TWC.2018.2794345.

[26] Rimal, B.P., Van, D.P. and Maier, M. (2017). Mobile edge computing empowered fiber-wireless access networks in the 5G Era. IEEE Communications Magazine 55(2): 192–200. doi: 10.1109/MCOM.2017.1600156CM.

[27] Varghese, B. and Buyya, R. (2018). Next generation cloud computing: New trends and research directions. Future Generation Computer Systems 79: 849–861. doi: 10.1016/J.FUTURE.2017.09.020.

[28] Meurisch, C., Seeliger, A., Schmidt, B., Schweizer, I., Kaup, F. and Mühlhäuser, M. (2015). Upgrading wireless home routers for enabling large-scale deployment of cloudlets. Lecture Notes of the Institute for Computer Sciences, Social-Informatics and Telecommunications Engineering, LNICST 162: 12–29. doi: 10.1007/978-3-319-29003-4_2.

[29] Wang, N., Varghese, B., Matthaiou, M. and Nikolopoulos, D.S. (2020). ENORM: A framework for edge NOde resource management. IEEE Trans. Serv. Comput., 13(6): 1086–1099. doi: 10.1109/TSC.2017.2753775.

[30] Case Studies of Edge Computing Solutions: NEC Technical Journal | NEC. https://www.nec.com/en/global/techrep/journal/g17/n01/170106.html (accessed Feb. 05, 2022).

Chapter 8
Edge Computing
Edge Network Layer Security

Parminder Singh Sethi and *Atishay Jain**

In today's computing world, The Internet of Things (IoT) is a rapidly growing and expanding domain. With far more data and data-producing gadgets, there is a need to shift from old computing technologies to newer and more optimized ones. IoT, coupled with Edge computing, is growing rapidly and drives promising results. There are numerous benefits in Edge computing in the performance and turnaround time for processing, but there are a few security challenges that come along with edge computing. A few such challenges are discussed in this chapter.

In this chapter, we have discussed implementations surrounding the security of edge networks.

1. Introduction

Edge computing entails bringing computing resources near to "edge" of the data source [1]. This reduces the latency due to data transfer over a network and offers reduced bandwidth and faster processing of data. Broadly speaking edge computing is transferring computing ability to the edge of the network. Autonomous Self Driving Vehicles, AI-based Virtual Assistants and 5G Telecom networks, are a few of the examples where edge computing finds vital and widespread utilization. In Edge Computing infrastructure tons of data is generated at the edge of the

Dell EMC, Dell EMC, India.
Email: singhsethi.parminder@gmail.com
* Corresponding author: atishayjain3098@gmail.com

network. Data being the most critical and cardinal component needs to be secured whether at rest or in motion. The data from the end-user device or sensor is always constantly flowing in edge deployments. This data can be intercepted or exposed to a malicious group and may pose major threats to an organization, it must be safeguarded both in transit and at rest.

A highly distributed edge infrastructure using numerous edge computing nodes opens up hundreds of possible entry points for DDoS assaults and other security breaches, which is a gruesome problem [2]. This chapter aims to provide awareness by discussing the security challenges of edge networks and applicable implementation to mitigate them.

2. Architecture of Edge, Cloud, and Fog Computing

Cloud, Fog, and Edge computing infrastructures enable businesses to interact with a wide range of computational and data storage resources. As presented in Figure 1 [3, 4], despite their affinities, these three computing technologies represent varying levels of IoT; each one builds on the preceding layer's capabilities [5, 6, 7]. These are distinct in terms of design and function, although they typically complement one another. Let's briefly look into each of these technologies.

2.1 Cloud Computing

Cloud computing is offering on-demand services or resources through the internet, allowing users to obtain seamless access to resources from remote places without having to invest additional time, money, or effort [8]. Cloud

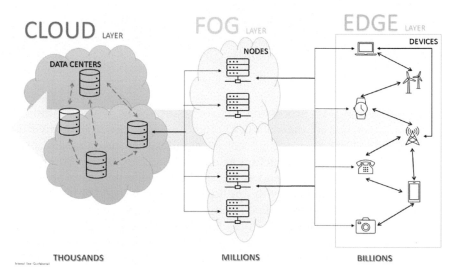

Fig. 1. Cloud, Fog, and Edge architecture.

computing architecture offers services on a pay-as-you-go basis. Cloud is generally a collection of data centers, and data is generally contained inside those data centers. Every cloud infrastructure has different types of security and privacy concerns. DoS attack, Injection of malware, and communication interception are to name a few. Despite these concerns, if any data breach occurs the teams managing the data center can control and manage the data movement in the data center. Moreover, traceability of leaks is also possible inside a contained data center environment, but this gets complicated in the fog and edge computing infrastructures. In Edge and Fog computing, the critical and valuable data of an entity is outside the data center's boundaries which becomes very difficult to manage and secure [9].

2.2 Fog Computing

Fog computing is a type of decentralized computing in which data, processing power, storage, and applications are distributed between the data source and the cloud. Rather than establishing in-cloud channels for utilization and storage, these resources are placed closer to devices where as a result, the overall bandwidth need is reduced. In a fog environment, intelligence is located on the local area network (LAN). This design sends data from endpoints to a gateway, where it is processed before being sent back to the endpoints. The goal of fog computing is to put basic analytical services through nodes on the edge of the network, much nearer to where they are required [10]. Reduced latency and support for real-time interaction are provided via these nodes. Despite its processing efficiency and reduced network latency fog computing has security and trust issues. Fog infrastructure is also susceptible to various attacks. DoS attacks, VM-based attacks, Session-hijacking, and Side-channel attacks are a few of the most critical and commonly occurring attacks.

2.3 Edge Computing

Edge computing is processing sensor data away from centralized nodes and nearer to the network's logical edge, closer to individual data sources. Data processing becomes significantly quicker with lower latency and bandwidth reduction as edge computing moves computing resources such as storage and servers closer to the end-user or source of data [8]. When dealing with applications that demand instantaneous responses with closely controlled latency, cloud or fog data is occasionally unreliable. Edge computing reduces the need to transport data back and forth from devices to the cloud leading to improved speeds and reduced latency. Edge devices are frequently installed outside of a centralized data infrastructure or data center, leaving them far more difficult to manage in terms of both digital and physical security. Data protection and storage is a major challenge in edge computing which eventually may lead to data sprawl. Edge networks can decrepit due to attacks like Eavesdropping, DoS, and Data Tampering attacks [11, 12].

3. Security Challenges of Edge Computing

Edge computing adds more network edges, resulting in greater complexity, which is difficult for businesses of all sizes to manage. Maintaining and managing the security of the extended and highly distributed edge network is a very complex and continuous task. There are various security challenges highlighted below that typically occur in an edge network [13]:

3.1 Data Storage and Protection

The devices present at edge networks generate a huge amount of data, from the edge computing infrastructure and this generated data is processed at the edge node which is generally stored in a lightweight database inside the node. The edge nodes miss the basic physical safeguards seen in most data centers. Vital information can be jeopardized easily by removing a disc drive from an edge resource or transferring data from a simple memory stick. Generally, the edge computing facilities typically have minimal local storage possibilities, backing up crucial information might be difficult, if not impossible. So, there may not be a backup copy of the database to restore if an incident happens [14].

3.2 Password and Authentication Risks

Local IT operations personnel that are security-sensitive rarely support edge computing services. Managing edge systems could be a secondary job for several people, and this situation encourages practicing lax passwords, such as accepting default credentials, using common passwords to remember, posting passwords for critical applications on sticky notes, and failing to change passwords frequently [15].

3.3 An Enlarged Attack Surface

Edge computing necessitates massive amounts of distributed computation and storage resources. Edge security policies must also account for the diverse range of edge computing nodes and systems, and a flexible solution that adjusts as needed within reasonable parameters must be devised. A physical threat as well as a virtual one/Perimeter defense risks exist [16].

3.4 Distributed Denial of Service (DDoS) Attacks

DDoS is a sort of cyber-attack that attempts to interrupt regular services offered by one or more servers using distributed resources such as a cluster of hacked edge devices. There are various types of DDoS attacks identified in edge computing such as, when an attack forces nodes to discontinue operating completely, it is called an outage attack. A Sleep deprivation assault occurs when attackers overwhelm nodes with valid requests, preventing them from entering a power-saving mode, resulting in a significant rise in power consumption. A battery-draining attack, also known as a barrage attack, can create disruption by depleting the battery life of certain nodes or sensors by repeatedly running energy-intensive programs or apps [17].

3.5 Connectivity Challenges (Routing Information Attacks)

Edge devices cannot be considered to have continual network access. Various routing attacks can disrupt the flow of data inside a network, potentially affecting throughput, latency, and communication pathways. To maintain optimal security even if the edge system is separated from the management console, whether for a short time or for a long time, security controls must continue to offer protection [18].

3.6 Beyond Traditional Information Security Visibility

In an edge-computing architecture, physical manipulation of devices is a likely possibility, depending on their location and amount of physical protection from attackers. Edge computing facilities are more vulnerable to physical manipulation and theft due to their lower size and variety. Remote edge locations generally lack IT professionals, security, and management strategies. Upon gaining physical access the attackers can alter node software and operating systems to extract sensitive and valuable cryptographic encrypted information and tamper with node circuits or damage the edge node causing a decrease in the efficiency of the network.

3.7 Malicious Hardware/Software Injections

Attackers can install illegitimate software and hardware components into the edge network, causing trouble with existing edge servers and devices and potentially allowing service provider exploitation. Node replication and camouflaging are a few of the common techniques used by attackers to gain access over the edge network.

4. Edge Node: Architecture and Security Considerations

The above figure represents the general architecture of a deployed edge node. Generally, the deployed node at an edge network has five core areas, i.e., data, deployed hardware, OS, the network of the node, and software. Securing each of these core areas is of crucial importance in edge networks to improve security. Let's discuss each of the core areas in detail [19]:

- *Securing Data*: The edge nodes are majorly deployed to collect, process, and extract various types of data through sensors and other devices. Data is the most valuable component in an edge network and securing data subsequently becomes very important. In an edge deployment generally, data is flowing from the end-user node. Techniques for securing data are listed below:

  o Using Encryption techniques for data flowing towards the master node.

  o Using encrypted secrets at rest, i.e., through the datastore.

  o Using volume encryption like TPM/vTPM to ensure tamper-proof encryption.

  o Using encryption for traffic flowing in cross directions, e.g., in the form of service meshes.

  o Using configures cipher suites.

- *Securing Network*: The network deployed in an edge is majorly hacked into through bad actors. These actors show themselves as genuine users and gain access to the network and then deploy various trojans to disrupt the services on an edge node. These actors are capable of launching a DoS (Denial of Service) attack on the edge node. Such attacks can overwhelm the system as edge nodes are highly resource-constrained and they cannot bear such attacks. A few methods to provide network security are listed below:

  o Maintaining the internal and external network access.

  o Separation and total isolation of network in a group of edge nodes.

  o Proactive analysis and monitoring of device health status.

  o Validation through authentication and authorization of an actor.

- *Securing OS Platform*: As OS platforms are widely available, bad actors may find a way into them, continuously looking for new methods to attack any vulnerabilities. Proactive CVE detection and instantaneous

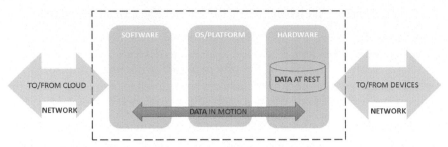

Fig. 2. Deployed Edge Node components.

patch fix are one of the ways that the OS platform can be secured. A few methods to provide security in OS platforms are listed below:

○ Using lesser to no third-party libraries to reduce the surface area for the attack.

○ Highly frequent and rigorous monitoring of system event logs.

• *Securing Software*: Using unlicensed and vulnerable software can lead to a highly vulnerable edge network. Not using industry-level secured coding practices and the development of software can expose doors for attackers to get into the system and gain control.

• *Securing Hardware*: Due to the non-confinement of hardware devices inside a secured perimeter in an edge network, the hardware components are at greater risk of being exploited. The attacker can launch an imposter device as genuine and gain access to the system. One of the efficient ways to deal with this is through device attestation.

5. Implementations of Edge Security

To understand the edge security implementations one first needs to understand various aspects involved in it [20, 21]:

1. *Perimeter security*: This aspect of edge security refers to maintaining optimized and secured access to edge resources through the use of encrypted tunnels, firewalls, and access control.

2. *Securing applications*: The application running on the edge network needs to be bug-free, tamper-resistant, and secured.

3. *Early Threat detection*: Edge computing technology is highly distributed and scalable; hence it becomes very crucial to use proactive threat detection technology to detect a potential breach as soon as possible.

4. *Managing vulnerabilities*: Monitoring Common Vulnerabilities and Exposures (CVEs), and role-based access control (RBAC) should be done proactively to identify and remove known and unknown vulnerabilities.

5. *Patching cycles*: Automated deployments to keep the nodes and devices updated with the latest patch for security requirements to minimize the potential surface attacks.

Based on the aspects of edge security various methods are discussed below to improve and optimize it:

1. *Zero trust approach*: Zero Trust is a security concept based on the premise that organizations should not trust anything within or outside their perimeters and should instead check anything attempting to connect to their systems before providing access. Professionals are granted only the bare minimum access to any device for it to function properly [22]. ZTE (Zero Trust Edge) networks are available from nearly everywhere, they provide a safer internet on-ramp, leveraging Zero Trust Network Access (ZTNA) to verify people and devices as they join.

Principles driving the ZTE security:

  i. Continuously monitoring and validating the users within and outside the organization, i.e., trusting no one.

  ii. Providing on-needs basis access to users.

  iii. Ensuring strict access control to the devices.

  iv. Using Multi-Factor Authentication to identify a genuine user.

A few of the benefits of using ZTE are:

  a. Risk Reduction

  b. Cost Reduction

  c. Enhanced user experience

2. *Secure access service edge (SASE)*: SASE is a network architecture that integrates VPN and SD-WAN capabilities with cloud-native security features including secure web gateways, cloud access security brokers, firewalls, and zero-trust network access. SASE is a cloud-delivered service paradigm that combines wide-area networking (WAN) with network security services such as CASB, FWaaS, and Zero Trust. SASE-based networks are adaptable and scalable, allowing globally dispersed employees and offices to join from any place on any device.

SASE includes four core security components:

  i. *Secure web gateways (SWG)*: By screening undesired information from web traffic, restricting illegal user activity, and enforcing enterprise security regulations, a SWG avoids cyber risks and data breaches.

  ii. *Cloud access security broker (CASB)*: To avoid data breaches, malware infection, regulatory violations, and a lack of visibility,

CASBs guarantee that cloud apps and services are used safely. CASBs protect cloud apps that are hosted in public clouds (IaaS), private clouds, or as software-as-a-service (SaaS).

iii. *Zero trust network access (ZTNA)*: ZTNA has a cutting-edge strategy to safeguard user application access. It follows a zero-trust approach, in which application access is adjusted dynamically based on user identification, location, device kind, and other factors.

iv. *Firewall-as-a-Service (FWaaS)*: Firewalls supplied as a service via the cloud are known as FWaaS. FWaaS guards against cyber threats on cloud-based platforms, infrastructure, and applications.

v. *Software-Defined WAN (SD-WAN)*: SD-WAN is an overlay architecture that chooses the optimum path for traffic to the internet, cloud apps, and the data center, reducing complexity and improving the user experience [23, 24].

3. *Ensuring the physical security of edge devices*: To improve physical security at the edge, use access control and monitoring. Software level controls to prevent physical security risks are as follows:

   a. *Segmentation of network*: The Edge network should be designed in such a manner that the interdependency of devices is minimum. This ensures very small impact on a device due to a physical security breach on another device.

   b. *Minimization of data*: Minimizing the storage and sharing of sensitive data in the edge network.

   c. *Highly advanced device authentication*: Using the highest possible level of authentication (like biometric) can ensure secure access to an extent, although it is not guaranteed.

4. *Applying 5 P's*:

   a. *People*: People are generally the most error-prone asset. Proper training and security practices must be ensured for maintaining edge security.

   b. *Policies and Procedures*: Edge security governance should be regular, and individuals should be reminded of how and when to be cautious.

   c. *Process*: It is critical to list the actions that individuals must take to properly limit the danger of edge security.

   d. *Products*: Organizations must be aware of the components that make up a complete cyber security solution.

   e. *Proof*: All the above must be tested regularly to identify and mitigate risks.

5. *Employing continuous and proactive audits and patching*: Setting up auditing processes to keep track of data and application hosting changes at the edge. All edge activity, particularly activity related to operations and configuration, should be monitored and logged. Regular audits must be performed to ensure the healthy status of devices/nodes in the edge network. Regular patching of devices based on the results of the audits should be put into the process.

6. Conclusion

The Internet of Things (IoT) is a rapidly expanding field. With far more data and data-producing gadgets, we'll need to shift away from old computing technologies toward new, more powerful ones. Edge computing is one of the technologies which is growing at a rapid pace and drives promising results. There are numerous benefits in Edge computing in the domain of performance and turnaround time for processing, but there are a few security challenges that come along with edge computing. Few such challenges are discussed in this chapter.

As Edge computing is more distributed than Cloud computing and has billions of endpoints as edge devices, there are far more security loopholes that can be explored and can exploit the edge network. For Edge Computing security must be considered from the beginning of the creation of an edge network. Although proper security implementation is a difficult and time-consuming operation, the sooner it is handled, the more likely the final product will be suitable.

In this chapter, we have discussed implementations surrounding the security of edge networks. Different implementations work effectively in a different type of edge environment, which makes the overall idea of security more challenging. For an Edge deployment, the physical security of the edge devices is one of the major security concerns.

References

[1] Definition of Edge Computing - IT Glossary | Gartner. https://www.gartner.com/en/information-technology/glossary/edge-computing (accessed Apr. 27, 2022).

[2] (PDF) Survey on Edge Computing Security. | Baydaa Hassan, Shavan Askar. https://www.researchgate.net/publication/349028144_Survey_on_Edge_Computing_Security (accessed Apr. 27, 2022).

[3] Practical Applications of Cloud, Edge and Fog Computing. | Oriol Rius. https://www.e-zigurat.com/innovation-school/blog/cloud-edge-fog-computing-practical-applications/ (accessed May 05, 2022).

[4] Page 2 of [Discussion post] Need of Cloud, Fog and Edge Computing - Huawei Enterprise Support Community. | MahMush. https://forum.huawei.com/enterprise/en/discussion-post-need-of-cloud-fog-and-edge-computing/thread/748771-893?page=2 (accessed May 05, 2022).

[5] The Three Layers of Computing – Cloud, Fog and Edge - SCC. https://www.scc.com/insights/it-solutions/data-centre-modernisation/the-three-layers-of-computing-cloud-fog-and-edge/ (accessed Apr. 27, 2022).

[6] Cloud computing vs fog computing vs edge computing: The future of IoT. | KARTIK WALI. https://analyticsindiamag.com/cloud-computing-vs-fog-computing-vs-edge-computing-the-future-of-iot/ (accessed Apr. 27, 2022).

[7] Al-Qamash, A., Soliman, I., Abulibdeh, R. and Saleh, M. (2018). Cloud, Fog, and Edge computing: A software engineering perspective. 2018 Int. Conf. Comput. Appl. ICCA 2018, pp. 276–284, Sep. 2018, doi: 10.1109/COMAPP.2018.8460443.

[8] The NIST Definition of Cloud Computing - Content Details -. https://www.govinfo.gov/app/details/GOVPUB-C13-74cdc274b1109a7e1ead7185dfec2ada (accessed Apr. 27, 2022).

[9] (PDF) Security and Privacy Issues in Cloud, Fog and Edge Computing. | Parikh, Shalin, Dave, Dharmin, Patel, Reema and Doshi, Nishant. https://www.researchgate.net/publication/337431584_Security_and_Privacy_Issues_in_Cloud_Fog_and_Edge_Computing (accessed Apr. 27, 2022).

[10] (PDF) Fog Computing and its Role in the Internet of Things. | Bonomi, Flavio and Milito, Rodolfo. https://www.researchgate.net/publication/235409978_Fog_Computing_and_its_Role_in_the_Internet_of_Things (accessed Apr. 27, 2022).

[11] Mohan, N. and Kangasharju, J. (2017). Edge-Fog cloud: A distributed cloud for Internet of Things computations. 2016 Cloudification Internet Things, CIoT 2016, Mar. 2017, doi: 10.1109/CIOT.2016.7872914.

[12] IEEE Xplore Full-Text. | Weisong Shi and Schahram Dustdar. PDF: https://ieeexplore.ieee.org/stamp/stamp.jsp?tp=&arnumber=7469991&tag=1 (accessed May 05, 2022).

[13] Xiao, Y. et al. (2019). Edge Computing Security: State-of-The-Art and Challenges. doi: 10.1109/JPROC.2019.2918437. (accessed Apr. 27, 2022).

[14] Edge computing security risks and how to overcome them. | Tom Nolle. https://www.techtarget.com/iotagenda/tip/Edge-computing-security-risks-and-how-to-overcome-them (accessed Apr. 27, 2022).

[15] Edge Computing Security Risk And Challenges in 2021. | Stuart Rauch. https://www.simplilearn.com/edge-computing-security-risk-and-challenges-article (accessed Apr. 27, 2022).

[16] Is Edge Computing Secure? Here Are 4 Security Risks to Be Aware Of. | Brett Daniel. https://www.trentonsystems.com/blog/is-edge-computing-secure (accessed Apr. 27, 2022).

[17] Li David Levine, M. (2020). A Survey on DDoS Attacks in Edge Servers.

[18] Security Challenges at the Edge of the Network | Section. https://www.section.io/blog/security-challenges-network-edge/ (accessed Apr. 27, 2022).

[19] 5 security considerations for edge implementations. | John Senegal. https://www.redhat.com/en/blog/5-security-considerations-edge-implementations (accessed Apr. 27, 2022).

[20] Edge Security: How to Secure the Edge of the Network. | Sean Michael Kerner. https://www.esecurityplanet.com/networks/edge-security-how-to-secure-the-edge-of-the-network/ (accessed Apr. 27, 2022).

[21] Edge Security, Edge Computing & Edge IoT Security | Forcepoint. https://www.forcepoint.com/cyber-edu/edge-security (accessed Apr. 27, 2022).

[22] Assunção, P. (2019). A Zero Trust Approach to Network Security. doi: 10.11228/dpsc.01.01.

[23] SASE: What is Secure Access Service Edge? | Cato Networks. https://www.catonetworks.com/sase/ (accessed Apr. 27, 2022).

[24] SASE: What is Secure Access Service Edge? | Zscaler. https://www.zscaler.com/resources/security-terms-glossary/what-is-sase (accessed Apr. 27, 2022).

Chapter 9

Current Status and Application of Data-Analytics in Cardiovascular Care

Dinesh C. Dobhal and *Bhawnesh Kumar**

Cardiovascular disease (CVD) is a generic term that is used for a class of diseases which are related to the functioning of the heart or blood vessels. It includes Coronary Artery Diseases (CAD), angina, Myocardial Infarction, Ventricular Fibrillation (Arrhythmia), Cardiomyopathy, Congenital Heart Disease (CHD), Mitral valve regurgitation, and Pulmonary stenosis. All these diseases are lethal that might be faced by a person with an unhealthy lifestyle. According to a report of World Health Organization CVD is fatal in nature and around 31% of all deaths worldwide are due to it. In India, it was observed that about 2 million people die annually because of CVD. Timely diagnosis of these diseases would assist the medical practitioner in the administration of appropriate treatment. Large and complex biomedical datasets need to be explored and compared to extract valuable insights that can be used to diagnose and take care of chronic diseases like Myocardial Infarction. Big Data analytics, which is widely used in cleaning, processing and managing voluminous datasets of structured as well as unstructured data, can be a useful tool to predict, manage and treat cardiovascular disease.

Associate Professor, Graphic Era University, Dehradun, UK, India.
Email: dineshdobhal@gmail.com
* Corresponding author: bhawneshmca@gmail.com

A systematic literature review methodology is used to explore the applicability of data analytics to cardiovascular care. Relevant articles were found from five major national and international scientific databases. A total of 62 articles were selected for the study. Most of the papers are experimental in nature and use machine-learning techniques to propose a solution for monitoring and taking care of cardiac disease. In this paper, we have presented various issues and challenges faced by Big Data Analytics (BDA) in healthcare. The current state of BDA in healthcare and cardiovascular disease prediction systems using machine-learning are also highlighted.

1. Introduction

A huge number of individuals follow an unhealthy and lethargic way of life. Therefore, they experience sickness, disability and even demise. Issues like metabolic infections, joint pain, cardiac problem, blood pressure, diabetes and excess weight, can occur due to an unhealthy lifestyle. Factors related to individual health and quality of life are profoundly correlated and ought to be considered by everyone [1–3, 4]. This unhealthy lifestyle reduces an individual's ability to fight diseases; thus it imposes a significant workload on healthcare systems, particularly at the time of pandemics. Healthcare practitioner rarely handle numerous ever growing healthcare issues and challenges that include a population with older age, constant sicknesses, uninsured cost of hospitalization, and the margin of clinical mistakes [5]. These healthcare systems can increase operational efficiency, treatment quality and patient care through regular up gradation of infrastructure, professional skills of employees, and adoption of data analytics technologies. Not doing so, however, can create a long list of technical and operational problems that can be difficult to recover from.

Data Analytics is a process of analyzing raw data to explore and derive valuable information that can be used to provide customized solutions to the individual customer. It includes identification and interpretation of patterns inside the data and is widely used by the different organizations of almost all sizes. The term Analytics in business was first used by Frederick Winslow Taylor, an American mechanical engineer, in 19th century, when he was working on time management exercises. In the late 1960s, with the advancement in computational machines, analytics started getting more consideration and evolved significantly with the development of data warehouses, data mining, big data, and cloud computing technologies. In present times, Data Analytics has grown to include: Big data Analytics, Cognitive Analytics, Predictive Analytics, Descriptive Analytics, Perspective Analytics, Augmented Analytics, Web Analytics, and more [6].

In the past few years, there has been, huge growth in data digitalization across industries. The healthcare industry is no exception, being touched by digital transformation [7]. The use of Electronic Medical Records (EMRs), handheld, wearable, and smart devices by the hospitals and healthcare providers, results in a massive amount of heterogeneous health-related digital data, which includes health profiles, administrative data, omics data, clinical trial data, and insurance claims data. In order to improve quality of life, diagnosis and care of critical diseases, vital information can be mined from healthcare big data, but the database is so large and complex that it is very hard to manage it with the help of traditional database management tools and computing machines [8]. The technologies, which were designed to process the big data, can be organized in the following four categories *'Big Data Storage', 'Big Data Mining', 'Big Data Analytics'*, and *'Big Data Visualization'*, shown in Table 1.

Big data analytics, such as predictive and descriptive analytics, are suitable for the analysis of structured data, such as text-based health records, and other unstructured data, such as genetic or molecular human profiles, hand written doctors' comments, instructions and medical images. These data analytics techniques can be used to collect, store, integrate, disseminate, clinical data to derive insights that can help healthcare organizations to improve the quality of patient health care and treatment cost [9]. A technical background of big data analytics is analyzed and presented by various researchers in [8, 10–13].

It is estimated that by using big data analytics, health care providers would save at least $300–450 billion per year. However, they keep on battling to pick up advantages from their investments in these analytical techniques and some of them are doubtful about their capacity [14].

The large, unstructured, and heterogeneous data set that is generated and analyzed in cardiovascular care and research include data from the patient's medical history, age, gender, weight, height, physical activities, work environment, lipid profile, Complete Blood Count (CBC), electrocardiogram (ECG), echocardiogram (ECHO), Computerized Tomography (CT) scan, *Magnetic Resonance Imaging (MRI)* scans, and Omics. These data sets can be processed and analyzed to identify the cause and care of various cardiac diseases and can also help to create "personalized medication" according to the unique biomedical profile of a patient.

The main objective of this paper is to explore the application and challenges of Big Data Analytics (BDA) in the prevention, diagnosis, and treatment of cardiovascular diseases. The paper is organized as follows: In Section 2, a methodology that is used to explore the previous research work on big data analytics in CVD and care is presented. Section 3 highlights the challenges for the applicability of Big Data Analytics in cardiovascular

Table 1. Big data technologies.

Category	Technology	Description
Big Data Storage	Hadoop framework	The data stored in different computing machines can be analyzed and processed in a distributed environment.
	MongoDB	It is an open-source document-based NoSQL database. It can be used to create and deploy a highly scalable database.
	Rainstor	It is designed to Manage and Analyze Big Data for large enterprises. The voluminous data is managed by using deduplication techniques.
	Hunk	Hunk is a relatively new product for exploring and visualizing Hadoop and other NoSQL data stores. It also provides support for Amazon's Elastic MapReduce.
Big Data Mining	Presto	It is an open-source Distributed SQL Query Engine tool, which is used for execution of Interactive Analytic Queries for small as well as large data sources.
	Rapid Miner	It is a Graphical User Interface based centralized solution that is used to explore big data for Predictive Analytics.
	Elasticsearch	It is a HTTP web interface based Distributed, Multi Tenant-capable, Full-Text Search Engine that is based on the Lucene Library.
Big Data Analytics	Apache Kafka	It is an open source distributed streaming platform that is designed to provide high-performance real-time data feeds written in Java and Scala.
	Splunk	Its application management tools capture, index and correlate real-time data; it is widely used in business and web analytics.
	KNIME	It is a Java based tool that can be used to create, view, and inspect data flows. It is extensible and also provides a mechanism to add plugins so that additional functionalities can be used.
	Spark	It is data analytics tools with in-Memory computing functionality, and provides a generalized execution model to support Java, Scala, and Python based application development.
	R	R is a programming environment for high-performance statistical computing and data mining. Although it is an open source language, some organizations are providing commercial support/extensions for their clients.
	BlockChain	It is a Distributed Ledger Technology (DLT), that uses decentralization and cryptographic hashing to make any digital asset transparent and non editable.
Big Data Visualization	Tableau	It is an end-to-end powerful and fast data analytics tool that is used to prepare, analyze, share and visualize valuable big data insights.
	Plotly	It is an open source, interactive Python library that can be used to plot a wide range of statistical, financial, scientific and geographical charts.

care. The healthcare issues that are addressed by BDA are discussed in Section 4. The Data Mining based Cardiovascular Disease Prediction System is reviewed in Section 5, and finally concluding remarks of the paper are presented in Section 6.

2. Review Methodology

Reviews papers that accumulate, explore, evaluate, and synthesize the previous accessible work done by researchers and academicians on a topic [15]. It also opens new possibilities for solving issues that have not been addressed yet. The objective of a Systematic Literature Review (SLR) is to explore a comprehensive list of research papers that are related to particular topics, whereas, the traditional reviews attempt to study and analyze the results of a number of papers [16]. A Systematic Literature Review (SLR) is recommended by many publications including [8, 16, 17], and in the present study, we also adopt a similar review procedure.

2.1 *Data Sources and Search Procedures*

A systematic keyword-based search of the research articles was carried out on online academic databases, such as Science Direct, *PubMed, Google Scholar, Mendeley, and IEEE Xplore,* which contain a significant number of notable pieces of work. Although, the articles were searched within a time-line of 2005–2020, most of the articles on the topic of big data were published after the year 2012. This may be due to the fact that BDA was globally recognized only after the year 2010 [8]. Although the study was focused on BDA applications in cardiovascular care, the search strings were composed of terms that included 'Big Data Analytics', 'Data Mining', 'Predictive Analytics', 'Machine Learning', 'Cardiovascular Disease', 'Cardiac Health', 'Healthcare', 'Quality of Life', 'Omics' and 'Medical Imaging'.

2.2 *Extraction Data (Inclusion and Exclusion of the Articles)*

Initially around 713 articles were downloaded as a result of keyword searches to ensure the quality of the publications taken for the review, the number was then reduced to 216 by excluding those papers which were either duplicate articles or non-journal based articles such as book chapters, master theses and editorial notes. Further, abstracts and keywords of the shortlisted articles were used as a preliminary filter to remove those articles that were not relevant to the objective of our review paper. The introduction and conclusion sections of a list of 112 articles were read to finalize the list of 62 articles to review the applications of big data in cardiovascular care. The majority of the most cited, high quality published articles were contributed by USA, England, and China.

Numerous opportunities are available in these countries to carry out research work on BDA applications in the healthcare segment.

3. Healthcare Issues Addressed by Big Data Analytics (Applications)

There are enormous applications of Big Data analytics (BDA) adopted by almost all types of organizations. One of the best examples of Big data analytics in our day to day lives is the Internet based path finder, which continually updates the data to show us the best route to the destination, and makes us aware of the accidents on the road [11]. In order to increase operational efficiency and productivity, organizations use different analytical techniques to get insights from big data; such as its heavy use by search engines to produce quick and highly informative responses; e-commerce and social media websites to predict user behaviors, and upcoming market trends. In this section, we are discussing some of the key areas where health-care organizations can be benefited by BDA.

3.1 Hospital Operations and Service Provided to the Patient

To enhance the overall operational efficiency and the productivity of their employees' health-care organizations like hospitals and pharmaceutical companies can collect and analyze their workforce data that will help them with efficient resource utilization their when and where required by making the best operational decisions. The insights which are derived from the collected data can be used by the organizations to predict the requirements of the patients and to manage them accordingly. Data analytics can also be used to reduce the operational cost and average patient service time duration. For example, the hospitals can predict the arrival rate of patients and can arrange the additional resources accordingly to manage the upcoming workload.

A number of hospitals have streamlined their operations by implementing a centralized command-and-control center, and a predictive analytics enabled platform which is able to learn continually, and use advanced optimization techniques to overcome various challenges. For example, these systems enhance the operational efficacy of hospitals by making an efficient utilization of resources by the Operation Theater (OT), assisting the emergency department in managing resources to balance queue loads of outpatient departments (OPD) and improving supply chain management. Apart from operational efficiency, BDA also improves the quality levels of care and services to patients, which they always expect at an affordable price with personalized treatment [18, 10].

Patients are now being advised to use wearable sensor based devices to monitor their blood pressure, pulse rate, body temperature, sleeping pattern, calorie burn, and so on. Doctors can monitor the health of their patients by accessing the data generated by these wearable devices which is saved in cloud storage. This would also help doctors to develop a personalized health program for the patient. Patients unable to visit the hospital, as we have seen recently at the time of the novel corona virus pandemic, can avail expert treatment using telemedicine services. In addition to personalized health programs and telemedicine services, BDA allows the patients to connect with social media platforms and different forums, to get more information such as disease symptoms, common treatment side-effects, post treatment care, and feedback on a particular hospital or medication [10, 19, 20].

3.2 Clinical Diagnosis and Research

Clinical diagnosis is an attempt made by physicians to diagnose a disease by analyzing medical signs and symptoms reported by patients. The volume and the complexity of the data provided to the physician makes it difficult for him/her to take a clinical decision. In such a situation, the use of the Healthcare Information System (HIS) could help the physician by processing data and making recommendations. Therefore, in order to enhance clinician performance and patient care, it is essential for healthcare organizations to implement and use computer-assisted decision support systems [21, 22].

There is a significant impact of BDA on reforming pharmaceutical and clinical research, where the omics, clinical, and other medical data is effectively integrated and analyzed by a predictive model to design and produce a drug [10, 23]. The pharmaceutical companies also use BDA to measure the effectiveness of designed drugs; in making strategic business decisions, and evaluating and visualizing their market position.

Medical research and drug designing are highly dependent on Omics data, which is extracted and collected during the comprehensive analysis of molecular profiles of human beings. It may include genomic, proteomic, transcriptomic, pharmacogenomic, and phenomic datasets. BDA allows the researcher to study the complex interactions between genes and molecules to analyze the disease symptoms in a patient. For example, human DNA may contain approximately 3 billion base pairs representing approximately 100 GB of data. In order to overcome these limitations and advancement in genomic research, a number of big data technologies based cost effective scalable solutions have been proposed [24, 25], which include Apache Hadoop based distributed data processing and analysis, Genomic sequence mapping [26, 27], Genomic sequencing analysis [28, 29], RNA sequence analysis [30, 31], Phylogenetic analysis [32, 33], and Statistical methods to analyze genomic data [34, 35, 36].

3.3 Medical Image and Signal Processing

Medical images are one of the components of a patient's electronic health record that are commonly used by physicians and radiologists to diagnose a disease [37]. It is a time consuming and complex process to analyze the series of different types of medical images, and requires years of experience for a radiologist to correctly identify anomalous parameters in these images. A delayed or incorrect identification of anomalous parameters of medical images may cause serious harm to the patient. Therefore, we can take advantage of data analytics techniques to design an efficient and automated system for medical image analysis. The potential application of BDA in medical imaging is discussed in [38, 39]. Application of deep-learning in medical imaging is highlighted in [40–43], whereas machine learning based solutions are presented in [44, 45, 46]. Machine learning algorithms can be used particularly in imaging analytics for pathological image diagnoses, which is a study of tissue diseases presented in [47, 48, 49].

3.4 Health Insurance

The Health insurance industry is one of the fastest growing industries in the Indian economy with approximately 1.3 billion beneficiaries. The gross premium that is collected by insurance companies in India has increased from Rs 2.56 trillion in the financial year 2012 to Rs 7.31 trillion in the financial year 2020 [50]. The development of cloud computing and big data analytics opens many opportunities for healthcare insurers [10, 51]. Like other industries, health insurance industries also can take benefits from big data technologies, by using predictive analytics models to understand the requirements of their customers. The insurers can introduce new and cost effective insurance plans for different classes of customers. They can use predictive modeling techniques to identify a pattern of fraud claims, which would help them to settle genuine claims on time. The innovative applications of data analytics in health insurance are discussed in [52, 53, 54].

4. Challenges for Big Data Applications in Cardiovascular Care

Despite numerous applications, there are many challenges also which need to be addressed first. In this section, the challenges that act as a major obstacle to the widespread acceptance of big data analytics by healthcare providers are discussed.

4.1 Source of Data

The healthcare data is generated by a number of sources and managed by different states, agencies and departments. The collaboration of medical data providers with each other would accelerate the research and innovation in health care. Development of infrastructure and a common standard that can be used to integrate these data sources is a challenge in itself.

4.2 Structuring of Data

Big Medical data combines a huge amount of data generated by hospitals and medical research from millions of patients. The data structure is heterogeneous and may vary from simple digital text to hand written doctor notes, medical images and highly complex sequences of genomes. There must be efficient and unpretentious algorithms to encode and decode such complex and unstructured data, so that it can be loaded in a computer's memory by using fewer system resources.

4.3 Data Storage

Magnetic Resonance Imaging (MRI), X-ray and photo-acoustic imaging, Computed Tomography (CT) scans, mammography, molecular, ultrasound and fluoroscope imaging, and Positron Emission Tomography-Computed Tomography (PET-CT), are some of the examples of medical imaging techniques that are widely and frequently used in diagnosis and care of a disease [55]. The medical image size depends on a number of factors such as the dimensions of the detector element, field of view, number of bits per pixel (pixel depth) and the resolution. A typical file sizes for images from different imaging modalities are given in Table 2.

The file size of the medical image can vary from a few kilobytes for a single image to several gigabytes for video file formats, which requires large and fast storage capacities. The facilitation of mass storage and designing fast and efficient algorithms to access medical image datasets becomes a challenge.

Table 2. File sizes of images from different imaging modalities [56].

Imaging Modality	Image matrix (in pixels)	Pixel Depth (bits per pixel)	File size (per image)
MRI	256 × 256	16	128 KB
CT Scan	512 × 512	16	512 KB
Ultrasound	512 × 512	8	256 KB
Color Doppler	768 × 576	8	432 KB
Digital radiography	Up to 3000 × 3000	Up to 16	Up to 18 MB
Digital mammography	Up to 3328 × 4096	14	27 MB
Computed radiography	3520 × 4280	12	Up to 22 MB

4.4 Quality of the Data

Data veracity is the accuracy and trustworthiness of the data set that is being prepared, and is directly related to different sources contributed to the data collection process, bias, abnormalities or inconsistencies, redundancies, rate of change and lifetime of the data. Poor or faulty data can reduce the data quality to the lowest level and may cause a number of real and abstract losses to organizations. Unluckily, most organizations don't actually understand their poor data quality [57]. Therefore, it is necessary for them to incorporate data quality assurance, which is a step-by-step process to identify inconsistencies, misinterpretations, inadequacies and other anomalies in the data to improve its quality.

In order to ensure the data quality for health care organizations, the different sources of errors along with their impact on the healthcare data life cycle are discussed and a systematic approach is presented in [58]. The importance and implication of the quality control of Electronic Health Records (EHRs) in clinical cardiology is highlighted by the authors in [59]. They have mentioned that coding inaccuracies in EHRs and data completeness, are the two main issues in large-scale datasets that we should focus on. As two groups of clinicians may define the same disease differently by using different sets of characteristics, the healthcare dataset generated by integration of their databases will be inconsistent. It is difficult and expensive to store continuous data streams, which are generated by monitoring medical devices, such as electrocardiogram, and lead to data incompleteness [60]. In addition, the disease information of patients, like medications and other biomedical conditions need to be recorded in the EHRs by healthcare practitioners, and this process may also result in erroneous data. According to a study conducted on [61], the inpatient medical record completeness of the Ethiopian Menelik II Referral Hospital was found to be 73% as opposed to the expected, 100%. The authors also highlighted that as these medical records are not only used for patient care but also support the clinical trials, and medical research, the quality of health care can be ensured by improving the completeness of such medical records.

Although a number of research articles addressing the assurance of data quality have been published in the past, most of them focus on the quality assurance of traditional data warehouses and big data in general. There is a growing requirement for conducting a comprehensive research on data quality issues in healthcare, particularly in cardiovascular care.

4.5 Real-Time Monitoring

Healthcare organizations and practitioners are looking forward to adopting more sophisticated tools and data analytics to offer better treatment by constantly monitoring the health of patients in real-time. Sensor enabled wearable devices can be used by doctors to monitor patients' health without unnecessary visits to the hospitals. A machine-learning based personalized healthcare system, using Bluetooth Low Energy (BLE) based sensor devices and real-time data processing to monitor the health of diabetic patients and assisting them in managing their life is discussed in [62]. ZigBee based embedded wireless health care monitoring systems are discussed in [63, 64, 65, 66] whereas Wi-Fi based systems are presented in [67, 68, 69, 70]. RFID, WSN, and IoT based, wireless sensing systems for monitoring and analyzing patient health conditions in real-time are proposed and discussed in [71, 72, 73, 74].

4.6 Patient Privacy and Data Security

With the adoption of big data analytics in health-care, almost every type of data, which is related to the medical history of patients, medications and medical research are available in an electronic format. Enhancing the availability of such data poses a serious concern of a higher risk for the loss of vital information including the personal information of a patient and organizations are unable to mine all benefits of analytics with their current resources [13]. Therefore, the security and privacy of information is another challenge for wide spread acceptance of big data analytics in healthcare.

In-depth analyses of the security and privacy issues in healthcare are presented in [75]. According to the given taxonomy, the solutions addressing the above mentioned issues are categorized as Processing based [76, 77, 78, 79, 80], Machine learning-based [81, 82, 83], Wearable device-based [84, 85, 86, 87], IoT-based [88, 89, 90], Tele-healthcare based [91, 92, 93], Policy or standard-based [94, 95], Authentication-based [96, 97, 98] and Network traffic-based schemes [99, 100]. A number of solutions have been proposed to address security and privacy issues [101], but Ethical challenges, User authentication, Confidentiality and Integrity, Data Ownership, Data Protection Policies and Misuse of Health Records are some of the issues, which are still open for research [75]. Blockchains for virtually incorruptible cryptographic databases, were originally designed for smaller sized linear transactions; their use for storing heterogeneous, voluminous medical data needs to be investigated further, particularly when legal issues are associated with the permanent storage of sensitive medical history of a patient [102]. Therefore, there is a scope to develop and implement a robust and secure infrastructure for collection, integration, access, and dissemination of health-care data [103].

Table 3. Summary of machine-learning based solutions for cardiovascular care.

S.No.	Year	Authors	Proposed Method	Technology/Algorithm used	Target disease	Data source used	Performance/Efficacy
1.	2008	Polat et al. [117]	Machine learning based computer-aided diagnosis system	Least Square Support Vector Machine (LSSVM)	Cardiac Arrhythmia	ECG Signal	Classification accuracy of 100% for all training and test data set.
2.	2011	Kutlu and Kuntalp [122]	Machine learning based automatic heartbeat recognition and classification system	Wrapper type feature selection algorithm, k-nearest neighbor algorithm	Cardiac Arrhythmia	ECG signals from MIT-BIH arrhythmia database	Average sensitivity, average selectivity, and average specificity, 85.59%, 95.46%, and 99.56% respectively
3.	2013	Javadi et al. [123]	Complementary features and Negatively Correlated Learning (NCL) based a arrhythmia classification method	Stationary wavelet transform (DWT), Negatively Correlated Learning (NCL), Neural Network	Cardiac Arrhythmia: premature ventricular contraction (PVC) arrhythmias	ECG signals from MIT-BIH arrhythmia database	Overall classification accuracy of 96.02%
4.	2013	Martis et al. [124]	A machine-learning based classification methodology	Classification And Regression Tree (CART), Artificial Neural Network, Independent Component Analysis (ICA), Random Forest (RF), and *k*-Nearest Neighbor (KNN)	Atrial Fibrillation (AF) and Atrial Flutter (AFL)	ECG records from MIT BIH atrial fibrillation database	Average accuracy for CART = 97.36% RF = 99.28%, ANN = 98.87%, and KNN = 99.50%

	Year	Author	Description	Method	Application	Data Source	Result
5.	2014	Ebrahimzaeh et al. [125]	A machine learning based three-step system to recognize the five types of Cardiac Arrhythmias	Stationary Wavelet Transform (SWT), hybrid Bees Algorithm-Radial Basis Function (RBF_BA)	Cardiac Arrhythmia	ECG Signal	Overall detection accuracy of 95.18% is achieved.
6.	2014	Zhang et al. [126]	A novel disease-specific feature selection method	Support Vector Machine (SVM) binary classifier	Cardiac Arrhythmia	ECG records from MIT-BIH-AR database	Average classification accuracy of 86.66%
7.	2015	Khalaf et al. [127]	Computer Aided Diagnosis (CAD) systems for early detection and diagnosis of cardiac arrhythmias	Principal Component Analysis (PCA), fisher scores algorithms, Support Vector Machine (SVM) with linear kernel.	Premature Ventricular Contraction (PVC), Premature Atrial Contraction (APC), Left Bundle Branch Block (LBBB), and Right Bundle Branch Block (RBBB).	ECG records	Classification accuracy of 98.60%
8.	2017	Shouval et al. [128]	A 30 days Predictive model for overall mortality after ST-elevation myocardial infarction (STEMI)	Naive Bayes, Logistic Regression, AD Tree, Random Forest, and ADAboost	Mortality rate after ST-elevation Myocardial Infarction	Acute Coronary Syndrome Israeli Survey (ACSIS) registry	Area Under the receiver operating characteristic curve (AUC) ranging from 0.64 to 0.91.
9.	2017	Mansoor et al. [109]	Predictive model for in-hospital mortality in women who are admitted with ST-elevation myocardial infarction (STEMI)	Logistic Regression (LR) and Random forest (RF) machine-learning algorithms	Mortality rate after ST-elevation Myocardial Infarction	National Inpatient Sample (NIS) data samples for the years 2011–2013	Average accuracy for LR = 88% and EF = 89%

Table 3 contd. ...

...Table 3 contd.

S.No.	Year	Authors	Proposed Method	Technology/Algorithm used	Target disease	Data source used	Performance/Efficacy
10.	2018	Yang et al. [110]	A novel analysis methodology to better classify regions of the left ventricle after myocardial infarction	Support Vector Machines Recursive Feature Elimination (SVM-RFE) algorithm, Linear Support Vector Machines (SVMs)	Infarction in regions of the left ventricle after Myocardial Infarction	Cardiac Magnetic Resonance Imaging (MRI)	Average accuracy for the following datasets; Basal = 83.9% Middle = 89.9% Apical = 81.5%
11.	2018	Mathews et al. [111]	A deep learning based, novel approach for the classification of single-lead ECG signals	Restricted Boltzmann Machine (RBM) and Deep Belief Networks (DBN)	Abnormalities in ventricular and supraventricular heartbeats	Single-lead ECG Signals	Average recognition accuracies of 93.63% for ventricular ectopic beats and 95.57% for supraventricular ectopic beats
12.	2018	Sannino et al. [112]	A novel deep learning approach for ECG beat classification	Deep Neural Network (DNN)	Cardiac Arrhythmia	MIT–BIH Arrhythmia Database	Average accuracy of 99.68%
13.	2019	Shashikant et al. [113]	Predictive model for prediction of heart attack in persons having the habit of smoking	Logistical Regression, Decision Tree, and Random Forest algorithms	Cardiac Arrest	Dataset received from the data science research group MITU Skillogies, Pune, India	Logistical Regression, Decision Tree, and Random Forest algorithms has achieved an accuracy of 88.50%, 92.59% and 93.61% respectively

14.	2019	Ibtehaz et al. [107]	VFPred: An efficient model for classification of Ventricular Fibrillation (VF).	Empirical Mode Decomposition and Discrete Fourier Transform for feature extraction, and a Support Vector Machine (SVM) for classification	Ventricular Fibrillation (VF)	The MIT-BIH Malignant Ventricular Arrhythmia Database, and Creighton University Ventricular Tachyarrhythmia Database	Sensitivity = 99.9%, and specificity = 98.4%
15.	2019	Akbar et al. [106]	A novel data mining method for coronary artery disease (CAD) diagnosis.	Genetic Algorithm and Particle Swarm Optimization for feature selection and SVM is employed for classification	Coronary Artery Disease (CAD)	Data collected from Iranian patients	Classification accuracy of 93.08% is obtained
16.	2019	Oksuz et al. [114]	Automatic detection of motion artifacts registered during in Cardiac Magnetic Resonance (CMR) cine images acquisition.	3D spatio-temporal Convolutional Neural Networks (3D-CNN), and Long-term Recurrent Convolutional Network (LRCN)	Motion-related artifacts in cardiac magnetic resonance (CMR) cine images	Cardiac MRI	Overall area under the ROC curve of 0.89 is achieved

Table 3 contd. ...

...Table 3 contd.

S.No.	Year	Authors	Proposed Method	Technology/Algorithm used	Target disease	Data source used	Performance/ Efficacy
17.	2020	Sharma et al. [115]	An accurate detection and localization of Myocardial Infarction (MI).	Stationary Wavelet Transform (SWT) for feature extraction and k-Nearest Neighbors with Mahalanobis distance function for classification	Myocardial Infarction	ECG records from Physikalisch-Technische Bundesanstalt (PTB) database	*For detection of MI:* An accuracy of 99.00% using multiple leads of ECG and an accuracy of 99.05% for a single ECG lead (i.e., lead V5). *For localization of MI:* An accuracy of 99.76% using multiple leads of ECG and an accuracy of 99.28% using a single ECG lead (i.e., lead V3).
18.	2020	Khan [116]	IoT based heart disease prediction system	Modified Deep Convolutional Neural Network	Abnormal heart function	Blood pressure and Electrocardiogram (ECG) signal from smart wearable monitoring devices	An accuracy of 98.2% is achieved
19.	2020	Gong et al. [118]	A 30-day mortality prediction model for patients with heart failure	Recurrent Attention Network	30-day mortality prediction, and prognostic factor after heart failure	Clinical and text data	An accuracy of 93.4% is achieved

20.	2020	Chang et al. [119]	A predictive model for classification of different types of cardiac arrhythmias	A Long Short-Term Memory (LSTM) deep-learning model	Cardiac arrhythmia	12-lead ECG signals from 38,899 patients	An accuracy of 95.2% is achieved
21.	2020	Wang et al. [120]	A left ventricle landmark localization and identification method	Deep distance metric learning and Convolutional Neural Network	Left ventricle landmark localization and identification	Cardiac Atlas Project: Cardiac MRI dataset	Identification rate of 95.82%
22.	2020	Muthunayaga et al. [121]	An efficient method for discrimination of subjects with normal, mild, moderate and severe abnormal ejection fraction (EF)	Optimized extreme learning machine	Abnormal ejection fraction (EF)	Cardiovascular magnetic resonance (CMR) images of 104 subjects	Multi-class a-curacy of 95.2% is achieved

5. Cardiovascular Disease Prediction System using Data Mining

Cardiovascular disease (CVD) is a generic term that is used for a class of diseases which are related to the functioning of the heart or blood vessels. It includes Coronary Artery Diseases (CAD), Angina, Myocardial Infarction, Ventricular Fibrillation (Arrhythmia), Cardiomyopathy, Congenital Heart Disease (CHD), Mitral valve regurgitation, and Pulmonary stenosis. According to a report of the World Health Organization around 31% of global deaths are due to cardiovascular disease (CVD) only. In India, nearly 20 lakh people lose their life annually just because of CVD [104, 105]. An early detection of CAD allows a physician to timely manage appropriate treatment and helps to reduce the rate of casualties [106]. Ventricular Fibrillation (VF) is a life threating cardiac arrhythmia, which is the one of the reasons for sudden cardiac arrests. A number of machine learning based solutions including Artificial Intelligence (AI) based solutions are designed and proposed in the literature to monitor and detect CVD [107, 108]. A tabular summary of these solutions is presented in Table 3.

6. Observations

1. A majority of the research work is focused on the application of machine learning to ECG-based heartbeat classifications of cardiovascular diseases, and less attention is given to the data from other sources such as Lipid profile, Echocardiogram (echo) and Cardiac Computerized Tomography (CT) scan. In order to increase classification accuracy an integrated dataset, that contains samples from multiple cardiac data sources, should be considered.

2. Machine learning based solutions are successfully used in many areas to solve complex problems accurately and efficiently by predicting the outcome on the basis of a number of features. However, "they currently lack the capacity to provide the context and causality for their predictions" [129].

3. Machine learning based algorithms just merge some parameters and draw a conclusion using those as features [107]. The feature selection process must be investigated further to identify an optimal set of features that identify the maximum number of CVDs.

4. According to the study of machine-learning (ML) algorithms on chronic heart patient datasets by the Almazov Medical Research Center, the algorithms perform better for a combination of temporal and non-temporal feature sets [130].

5. The application of ML based solutions to datasets is highly imbalanced, and can lead to biased results and inaccurate predictions [131].

6. The efficiency of machine learning techniques is limited by the quality of the medical data, which is a challenging issue and is a prerequisite for the analysis [114, 132, 133].

Deep Neural Networks (DNNs) can efficiently process big data that is generated though wearable devices, and is ideal for real-time monitoring of ECG signals [132].

7. Conclusion

Cardiovascular diseases are life threatening disease and cause a significant number of deaths worldwide. For the past few years, there was huge a growth in the digitalization of data across industries. The healthcare industry is also not untouched with this digital transformation. The use of Electronic Medical Records (EMRs) handheld, wearable, and smart devices by hospitals and healthcare providers, results in a massive amount of heterogeneous health-related digital data. In order to improve quality of life, diagnosis and care of critical diseases, vital information can be mined from big healthcare data, but the database is so large and complex that it is very hard to manage it with the help of traditional database management tools and computing machines.

Big data analytics, such as descriptive analytics and predictive analytics, are suitable for analysis of structured data, such as text-based health records, and other unstructured data, such as genetic or molecular profiles of humans, a doctor's hand written comments, instructions and medical images. These data analytics techniques can be used to collect, store, integrate, disseminate, clinical data to derive insights that can help healthcare organizations detect CVDs at an early stage and improve the quality of patient health care and treatment cost.

In this paper, we highlighted the key issues has to be addressed before widespread acceptance of BDA in healthcare. We analyzed big data technology enabled solutions for early diagnosis of CVD and presented a critical review. This observation offers a future direction for researchers and will be helpful in developing an efficient computer assisted healthcare system.

References

[1] Farhud, D.D. (2015). Impact of lifestyle on health. Iranian Journal of Public Health 44(11): 1442–1444.

[2] St-Onge, M.-P., Grandner, M.A., Brown, D., Conroy, M.B. and Syaputra, H. (2016). Sleep duration and quality: Impact on lifestyle behaviors and cardiometabolic health: A scientific statement from the american heart association. Circulation 134(18): e367–e386, Nov. 2016, doi: 10.1161/CIR.0000000000000444.

[3] Woo, K.S., Hu, Y.J., Chook, P., Wei, A.N. and Wu, M.J. (2020). The impact of lifestyle changes on cardiometabolic health in modernizing China: A tale of three gorges in the

Yangtze river. Metabolic Syndrome and Related Disorders 18(1): 65–71, Feb. 2020, doi: 10.1089/met.2019.0027.

[4] Ziglio, E., Currie, C. and Rasmussen, V.B. (2004). The WHO cross-national study of health behavior in school-aged children from 35 Countries: Findings from 2001–2002. Journal of School Health 74(6): 204–206, Aug. 2004, doi: 10.1111/j.1746-1561.2004. tb07933.x.

[5] Baig, M.M., GholamHosseini, H., Moqeem, A.A., Mirza, F., Lindén, M. et al. (2017). A systematic review of wearable patient monitoring systems – current challenges and opportunities for clinical adoption. Journal of Medical Systems 41(7): 115, Jul. 2017, doi: 10.1007/s10916-017-0760-1.

[6] Keith D. Foote. (2018). A brief history of analytics. Dataversity. [Online]. Available: https://www.dataversity.net/brief-history-analytics/.

[7] Mehta, N. and Pandit, A. (2018). Concurrence of big data analytics and healthcare: A systematic review. International Journal of Medical Informatics 114: 57–65, Jun. 2018, doi: 10.1016/j.ijmedinf.2018.03.013.

[8] Kamble, S.S., Gunasekaran, A., Goswami, M. and Manda, J. (2019). A systematic perspective on the applications of big data analytics in healthcare management. International Journal of Healthcare Management 12(3): 226–240, Jul. 2019, doi: 10.1080/20479700.2018.1531606.

[9] Wang, Y., Kung, L. and Byrd, T.A. (2018). Big data analytics: Understanding its capabilities and potential benefits for healthcare organizations. Technological Forecasting and Social Change 126: 3–13, Jan. 2018, doi: 10.1016/j.techfore.2015.12.019.

[10] Palanisamy, V. and Thirunavukarasu, R. (2019). Implications of big data analytics in developing healthcare frameworks—A review. Journal of King Saud University - Computer and Information Sciences 31(4): 415–425, Oct. 2019, doi: 10.1016/j. jksuci.2017.12.007.

[11] Weintraub, W.S. (2019). Role of big data in cardiovascular research. Journal of the American Heart Association 8(14), Jul. 2019, doi: 10.1161/JAHA.119.012791.

[12] Ismail, A., Shehab, A. and El-Henawy, I.M. (2019). Healthcare analysis in smart big data analytics: reviews, challenges and recommendations. pp. 27–45. *In*: Security in Smart Cities: Models, Applications, and Challenges.

[13] Abouelmehdi, K., Beni-Hessane, A. and Khaloufi, H. (2018). Big healthcare data: preserving security and privacy. Journal of Big Data 5(1): 1, Dec. 2018, doi: 10.1186/ s40537-017-0110-7.

[14] Asante-Korang, A. and Jacobs, J.P. (2016). Big Data and paediatric cardiovascular disease in the era of transparency in healthcare. Cardiology in the Young 26(8): 1597–1602, Dec. 2016, doi: 10.1017/S1047951116001736.

[15] Suter, G.W. (2013). Review papers are important and worth writing. Environmental Toxicology and Chemistry 32(9). doi: 10.1002/etc.2316.

[16] Panjaitan, F., Nurmaini, S., Akbar, M., Mirza, A.H. and Syaputra, H. (2019). Identification of classification method for sudden cardiac death: A review. pp. 93–97. *In*: 2019 International Conference on Electrical Engineering and Computer Science (ICECOS), Oct. 2019, doi: 10.1109/ICECOS47637.2019.8984465.

[17] Saheb, T. and Izadi, L. (2019). Paradigm of IoT big data analytics in the healthcare industry: A review of scientific literature and mapping of research trends. Telematics and Informatics 41: 70–85, Aug. 2019, doi: 10.1016/j.tele.2019.03.005.

[18] Mancini, M. (2014). Exploiting big data for improving healthcare services. Journal of E-Learning and Knowledge Society 10(2): 23–33, doi: 10.20368/1971-8829/929.

[19] Mounia, B. and Habiba, C. (2015). Big Data privacy in healthcare moroccan context. Procedia Computer Science 63: 575–580, doi: 10.1016/j.procs.2015.08.387.

[20] Kupwade Patil, H. and Seshadri, R. (2014). Big Data security and privacy issues in healthcare. pp. 762–765. *In*: 2014 IEEE International Congress on Big Data, Jun. 2014, doi: 10.1109/BigData.Congress.2014.112.

[21] Belle, A., Kon, M.A. and Najarian, K. (2013). Biomedical informatics for computer-aided decision support systems: a survey. The Scientific World Journal, pp. 1–8, doi: 10.1155/2013/769639.

[22] Johnston, M.E. (1994). Effects of computer-based clinical decision support systems on clinician performance and patient outcome: a critical appraisal of research. Annals of Internal Medicine 120(2): 135, Jan. 1994, doi: 10.7326/0003-4819-120-2-199401150-00007.

[23] Wu, P., Cheng, C., Kaddi, C.D., Venugopalan, J., Hoffman, R. et al. (2017). Omic and electronic health record big data analytics for precision medicine. IEEE Transactions on Biomedical Engineering 64(2): 263–273, Feb. 2017, doi: 10.1109/TBME.2016.2573285.

[24] O'Driscoll, A., Daugelaite, J. and Sleator, R.D. (2013). 'Big data', Hadoop and cloud computing in genomics. Journal of Biomedical Informatics 46(5): 774–781, Oct. 2013, doi: 10.1016/j.jbi.2013.07.001.

[25] Stephens, Z.D., Lee, S.Y., Faghri, F., Campbell, R.H. and Zhai, C. (2015). Big Data: astronomical or genomical? PLOS Biology 13(7): e1002195, Jul. 2015, doi: 10.1371/journal.pbio.1002195.

[26] Nguyen, T., Shi, W. and Ruden, D. (2011). CloudAligner: A fast and full-featured MapReduce based tool for sequence mapping. BMC Research Notes 4(1): 171, Dec. 2011, doi: 10.1186/1756-0500-4-171.

[27] Pireddu, L., Leo, S. and Zanetti, G. (2011). SEAL: a distributed short read mapping and duplicate removal tool. Bioinformatics 27(15): 2159–2160, Aug. 2011, doi: 10.1093/bioinformatics/btr325.

[28] Langmead, B., Schatz, M.C., Lin, J., Pop, M., Salzberg, S.L. et al. (2009). Searching for SNPs with cloud computing. Genome Biology 10(11): R134, doi: 10.1186/gb-2009-10-11-r134.

[29] Chang, Y.-J., Chen, C.-C., Chen, C.-L. and Ho, J.-M. (2012). A *de novo* next generation genomic sequence assembler based on string graph and MapReduce cloud computing framework. BMC Genomics 13(S7): S28, Dec. 2012, doi: 10.1186/1471-2164-13-S7-S28.

[30] Hong, D., Rhie, A., Park, S., Lee, J. and Ju, Y.S. (2012). FX: An RNA-Seq analysis tool on the cloud. Bioinformatics 28(5): 721–723, Mar. 2012, doi: 10.1093/bioinformatics/bts023.

[31] Jourdren, L., Bernard, M., Dillies, M.-A. and Le Crom, S. (2012). Eoulsan: a cloud computing-based framework facilitating high throughput sequencing analyses. Bioinformatics 28(11): 1542–1543, Jun. 2012, doi: 10.1093/bioinformatics/bts165.

[32] Matthews, S.J. and Williams, T.L. (2010). MrsRF: an efficient MapReduce algorithm for analyzing large collections of evolutionary trees. BMC Bioinformatics 11(S1): S15, Jan. 2010, doi: 10.1186/1471-2105-11-S1-S15.

[33] Colosimo, M.E., Peterson, M.W., Mardis, S. and Hirschman, L. (2011). Nephele: genotyping via complete composition vectors and MapReduce. Source Code for Biology and Medicine 6(1): 13, Dec. 2011, doi: 10.1186/1751-0473-6-13.

[34] Liu, H. and Guo, G. (2016). Opportunities and challenges of big data for the social sciences: The case of genomic data. Social Science Research 59: 13–22, Sep. 2016, doi: 10.1016/j.ssresearch.2016.04.016.

[35] Xu, H. (2020). Big data challenges in genomics. pp. 337–348. *In*: Handbook of Statistics.

[36] Cała, J. and Missier, P. (2018). Selective and recurring re-computation of big data analytics tasks: insights from a genomics case study. Big Data Research 13: 76–94, Sep. 2018, doi: 10.1016/j.bdr.2018.06.001.

[37] Ker, J., Wang, L., Rao, J. and Lim, T. (2018). Deep learning applications in medical image analysis. IEEE Access 6: 9375–9389, doi: 10.1109/ACCESS.2017.2788044.

[38] Vidhyalakshmi, A. and Priya, C. (2020). Medical big data mining and processing in e-health care. pp. 1–30. *In*: An Industrial IoT Approach for Pharmaceutical Industry Growth, Elsevier.

[39] Yaffe, M.J. (2019). Emergence of 'Big Data' and its potential and current limitations in medical imaging. Seminars in Nuclear Medicine 49(2): 94–104, Mar. 2019, doi: 10.1053/j.semnuclmed.2018.11.010.

[40] Maier, A., Syben, C., Lasser, T. and Riess, C. (2019). A gentle introduction to deep learning in medical image processing. Zeitschrift für Medizinische Physik 29(2): 86–101, May 2019, doi: 10.1016/j.zemedi.2018.12.003.

[41] Lundervold, A.S. and Lundervold, A. (2019). An overview of deep learning in medical imaging focusing on MRI. Zeitschrift für Medizinische Physik 29(2): 102–127, May 2019, doi: 10.1016/j.zemedi.2018.11.002.

[42] Indraswari, R., Kurita, T., Arifin, A.Z., Suciati, N., Astuti, E.R. et al. (2019). Multi-projection deep learning network for segmentation of 3D medical images. Pattern Recognition Letters 125: 791–797, Jul. 2019, doi: 10.1016/j.patrec.2019.08.003.

[43] Faes, L., Wagner, S.K., Fu, D.J., Liu, X. and Korot, E. (2019). Automated deep learning design for medical image classification by health-care professionals with no coding experience: A feasibility study. The Lancet Digital Health 1(5): e232–e242, Sep. 2019, doi: 10.1016/S2589-7500(19)30108-6.

[44] Shin, H.-C., Roth, H.R., Gao, M., Lu, L. and Xu, Z. (2016). Deep convolutional neural networks for computer-aided detection: CNN architectures, dataset characteristics and transfer learning. IEEE Transactions on Medical Imaging 35(5): 1285–1298, May 2016, doi: 10.1109/TMI.2016.2528162.

[45] Kamnitsas, K., Ledig, C., Newcombe, V.F.J., Simpson, J.P. and Kane, A.D. (2017). Efficient multi-scale 3D CNN with fully connected CRF for accurate brain lesion segmentation. Medical Image Analysis 36: 61–78, Feb. 2017, doi: 10.1016/j.media.2016.10.004.

[46] Ciompi, F., Jacobs, C., Scholten, E.T., Wille, M.W. and Jong, P.A. (2015). Bag-of-frequencies: A descriptor of pulmonary nodules in computed tomography images. IEEE Transactions on Medical Imaging 34(4), doi: 10.1109/TMI.2014.2371821.

[47] Yu, Y., Jiahao, W., Chun, H.E., Yumeng, X. and Fong, E.L.S. (2021). Implementation of machine learning-aided imaging analytics for histopathological image diagnosis. pp. 208–221. *In*: Systems Medicine, vol. 322, Elsevier.

[48] Kaushal, C., Bhat, S., Koundal, D. and Singla, A. (2019). Recent trends in computer assisted diagnosis (CAD) system for breast cancer diagnosis using histopathological images. IRBM 40(4): 211–227, Aug. 2019, doi: 10.1016/j.irbm.2019.06.001.

[49] Yan, R., Ren, F., Wang, Z., Wang, L. and Zhang, T. (2020). Breast cancer histopathological image classification using a hybrid deep neural network. Methods 173: 52–60, Feb. 2020, doi: 10.1016/j.ymeth.2019.06.014.

[50] IBEF. Indian Insurance Industry Overview & Market Development Analysis. [Online]. Available: www.ibef.org.

[51] Gupta, S. and Tripathi, P. (2016). An emerging trend of big data analytics with health insurance in India. pp. 64–69. *In*: 2016 International Conference on Innovation and Challenges in Cyber Security (ICICCS-INBUSH), Feb. 2016, doi: 10.1109/ICICCS.2016.7542360.

[52] Rumson, A.G. and Hallett, S.H. (2019). Innovations in the use of data facilitating insurance as a resilience mechanism for coastal flood risk. Science of The Total Environment 661: 598–612, Apr. 2019, doi: 10.1016/j.scitotenv.2019.01.114.

[53] Ko, I. and Chang, H. (2018). Interactive data visualization based on conventional statistical findings for antihypertensive prescriptions using National Health Insurance claims data. International Journal of Medical Informatics 116: 1–8, Aug. 2018, doi: 10.1016/j.ijmedinf.2018.05.003.

[54] Fang, K., Jiang, Y. and Song, M. (2016). Customer profitability forecasting using Big Data analytics: A case study of the insurance industry. Computers & Industrial Engineering 101: 554–564, Nov. 2016, doi: 10.1016/j.cie.2016.09.011.

[55] Belle, A., Thiagarajan, R., Soroushmehr, S.M.R., Navidi, F., Beard, D.A. et al. (2015). Big Data analytics in healthcare. BioMed Research International pp. 1–16, doi: 10.1155/2015/370194.

[56] Ravi Varma Dandu. (2008). Storage media for computers in radiology. Indian Journal of Radiology and Imaging 18(4): 287–289.

[57] Gao, J., Xie, C. and Tao, C. (2016). Big Data validation and quality assurance—issuses, challenges, and needs. pp. 433–441. *In*: 2016 IEEE Symposium on Service-Oriented System Engineering (SOSE), Mar. 2016, doi: 10.1109/SOSE.2016.63.

[58] Sukumar, S.R., Natarajan, R. and Ferrell, R.K. (2015). Quality of Big Data in health care. International Journal of Health Care Quality Assurance 28(6): 621–634, Jul. 2015, doi: 10.1108/IJHCQA-07-2014-0080.

[59] Martin, G.P. and Mamas, M.A. (2019). Importance of quality control in 'big data': implications for statistical inference of electronic health records in clinical cardiology. Cardiovascular Research 115(6): e63–e65, May 2019, doi: 10.1093/cvr/cvy290.

[60] Hong, L., Luo, M., Wang, R., Lu, P., Lu, W. et al. (2018). Big Data in health care: applications and challenges. Data and Information Management 2(3): 175–197, Dec. 2018, doi: 10.2478/dim-2018-0014.

[61] Tola, K., Abebe, H., Gebremariam, Y. and Jikamo, B. (2017). Improving completeness of inpatient medical records in Menelik II Referral Hospital, Addis Ababa, Ethiopia. Advances in Public Health pp. 1–5, doi: 10.1155/2017/8389414.

[62] Alfian, G., Syafrudin, M., Ijaz, M., Syaekhoni, M., Fitriyani, N. et al. (2018). A personalized healthcare monitoring system for diabetic patients by utilizing ble-based sensors and real-time data processing. Sensors 18(7): 2183, Jul. 2018, doi: 10.3390/s18072183.

[63] Alwan, O.S. and Prahald Rao, K. (2017). Dedicated real-time monitoring system for health care using ZigBee. Healthcare Technology Letters 4(4): 142–144, Aug. 2017, doi: 10.1049/htl.2017.0030.

[64] Lee, H.J., Lee, S.H., Ha, K.S., Jang, H.C., Jang and Chung, W.Y. (2009). Ubiquitous healthcare service using Zigbee and mobile phone for elderly patients. International Journal of Medical Informatics 78(3): 193–198, Mar. 2009, doi: 10.1016/j.ijmedinf.2008.07.005.

[65] Pathak, S., Kumar, M., Mohan, A. and Kumar, B. (2015). Energy optimization of ZigBee Based WBAN for patient monitoring. Procedia Computer Science 70: 414–420, doi: 10.1016/j.procs.2015.10.055.

[66] Huang, C.-N. and Chan, C.-T. (2011). ZigBee-based indoor location system by k-nearest neighbor algorithm with weighted RSSI. Procedia Computer Science 5: 58–65, doi: 10.1016/j.procs.2011.07.010.

[67] Swaroop, K.N., Chandu, K., Gorrepotu, R. and Deb, S. (2019). A health monitoring system for vital signs using IoT. Internet of Things 5: 116–129, Mar. 2019, doi: 10.1016/j.iot.2019.01.004.

[68] Tan, B., Chen, Q., Chetty, K., Woodbridge, K., Li, W. et al. (2018). Exploiting WiFi channel state information for residential healthcare informatics. IEEE Communications Magazine 56(5): 130–137, doi: 10.1109/MCOM.2018.1700064.

[69] Kim, Y., Lee, S.S. and Lee, S.K. (2016). Coexistence of ZigBee-based WBAN and WiFi for health telemonitoring systems. IEEE Journal of Biomedical and Health Informatics 20(1): 222–230, doi: 10.1109/JBHI.2014.2387867.

[70] Karthikamani, R., Prasath, P.S.Y., Sree, M.V. and Sangeetha, J. (2019). Wireless patient monitoring system. International Journal of Scientific and Technology Research 8(8): 1081–1084.

[71] Adame, T., Bel, A., Carreras, A., Melià-Seguí, J., Oliver, M. et al. (2018). CUIDATS: An RFID–WSN hybrid monitoring system for smart health care environments. Future Generation Computer Systems 78: 602–615, Jan. 2018, doi: 10.1016/j.future.2016.12.023.

[72] Ren, H., Jin, H., Chen, C., Ghayvat, H., Chen, W. et al. (2018). A novel cardiac auscultation monitoring system based on wireless sensing for healthcare. IEEE Journal of Translational Engineering in Health and Medicine 6: 1–12, doi: 10.1109/JTEHM.2018.2847329.

[73] Nayyar, A., Puri, V. and Nguyen, N.G. (2019). BioSenHealth 1.0: A novel Internet of Medical Things (IoMT)-based patient health monitoring system, pp. 155–164.

[74] Syafrudin, M., Alfian, G., Fitriyani, N. and Rhee, J. (2018). Performance analysis of IoT-based sensor, big data processing, and machine learning model for real-time monitoring system in automotive manufacturing. Sensors 18(9): 2946, Sep. 2018, doi: 10.3390/s18092946.

[75] Hathaliya, J.J. and Tanwar, S. (2020). An exhaustive survey on security and privacy issues in Healthcare 4.0. Computer Communications 153: 311–335, Mar. 2020, doi: 10.1016/j.comcom.2020.02.018.

[76] Al Hamid, H.A., Rahman, S.M.M., Hossain, M.S., Almogren, A., Alamri, A. et al. (2017). A security model for preserving the privacy of medical big data in a healthcare cloud using a fog computing facility with pairing-based cryptography. IEEE Access 5: 22313–22328, doi: 10.1109/ACCESS.2017.2757844.

[77] Zhou, J., Cao, Z., Dong, X. and Lin, X. (2015). TR-MABE: White-box traceable and revocable multi-authority attribute-based encryption and its applications to multi-level privacy-preserving e-healthcare cloud computing systems. pp. 2398–2406. *In*: 2015 IEEE Conference on Computer Communications (INFOCOM), Apr. 2015, doi: 10.1109/INFOCOM.2015.7218628.

[78] Yang, J., Onik, M., Lee, N.-Y., Ahmed, M., Kim, C.-S. et al. (2019). Proof-of-familiarity: a privacy-preserved blockchain scheme for collaborative medical decision-making. Applied Sciences 9(7): 1370–1395, Apr. 2019, doi: 10.3390/app9071370.

[79] Hölbl, M., Kompara, M., Kamišalić, A. and Nemec Zlatolas, L. (2018). A systematic review of the use of blockchain in healthcare. Symmetry 10(10): 470–492, Oct. 2018, doi: 10.3390/sym10100470.

[80] Agbo, C., Mahmoud, Q. and Eklund, J. (2019). Blockchain technology in healthcare: a systematic review. Healthcare 7(2): 56–86, Apr. 2019, doi: 10.3390/healthcare7020056.

[81] Kaur, P., Sharma, M. and Mittal, M. (2018). Big Data and machine learning based secure healthcare framework. Procedia Computer Science 132: 1049–1059, doi: 10.1016/j.procs.2018.05.020.

[82] Marwan, M., Kartit, A. and Ouahmane, H. (2018). Security enhancement in healthcare cloud using machine learning. Procedia Computer Science 127: 388–397, doi: 10.1016/j.procs.2018.01.136.

[83] Nagamani, T., Logeswari, S. and Gomathy, B. (2019). Heart disease prediction using data mining with mapreduce algorithm. International Journal of Innovative Technology and Exploring Engineering 8(3): 137–140.

[84] Jangirala, S., Das, A.K., Kumar, N. and Rodrigues, J.J.P.C. (2020). Cloud centric authentication for wearable healthcare monitoring system. IEEE Transactions on Dependable and Secure Computing 17(5): 942–956, Sep. 2020, doi: 10.1109/TDSC.2018.2828306.

[85] Gao, Y., Li, H. and Luo, Y. (2015). An empirical study of wearable technology acceptance in healthcare. Industrial Management & Data Systems 115(9): 1704–1723, Oct. 2015, doi: 10.1108/IMDS-03-2015-0087.

[86] Erdmier, C., Hatcher, J. and Lee, M. (2016). Wearable device implications in the healthcare industry. Journal of Medical Engineering & Technology 40(4): 141–148, May 2016, doi: 10.3109/03091902.2016.1153738.

[87] Lee, S.Y. and Lee, K. (2018). Factors that influence an individual's intention to adopt a wearable healthcare device: The case of a wearable fitness tracker. Technological Forecasting and Social Change 129: 154–163, Apr. 2018, doi: 10.1016/j.techfore.2018.01.002.

[88] Strielkina, A., Illiashenko, O., Zhydenko, M. and Uzun, D. (2018). Cybersecurity of healthcare IoT-based systems: Regulation and case-oriented assessment. pp. 67–73. *In*: 2018 IEEE 9th International Conference on Dependable Systems, Services and Technologies (DESSERT), May 2018, doi: 10.1109/DESSERT.2018.8409101.

[89] Poongodi, T., Krishnamurthi, R., Indrakumari, R., Suresh, P., Balusamy, B. et al. (2020). Wearable devices and IoT. pp. 245–273. *In*: Intelligent Systems Reference Library, vol. 165, Springer Science and Business Media Deutschland GmbH.

[90] Qi, J., Yang, P., Min, G., Amft, O., Dong, F. et al. (2017). Advanced internet of things for personalised healthcare systems: A survey. Pervasive and Mobile Computing 41: 132–149, Oct. 2017, doi: 10.1016/j.pmcj.2017.06.018.

[91] Khosla, S. (2020). Implementation of synchronous telemedicine into clinical practice. Sleep Medicine Clinics 15(3): 347–358, Sep. 2020, doi: 10.1016/j.jsmc.2020.05.002.

[92] Alexandru, C.A. (2016). Considerations of interface efficiency in scaling up telehealthcare systems. Procedia Computer Science 98: 308–315, doi: 10.1016/j.procs.2016.09.047.

[93] Gaveikaite, V., Grundstrom, C., Winter, S., Chouvarda, I., Maglaveras, N. et al. (2019). A systematic map and in-depth review of European telehealth interventions efficacy for chronic obstructive pulmonary disease. Respiratory Medicine 158: 78–88, Oct. 2019, doi: 10.1016/j.rmed.2019.09.005.

[94] Seymour, D.M., McCall, K.R. and DiPaola, L. (2004). Security and interconnection of medical devices to healthcare networks. International Congress Series 1268: 131–134, Jun. 2004, doi: 10.1016/j.ics.2004.03.242.

[95] Martínez, S., Sánchez, D. and Valls, A. (2013). A semantic framework to protect the privacy of electronic health records with non-numerical attributes. Journal of Biomedical Informatics 46(2): 294–303, Apr. 2013, doi: 10.1016/j.jbi.2012.11.005.

[96] Li, X., Ibrahim, M.H., Kumari, S., Sangaiah, A.K., Gupta, V. et al. (2017). Anonymous mutual authentication and key agreement scheme for wearable sensors in wireless body area networks. Computer Networks 129: 429–443, Dec. 2017, doi: 10.1016/j.comnet.2017.03.013.

[97] Koya, A.M. and Deepthi, P.P. (2018). Anonymous hybrid mutual authentication and key agreement scheme for wireless body area network. Computer Networks 140: 138–151, Jul. 2018, doi: 10.1016/j.comnet.2018.05.006.

[98] Gupta, A., Tripathi, M. and Sharma, A. (2020). A provably secure and efficient anonymous mutual authentication and key agreement protocol for wearable devices in WBAN. Computer Communications 160: 311–325, Jul. 2020, doi: 10.1016/j.comcom.2020.06.010.

[99] Tewari, A. and Gupta, B.B. (2020). Security, privacy and trust of different layers in Internet-of-Things (IoTs) framework. Future Generation Computer Systems 108: 909–920, Jul. 2020, doi: 10.1016/j.future.2018.04.027.

[100] McLeod, A. and Dolezel, D. (2018). Cyber-analytics: Modeling factors associated with healthcare data breaches. Decision Support Systems 108: 57–68, Apr. 2018, doi: 10.1016/j.dss.2018.02.007.

[101] Abouelmehdi, K., Beni-Hssane, A., Khaloufi, H. and Saadi, M. (2017). Big data security and privacy in healthcare: A review. Procedia Computer Science 113: 73–80, doi: 10.1016/j.procs.2017.08.292.

[102] Esposito, C., De Santis, A., Tortora, G., Chang, H., Choo, K.-K.R. et al. (2018). Blockchain: A panacea for healthcare cloud-based data security and privacy? IEEE Cloud Computing 5(1): 31–37, Jan. 2018, doi: 10.1109/MCC.2018.011791712.

[103] Blobel, B., Lopez, D.M. and Gonzalez, C. (2016). Patient privacy and security concerns on big data for personalized medicine. Health and Technology 6(1): 75–81, Jun. 2016, doi: 10.1007/s12553-016-0127-5.

[104] Banu, N.K.S. and Swamy, S. (2016). Prediction of heart disease at early stage using data mining and big data analytics: A survey. pp. 256–261. *In*: 2016 International Conference on Electrical, Electronics, Communication, Computer and Optimization Techniques (ICEECCOT), Dec. 2016, doi: 10.1109/ICEECCOT.2016.7955226.

[105] Ekta, M., Bondu, V. and Arbind, G. (2018). Data lake-an optimum solution for storage and analytics of big data in cardiovascular disease prediction system. International Journal of Computational Engineering & Management 21(6): 33–39.

[106] Abdar, M., Książek, W., Acharya, U.R., Tan, R.-S., Makarenkov, V. et al. (2019). A new machine learning technique for an accurate diagnosis of coronary artery disease. Computer Methods and Programs in Biomedicine 179: 104992, Oct. 2019, doi: 10.1016/j.cmpb.2019.104992.

[107] Ibtehaz, N., Rahman, M.S. and Rahman, M.S. (2019). VFPred: A fusion of signal processing and machine learning techniques in detecting ventricular fibrillation from ECG signals. Biomedical Signal Processing and Control 49: 349–359, Mar. 2019, doi: 10.1016/j.bspc.2018.12.016.

[108] Bashir, M. and Harky, A. (2019). Artificial intelligence in aortic surgery: the rise of the machine. Seminars in Thoracic and Cardiovascular Surgery 31(4): 635–637, doi: 10.1053/j.semtcvs.2019.05.040.

[109] Mansoor, H., Elgendy, I.Y., Segal, R., Bavry, A.A., Bian, J. et al. (2017). Risk prediction model for in-hospital mortality in women with ST-elevation myocardial infarction: A machine learning approach. Heart & Lung 46(6): 405–411, Nov. 2017, doi: 10.1016/j.hrtlng.2017.09.003.

[110] Yang, F., Xulei, Y., Kng, T.S., Lee, G. and Liang, Z. (2018). Multi-dimensional proprio-proximus machine learning for assessment of myocardial infarction. Computerized Medical Imaging and Graphics 70: 63–72, Dec. 2018, doi: 10.1016/j.compmedimag.2018.09.007.

[111] Mathews, S.M., Kambhamettu, C. and Barner, K.E. (2018). A novel application of deep learning for single-lead ECG classification. Computers in Biology and Medicine 99: 53–62, Aug. 2018, doi: 10.1016/j.compbiomed.2018.05.013.

[112] Sannino, G. and De Pietro, G. (2018). A deep learning approach for ECG-based heartbeat classification for arrhythmia detection. Future Generation Computer Systems 86: 446–455, Sep. 2018, doi: 10.1016/j.future.2018.03.057.

[113] Shashikant, R. and Chetankumar, P. (2019). Predictive model of cardiac arrest in smokers using machine learning technique based on Heart Rate Variability parameter. Applied Computing and Informatics, Jun. 2019, doi: 10.1016/j.aci.2019.06.002.

[114] Oksuz, I., Ruijsink, B., Antón, E.P., Clough, J.R. and Cruz, G. (2019). Automatic CNN-based detection of cardiac MR motion artefacts using k-space data augmentation and curriculum learning. Medical Image Analysis 55: 136–147, Jul. 2019, doi: 10.1016/j.media.2019.04.009.

[115] Sharma, L.D. and Sunkaria, R.K. (2020). Myocardial infarction detection and localization using optimal features based lead specific approach. IRBM 41(1): 58–70, Feb. 2020, doi: 10.1016/j.irbm.2019.09.003.

[116] Khan, M.A. (2020). An IoT framework for heart disease prediction based on MDCNN classifier. IEEE Access 8: 34717–34727, doi: 10.1109/ACCESS.2020.2974687.

[117] Polat, K., Akdemir, B. and Güneş, S. (2008). Computer aided diagnosis of ECG data on the least square support vector machine. Digital Signal Processing 18(1): 25–32, Jan. 2008, doi: 10.1016/j.dsp.2007.05.006.

[118] Gong, J., Bai, X., Li, D.-a., Zhao, J. and Li, X. (2020). Prognosis analysis of heart failure based on recurrent attention model. IRBM 41(2): 71–79, Apr. 2020, doi: 10.1016/j.irbm.2019.08.002.

[119] Chang, K.-C., Hsieh, P.H., Wu, M.Y., Wang, Y.C. and Chen, J.Y. (2020). Usefulness of machine learning-based detection and classification of cardiac arrhythmias with 12-

lead electrocardiograms. Canadian Journal of Cardiology, In press, Mar. 2020, doi: 10.1016/j.cjca.2020.02.096.

[120] Wang, X., Zhai, S. and Niu, Y. (2020). Left ventricle landmark localization and identification in cardiac MRI by deep metric learning-assisted CNN regression. Neurocomputing 399: 153–170, Jul. 2020, doi: 10.1016/j.neucom.2020.02.069.

[121] Muthunayagam, M. and Ganesan, K. (2020). Cardiovascular disorder severity detection using myocardial anatomic features based optimized extreme learning machine approach. IRBM, In press, Jun. 2020, doi: 10.1016/j.irbm.2020.06.004.

[122] Kutlu, Y. and Kuntalp, D. (2011). A multi-stage automatic arrhythmia recognition and classification system. Computers in Biology and Medicine 41(1): 37–45, Jan. 2011, doi: 10.1016/j.compbiomed.2010.11.003.

[123] Javadi, M., Arani, S.A.A.A., Sajedin, A. and Ebrahimpour, R. (2013). Classification of ECG arrhythmia by a modular neural network based on mixture of experts and negatively correlated learning. Biomedical Signal Processing and Control 8(3): 289–296, May 2013, doi: 10.1016/j.bspc.2012.10.005.

[124] Martis, R.J., Acharya, U.R., Prasad, H., Chua, C.K., Lim, C.M. et al. (2013). Application of higher order statistics for atrial arrhythmia classification. Biomedical Signal Processing and Control 8(6): 888–900, Nov. 2013, doi: 10.1016/j.bspc.2013.08.008.

[125] Ebrahimzadeh, A., Shakiba, B. and Khazaee, A. (2014). Detection of electrocardiogram signals using an efficient method. Applied Soft Computing 22: 108–117, Sep. 2014, doi: 10.1016/j.asoc.2014.05.003.

[126] Zhang, Z., Dong, J., Luo, X., Choi, K.-S., Wu, X. et al. (2014). Heartbeat classification using disease-specific feature selection. Computers in Biology and Medicine 46: 79–89, Mar. 2014, doi: 10.1016/j.compbiomed.2013.11.019.

[127] Khalaf, A.F., Owis, M.I. and Yassine, I.A. (2015). A novel technique for cardiac arrhythmia classification using spectral correlation and support vector machines. Expert Systems with Applications 42(21): 8361–8368, Nov. 2015, doi: 10.1016/j. eswa.2015.06.046.

[128] Shouval, R., Hadanny, A., Shlomo, N., Iakobishvili, Z. and Unger, R. (2017). Machine learning for prediction of 30-day mortality after ST elevation myocardial infraction: An Acute Coronary Syndrome Israeli Survey data mining study. International Journal of Cardiology 246: 7–13, Nov. 2017, doi: 10.1016/j.ijcard.2017.05.067.

[129] Varga-Szemes, A., Jacobs, B.E. and Schoepf, U.J. (2018). The power and limitations of machine learning and artificial intelligence in cardiac CT. Journal of Cardiovascular Computed Tomography 12(3): 202–203, May 2018, doi: 10.1016/j.jcct.2018.05.007.

[130] Balabaeva, K. and Kovalchuk, S. (2019). Comparison of temporal and non-temporal features effect on machine learning models quality and interpretability for chronic heart failure patients. Procedia Computer Science 156: 87–96, doi: 10.1016/j. procs.2019.08.183.

[131] Kolossváry, M., De Cecco, C.N., Feuchtner, G. and Maurovich-Horvat, P. (2019). Advanced atherosclerosis imaging by CT: Radiomics, machine learning and deep learning. Journal of Cardiovascular Computed Tomography 13(5): 274–280, Sep. 2019, doi: 10.1016/j.jcct.2019.04.007.

[132] Mincholé, A., Camps, J., Lyon, A. and Rodríguez, B. (2019). Machine learning in the electrocardiogram. Journal of Electrocardiology 57: S61–S64, Nov. 2019, doi: 10.1016/j. jelectrocard.2019.08.008.

[133] Miller, P.E., Pawar, S., Vaccaro, B., McCullough, M. and Rao, P. (2019). Predictive abilities of machine learning techniques may be limited by dataset characteristics: insights from the UNOS database. Journal of Cardiac Failure 25(6): 479–483, Jun. 2019, doi: 10.1016/j.cardfail.2019.01.018.

Chapter 10
Edge Computing in Smart Agriculture

Bikram Pratim Bhuyan,[1,*] *Ravi Tomar*[2] and *Anuj Kumar Yadav*[3]

Food security is one of the UN's Sustainable Development Goals for 2030. To address this challenge, farmers must be able to produce food profitably and sustainably. Smart agriculture is typically considered as a key facilitator in alleviating hunger and malnutrition globally. Due to the confluence of technological, social, and economic components, smart agricultural systems are still under development. Edge computing may assist mainstream smart agriculture. Using this synergistic relationship, majorities and minorities worldwide may adopt smart agricultural technologies. Smart agriculture is highlighted, as is the present worldwide challenge of internet access. The current state of computer assisted agricultural research is assessed. The Edge model is being tried in various agricultural sectors. Because research is currently in the prototype stage, there are no in-depth studies. To have a substantial impact on farms, a variety of structural issues must be addressed.

1. Introduction

Agriculture, along with its related industries, is without a doubt the most important support provider in our country. Many of these activities can

---
[1] Department of Informatics, School of Computer Science, University of Petroleum and Energy Studies, India.
[2] Senior Architect, Persistent Systems, India.
[3] School of Computing, DIT University Dehradun, India.
Emails: rtomar@ddn.upes.ac.in; anujbit@gmail.com
* Corresponding author: bikram23bhuyan@gmail.com

only be carried out in rural regions because of the sheer size of the cities. Using technology to replace humans may be a growing trend in many sectors, and this should not be any different in agriculture. Any other form of automation, such as a tractor equipped with a Global Positioning System (GPS) system that allows it to navigate the field on its own, such as the Driverless tractor may be used effectively. In terms of digitalization and process automation, modern agriculture has made very modest progress.

Farmers must visit their plants on a regular basis in order to carry out tasks such as watering and fertilizing. It is possible that a farmer's livelihood and harvests may be jeopardized if he or she has isolated fields too far away. When the farmland is large, accomplishing these tasks becomes more difficult and necessitates the use of more human resources. Although operational expenditures are anticipated to increase dramatically, productivity is unlikely to decrease as a result.

Because of the Internet of Things (IoT), it is now feasible to construct remote monitoring and management systems for these isolated farms. Smart farms, which are enabled by the Internet of Things, are becoming more popular. However, because of the poor Internet connection speeds, remote farm monitoring and management has only a limited impact [1]. This is an issue in industrialized countries as well as developing ones.

The Internet of Things (IoT) connects and allows real and virtual objects to communicate and interact with one another. IoT systems are comprised of many components, including wireless sensor networks, cloud computing, and embedded intelligence. Only a few of the complex capabilities available through these systems include real-time monitoring, online analytics, and remote management, among others. When it comes to improving efficiency and lowering costs, the Internet of Things (IoT) is being utilized in a broad variety of sectors, from healthcare to smart manufacturing, smart homes, cities, and agriculture, to name a few [2]. Automation and remote farming systems may be able to benefit from some of them provided by the Internet of Things (IoT). For example, relying only on cloud-centric Internet of Things designs for remote farm monitoring and management does not ensure that the systems will operate properly since the Internet of Things now faces a number of challenges. When it comes to cloud-based IoT solutions, for example, they cannot be deployed in remote areas where the internet connection is inconsistent or coverage is limited. Consequently, data cannot be monitored in real time, and countermeasures against anomalies may be placed on hold until the situation is rectified. During an emergency, such as a sudden fire or a wild animal assault on crops, the system cannot react rapidly enough to prevent harm from occurring.

So far, there's a lot of evidence that smart agriculture has the potential to be both cost-effective and long-lasting. When it comes to smart agriculture, one thing is clear: these services are almost always dependent upon constant internet access to work correctly. Farmers are particularly vulnerable to this kind of access problem, which is made worse by the fact that they are geographically isolated. In general, the problem is two-fold: some individuals do not have access to the internet, while others have access to a connection that is unstable and of poor quality. As a result, those who might benefit the most from even the most basic services are unable to use them because they are not easily accessible.

With the use of edge computing, farmers may be able to access and employ smart agricultural services that were previously difficult to get. Although it will help in certain ways, it will not be able to totally address the problem of poor internet access. The successful incorporation of an Edge model into service provider designs would be challenging. Agriculture, particularly at the farm level, provides a good test case for Edge computing's smart service delivery paradigm, which may be found in a variety of settings. Because of this, the purpose of this paper is to investigate how agricultural researchers are using Edge computing technology in their research.

2. Food as a Global Problem

A major contributing factor to the world's food issue is the fact that there is not enough food to feed everyone on the earth. As their populations continue to grow, it is becoming increasingly common in the poorest countries of the Third World, particularly in Africa. Approximately one billion people throughout the world are starving to death as a result of a scarcity of food supplies [3]. In recent years, it has been established fact that agricultural productivity and technological progress are surpassing population growth. However, even at the present level of agricultural and cattle breeding systems, some experts think that we could feed more than 10 billion people if we utilized existing resources properly and distributed the resulting commodities equally.

A consequence of the COVID-19 pandemic's long-term impact on global food security, an estimated 660 million people may still be at danger of starvation in 2030—30 million more people than would have been at risk if the pandemic had not occurred [4]. People in 2030 may be suffering from hunger at a rate that is almost double that of the United States and three times more than the rate experienced in Brazil. Hunger will not be eradicated by 2030 unless significant progress is achieved in addressing the root causes of food insecurity and malnutrition, as well as the discrepancies that affect millions of peoples' access to nutritious food [5].

Obesity is becoming more prevalent among children, despite the fact that it has traditionally been considered a disease of the elderly. Globally, more than 1.9 billion people aged 18 and older were overweight in 2016, with more than 650 million adults being obese, according to the World Health Organization [6]. According to current estimates, there are around 41 million overweight or obese children under the age of five in the United States. Obesity is becoming more prevalent in low- and middle-income countries. A complex illness with heredity, hormonal imbalances, and the environment all contributing factors, obesity is a serious public health problem in America. Because maintaining a healthy diet may be prohibitively expensive for individuals with little financial resources in rich countries, obesity may be considered a sign of food insecurity [7].

Factors that contribute to food insecurity in terms of both production and supply are complex and multifaceted. There is a wide range of causes that contribute to this, including political instability, violence, low economic prospects, and natural disasters, to name a few [8]. Floods, droughts, and tropical storms are the natural disasters that have the greatest impact on food production. Drought, in particular, is responsible for more than 80% of the overall damage and losses in agriculture, with the livestock and agricultural production subsectors being especially hard hit [9]. Given that there is no one cause why the food supply is insufficient, there can be no single solution to the issue. It is possible that numerous variables are contributing to the insecurity of food production and distribution. All these factors contribute to political instability, violence, a lack of economic opportunity, and natural calamities. Natural catastrophes such as floods, droughts, and tropical storms have a detrimental influence on the majority of food production, with the livestock and agricultural production sectors being particularly heavily affected. In the agricultural sector, drought is responsible for more than 80 percent of losses and damage [8]. Because there is no one source of the food supply crisis, there is no single solution to the problem of food scarcity that is feasible. In its place, a varied range of approaches should be used.

Sustainable food production is one of the most often mentioned topics when addressing food security. Any way you look at it, it's a controversial and polarizing concept. According to [10], although many communities have adopted the word "sustainable," the phrase is ill-defined and poorly used in many cases. For as long as we cling to a single interpretation, the unavoidable trade-offs between nutrition, energy consumption, water usage, and greenhouse gas emissions will become even more difficult to reconcile than they are today [11]. When it comes to food security, it is a problem that must be addressed, and the awareness of its wickedness may assist in defining its scale and complexity, as well as stimulating the consideration of disruptive alternatives to addressing it [12]. Instead, a diversified portfolio of techniques should be used to address the issue.

Despite the fact that Information and Communication Technologies (ICT) adoption in agriculture has traditionally been gradual, with a number of reasons provided for this, an underlying lack of infrastructure continues to be a key hurdle to progress [13]. Despite the fact that many farmers in the United States are still uncertain about the value proposition, this is a big component of the country's socioeconomic problems [14]. Consequently, governments have an obligation to ensure that the value proposition is meaningful to all stakeholders in the value chain, not only farmers, in order to achieve sustainability. According to the World Economic Forum (WEF), if Internet of Things (IoT) technologies were integrated across 50–75 percent of supply chains in industrialized countries by 2020, they might save 10–50 million tons of food in such countries [15].

One method in which technology will influence agricultural practices is via the implementation of "smart agriculture." The farm is where food is produced, and it is on the farm that sustainable solutions to the global food supply dilemma must be implemented first. A broad variety of agricultural systems, rather than a single global solution for the farm, is required for smart agriculture to be successful [16]. It is possible that farmers taking on a R&D role, would contribute to enhancing innovation and validating ideas in the agricultural sector.

3. Smart Farming

Since the beginning of civilization, farmers have served as the backbone of the agricultural industry. Farmers toiling tirelessly in the fields do, in fact, supply food for the whole planet. In ancient times, farming was a time-consuming and labor-intensive operation that required a lot of effort. During the course of time, labor-intensive operations have been replaced with capital-intensive ones, which has resulted in improved production while demanding less efforts from the employees. Smart farming, also known as smart agriculture, is vital for assisting farmers in India in increasing their production and income [17].

In agriculture, when we speak about "smart farming," we are referring to the use of ICT (information and communication technologies) to increase accuracy and efficiency, regardless of the size of the field. In the definition of precision agriculture, it is "the control of spatial and temporal variation in the fields with reference to the soil, the atmosphere, and the plants" [18]. It's not a new notion, and little farmers have been tending their crops with pinpoint accuracy since the dawn of civilization. Old-style precision farming, on the other hand, is dependent mostly on the farmer's own assessment of the field and on his or her own personal experience, rendering it inapplicable on a broader scale. Using information and communication technology (ICT) in order to allow precision agriculture with better accuracy, regardless of the size of the field, is referred to as "smart farming" [19]. The idea of precision cultivation is not new, as small farms aim to tailor their efforts for each particular crop in each specific field since time immemorial. However, the old-style precision cultivation relies mostly on the farmer's personal inspection of the field and draws on individual experience, which makes it inapplicable on a greater scale.

In order to achieve precision cultivation at any scale, intelligent agriculture technology is essential. Smart farming is defined as farming that "draws on studies in precision farming, farm management information systems (FMIS), agricultural automation and robotics," and as a result, "drawing on studies in precision farming, farm management information systems (FMIS), and agricultural automation and robotics" [20]. It is possible to handle a broad variety of agricultural production issues by using the large range of technologies contained in "smart farming" [64].

In the early days of smart farming technology, data capture technology was one of the first forms of smart farming technologies that made it possible to greatly enhance agricultural productivity (DAT). With the aid of the goods in this category, it is possible to measure and record the features of crops and fields. Data acquisition for mapping is mostly accomplished via the use of unmanned aerial vehicles (UAVs) and satellite imagery, which are two of the most common ways [21].

Through the use of mapping technology, the farmer may quickly and fairly investigate tendencies that would be far more difficult to detect if monitoring the fields on foot were to be discovered. Additionally, the evaluation of environmental characteristics, such as the normalized difference vegetation index (NDVI) or soil moisture, is a kind of data collection that allows farmers to continuously and efficiently monitor the state of their crops and soils [22]. Additionally, data collecting technologies such as GNSS (global positioning satellite systems), which are often used in self-driving agricultural equipment, are available. When it comes to gathering information on fields and soils, as well as crops and agricultural gear, there are several benefits [23].

Another possible use for smart farming technology is data evaluation, which is necessary since the data obtained may only be helpful if it is thoroughly processed and the appropriate conclusions formed. This is one area where technology may aid farmers. Management zone delineation, which allows for the designation of "parts of the field with common characteristics that can be treated independently," is one means by which technology can assist farmers in this area [24].

As the name indicates, decision support systems assist farmers in making more informed decisions regarding the operations of their farms. Some of these technologies enable "extensive and scalable analysis, recommendation/visualization, or sharing of agricultural performance data among farmers, producers, biologists, government officials, and commercial organizations" under specific conditions [25]. For better or worse, smart farming provides farmers with a wealth of information about their fields and crops, as well as the ability to make informed choices based on that information, as explained above.

The last kind of application is precision agriculture, which refers to the high-accuracy digital performance of a broad variety of agricultural tasks. By using a wireless network, which contains temperature and moisture sensors, it is feasible to execute exact irrigation while wasting no water. Using variable-rate "tilling and fertilizer application devices," it is also feasible to apply precise quantities of granulated fertilizer, lime, manure, and pesticides to specific areas of the field [26].

4. Edge Computing

Client data is handled at the edge of the network in a distributed IT architecture known as "edge computing," in order to process it as close to the source as is practical.

Companies can get insight into their operations and manage critical activities in real time thanks to data, which is considered to be the lifeblood of modern business. Sensors and Internet of Things devices running in real time from remote locations and tough operating environments almost everywhere on the planet may gather large amounts of data on a daily basis, and today's organizations are drowning in a sea of information [27].

However, this deluge of information is also altering the manner in which organizations manage their computer systems and networks. The previous computer paradigm has been abandoned because of its incapacity to cope with the ever-increasing streams of real-world datasets that are being generated. Broadband limits, latency problems, and network disruptions may make such initiatives difficult to complete successfully. Several firms are using edge computing architectures in order to solve these data problems [28].

The most straightforward way to explain it is that edge computing transfers certain storage and computing resources from central data centers to the locations where information is created and utilized. As opposed to sending information to an off-site data center, that job is completed at the spot where the information is generated, whether it is a retail store, a factory, a utility, or an intelligent city. Example: After the computing work at the edge has been performed, real-time business insights and equipment maintenance estimates are provided back to the main data center for analysis and human involvement [29].

A content delivery network (CDN) was built in the 1990s, which allowed data gathering nodes to be located closer to the end user. Images and videos, on the other hand, were the only things that this technology was capable of processing. Newer mobile gadgets, such as smartphones and early smart devices, strained the capabilities of existing information technology systems. As a result, ubiquitous computing and peer-to-peer overlay networks were developed in an attempt to alleviate some of the burden [30].

However, it was not until the widespread adoption of cloud computing that true decentralization of information technology could be achieved, as cloud computing provides end users with enterprise-level processing capacity with improved flexibility, on-demand scalability, and collaboration from anywhere in the world [31].

A growing demand for cloud-based applications, as well as the increasing number of organizations operating from many places at the same time, prompted the need to handle more data outside of the data center and manage it from a single centralized location. In other words, it was at this moment that the possibility of mobile edge computing became a reality [32].

As a result of the "Internet of Things," which makes previously complex data collection activities more manageable, businesses' IT budgeting tactics are being revolutionized [33].

Because the Internet of Things (IoT) and edge computing are still in their early stages of development, their full potential has not yet been realized. Meanwhile, they are hastening digital change across a broad variety of businesses and having an influence on people's everyday lives all around the world [34].

The only difference between edge computing and fog computing is that the process takes place on the IOT device's edge and the results are created quickly rather than having to go to the cloud and then return with the results. In edge computing, like in fog computing, the user or organization has the option of choosing from a comparable set of framework options. The data acquired by cloud or fog-based platforms is normally sent to the cloud for processing, but with edge computing, the data is collected and processed directly on the edge of the network. It is not possible to steal information since it is not transported to the cloud [35]. There is also no problem with network traffic because the result is created at the edge, so even if network traffic grows, it does not hamper edge computing. It is possible to respond to real-time data without any delay due to the fact that data is taken and processed only at the edge of a smart device, rather than in the center. Due to the fact that the response time is minimum, there is no trouble with network traffic, and it has a better connection between devices and the cloud at a faster speed than other platforms such as cloud and fog computing; edge computing has more advantages than the other mentioned platforms. Edge computing is preferable for the Internet of Things for the following reasons: Because of the reduced latency, IoT devices will have a longer battery life.

By using edge computing, businesses and organizations are able to manage much more data in significantly less time, allowing them to learn and find new information at an astonishingly fast rate. As a result of more comprehensive data from a variety of multi-access edge computing sites, businesses will be able to more accurately forecast, manage, plan, and respond to future needs by utilizing historical and near-real-time data, scalable and flexible processing, and scalable and flexible data storage without the costs and limitations of earlier IT alternatives [33].

Edge computing enables the development of new and innovative technologies such as faster and more powerful mobile devices, online collaboration, as well as more fun and engaging gaming and content production. These technologies are made possible by the data acceleration and ease of use that edge computing provides. Automobiles that are driverless in particular are a great example of edge computing in action, since they are able to react and adapt in real time rather than waiting for commands from a data center that is hundreds of miles away [34].

Edge computing is employed in a broad variety of entertainment and business technologies today, including content delivery systems, smart technology, gaming, 5G, and predictive maintenance, to name a few examples.

Caching information in order to minimize latency has enabled streaming music and video businesses to better handle customer traffic demands as a consequence.

Because of edge computing, manufacturers are better equipped to keep tabs on their business activities. Edge computing enables organizations to maintain a close check on their equipment and manufacturing processes, and even identify possible issues before they arise, allowing them to save money in the process. It is possible to see a comparable use of edge computing in the healthcare industry, where it provides clinicians with more rapid access to patient health conditions without having them to transport their data offshore for processing. Oil and gas companies should maintain a close check on their assets in other parts of the world in order to avoid costly blunders.

Additionally, edge computing technologies are being applied in the development of smart houses. When it comes to transmitting and interpreting data, voice assistants, in particular, are becoming more dependent on local networks. If decentralized computing power were not available to aid Amazon Alexa and Google Assistant in discovering sought-after answers for customers, it would take significantly longer for them to do so.

5. Edge Computing in Smart Agriculture

It has been suggested that edge mining (EM) may be used to predict heat stress in dairy cows [35]. *In-situ* temperature and humidity sensors collect data that is used to calculate the Temperature Humidity Index (THI). The THI as well as the chance of heat stress in each cow are calculated based on data obtained from the collars of each cow. The farmer is then made aware of any possible dangers that may exist in his operation. This case study focuses on dairy cows, however the approaches discussed here may be applied to a variety of other agricultural situations as well [36].

A modified version of the EM approach is presented in this scenario, the authors' Interactive Edge Mining classification technique is utilized to categorize the movements of the dairy cow on the collar device, which is described in more detail below (IEM) [37]. The signal is categorized using a decision tree that employs two classification methods: Bare Necessities and Class Act, respectively. An accelerometer is used to assess the present status of an item by analyzing the signals it generates. The movements of the animal will be tracked and analyzed in the Cloud before any contact with the farmer is established. It is only during this time that the cow is at the milking station where the uploading takes place. The Linear Spanish Inquisition Protocol (LSIP) has been subjected to a second round of review [38]. Another version of the EM study looks at both the IEM algorithm (IEM2.0) and the Cooperative Activity Sequence-based Map Matching (CASMM)—an extension of the ASMM [39] to provide a Fog analytics solution for activity detection and localization in dairy cows. The IEM algorithm (IEM2.0) is used to detect and localize activity in dairy cows. So far, the findings have been positive, with accuracy in localization reaching up to 99 percent in certain cases. Once again, the essential approaches are universal and easily applicable to any situation.

A demonstration of the use of fog nodes and pedometers connected to each cow in the herd using Edge computing for herd health monitoring was done in [40]. It is at the node level that data aggregation, pre-processing, classification, and feature selection are carried out. Deviations from norms, for example, may be employed as a signal of illness in the context of behavioral analytics. When a farmer's animal is found to be lame, for example, an alarm is sent to the farmer. In their papers, they provide generic designs that may be used for animal welfare monitoring at the edge of the network.

It is possible to study animal behavior utilizing a smartphone platform (the iPhone) as an Edge node. When the gadget was installed on a halter, it was possible to measure five distinct parameters using the IMU on the device. As a result of the processing of these, a total of 41 parameters were generated for analysis. When dealing with data management challenges that arise as a result of the sheer amount and diversity of data that is created, a lambda Cloud architecture may be used (referred to as "cows"). With the implementation of Edge Computing on the iPhone, the amount of raw data required for transmission was reduced by 43.5 percent, resulting in lower transmission costs [41].

In [42] the authors offer a low-cost, integrated cloud-to-fog architecture for smart farming that is inexpensive and high in functionality. A unique characteristic of this design is that it incorporates a heterogeneous array of sensors for both monitoring animals and their interior physical environments; nonetheless, the Raspberry Pi is the platform of choice for the majority of users. It exhibits lower latency and enhanced support for scalability, flexibility, and dependability when using Edge computing to its full potential. Future-proofing sensor infrastructure via the application of machine learning is seen as an achievable goal, as well as a foundation for more sustainable unobtrusive sensing. On the same topic, the authors in [43] address the problem of indoor environmental monitoring, this time in the context of chicken houses. Climate variables such as temperature, humidity, and light intensity are monitored, allowing for management in near real time. The analysis of data from the sensors is carried out on a gateway (Edge) node, which is responsible for controlling both the fan and the lighting [44].

A variety of meteorological and soil properties may be monitored in a vineyard environment via the use of an Internet of Things based monitoring system. Planned disease outbreaks in vineyards are strongly related to weather patterns, thus it is critical to be aware of weather trends in advance of any planned disease outbreaks. The diseases downy mildew and black rot are two examples of this. In a Cloud-centric design, data from a dispersed sensor network is gathered by an Edge computing node, which is located at the edge of the network [45].

Precision viticulture monitoring applications were the inspiration for the development of a generic platform called mySense [45]. Sensors/actuators, WSN/gateway, Web/Cloud, and applications are all grouped together under one roof. Fog computing at the WSN/Gateway layer facilitates the completion of local tasks as well as the generation of real-time notifications. Using the platform in a vineyard, researchers have been able to investigate disease dynamics in connection with particular microclimates [46].

According to [47], an exemplary case study highlights how Edge computing may be used to demonstrate scalable data analytics. The Raspberry Pi fulfils this function by acting as a sensor configuration base station as well as an edge node for the network. The Edge node generates projections of cherry tomato growth status, which are then forwarded to a Cloud server for conflation, model integration, and analysis, among other things. As a consequence, yield forecasts may be made. Farmers may keep their data private and only share the information they choose to share with others using this technique, which also helps to reduce data traffic.

RAS in conventional aquaculture has the potential to drastically reduce the quantity of fresh water needed by using modern biofiltration technologies; nevertheless, near real-time management and monitoring are necessary. Roddek et al. [48] developed a data collection and monitoring technique for the RAS that makes use of a Raspberry Pi acting as a fog node. In order to control the water level in a growbed tank, it has been shown that a similar mechanism may be utilized [48]. A NodeMCU is utilized to monitor water speed at the input and outflow of the system, with the Raspberry Pi acting as a broker. In later years, as an alternative method of measuring water level, an ultrasonic sensor was used [49].

A low-cost sensor/actuator platform based on the Internet of Things has been developed by [50] for precision agriculture (IoT). In process management, edge computing, which is based on the Internet of Things, enables a multi-protocol approach to be taken into consideration. The platform was tested using hydroponic veggies produced in a greenhouse, according to the researchers. An aeroponic-style greenhouse growth system, described by [51], is controlled by a fog-enabled controller. The ThingSpeak9 platform [51], which is hosted in the cloud, is utilized at the application layer.

Forestry in agriculture includes the cultivation of trees and shrubs alongside arable and grazing land, which is an essential aspect of the overall picture [54]. Agroforestry has a number of benefits, including enhanced agricultural production and protection for animals in both the winter and summer months, among other things [52].

The research [53] illustrated how drones equipped with a Raspberry Pi may be used to collect data on forest fires by using a Raspberry Pi as a sensor. In this case study, many data processing strategies are evaluated, including one that makes use of an unmanned aerial vehicle (UAV) with a Raspberry Pi serving as an Edge node [55]. It's interesting to think about the trade-offs involved. It is necessary to balance the power consumption of a UAV with the computational needs of image processing in order to maximize flying endurance. Given that images are processed on the Edge node, just a decided risk-index has to be transmitted when photos are handled on the Edge node. In contrast, off-loading has been proved to be the most effective long-term option in the long run [56].

Neumann and colleagues were the ones who pioneered a fresh approach to the problem of fire detection [57]. The implementation of a participatory data collection paradigm is made possible via the usage of Edge computing technologies. A forest was utilized to test Bluetooth Low Energy (BLE) sensors, which were used to communicate with one another and gather data on temperature and humidity (BLE). Guards and visitors alike utilize their cellphones as mobile hubs to communicate with one another. All these features are then communicated to a host server, where they serve as an indication of fire threats, allowing for more accurate risk assessment as well as improved planning and response strategies to be put into effect [58].

Forest fire outbreaks might be forecasted with the use of data mining [59]. A Support Vector Machine (SVM) prediction model is hosted by a local Fog node, and it makes use of wind speed, precipitation, relative humidity, and temperature parameters to predict the weather. These predictions are received by the Cloud. Avgeris and colleagues present a fire detection edge computing architecture that incorporates Internet of Things (IoT), the Cloud, and participatory sensing capabilities. Time criticality and swift decision making in the core model are ensured by offloading to the network edge, which is critical [59].

People (and, indirectly, domesticated and farmed cattle) are more likely than ever before to come into touch with wild animals as animal habitats become more confined. Difficulties with disease transmission (such as bovine tuberculosis, for example) and human safety are other constant concerns that might arise as a consequence of animal-vehicle collisions. Even while solutions such as fences and boundary walls would always reduce the number of contacts, their large sizes and challenging terrains sometimes make them uneconomical and impracticable in a large number of situations.

Singh et al. [60] propose an early warning system based on the Internet of Things (IoT) and Edge technologies to address the issue of animal-human cohabitation in the context of urbanization. Using a hybrid Fiber-Wireless (FiWi) network, edge nodes (wireless sensors) are linked to the Cloud for data collection and analysis. The movement of an animal is detected by a PIR sensor, which activates a camera module, which takes an image of the animal [61]. Because of their better accuracy and speed, CNNs are often employed in image processing applications. The results of simulations demonstrated that by dynamically assigning bandwidth and processing data at the source, end-to-end latency could be reduced, and energy consumption may be reduced as well. Understanding the trade-offs between computation and communication has been a recurring topic in WSN research for many years, and it continues to be so. Regardless of the domain, effective WSN implementation requires a thorough understanding of available resources and power constraints. A related architecture, presented by [62], includes Internet of Things (IoT) and an Edge Cloud model; in this instance, particular species (such as bears, deer, and coyotes) may be recognized. It is intended to automate wildlife monitoring, but it is possible to apply the idea to a variety of other security related scenarios as well.

Edge Computing and similar ideas have just lately started to gain traction, having been around for less than five years at the time of writing. Many challenges must be met before major services for agricultural value chain players can be made widely available to the general public. Put in another way, all of the systems outlined before are prototypes, ranging from TRL 4 (which have been evaluated in a laboratory setting) to TRL 5, which have been confirmed in a real-world situation [63, 64]. In agriculture, it is possible that edge computing is more ubiquitous than previously imagined, due to the fact that it is often a sub-component of other research topics, such as the Internet of Things [65, 66].

The possibility of exploring two types of Edge-enabled services is being investigated: node-centric services that run independently of the Cloud and cloudcentric services that need at least one service from the Cloud to function [67]. All the systems outlined in the previous paragraph may be categorized as cloud-based systems. Some of the benefits of Edge Computing, such as minimizing latency, maximizing bandwidth use, and delegating work, were utilized in varying degrees during the study period [68, 69]. The local Edge was responsible for the initial level of data processing, while core Cloud services were used for the second level of data processing, which included offloading, storing, and producing alerts. As in the rest of the world, edge computing in agriculture is dominated by physical edge servers and locally installed sensors and sensor networks, which are commonplace in this industry.

6. Conclusion

Edge computing may help smart agriculture. The Edge idea is still in its infancy in agricultural systems. Prototype systems representing several agricultural fields show the notion of Edge Computing in operation. Interoperability and scalability are two important issues that remain unresolved. Rather than depending on custom solutions, Edge-enabled services should employ proven platforms. In many rural locations, where even modest smart agricultural services may have a tremendous impact, there is a serious shortage of adequate internet connectivity. It is critical to recognize this state and suggest remedies before providing farmers with sustainable tools and tackling the global food insecurity challenge.

References

[1] Gowda, C.L. and Nagaraj, S. Challenges and opportunities for IoT applications in smart agriculture.

[2] Mohamed, K.S. (2022). An Introduction to IoT. InBluetooth 5.0 Modem Design for IoT Devices, pp. 33–43. Springer, Cham.

[3] Ahmed, M.H., Vasas, D., Hassan, A. and Molna´r, J. (2022). The impact of functional food in prevention of malnutrition. PharmaNutrition. 2022 Jan 15: 100288.

[4] Manca, R., Bombillar, F., Glomski, C. and Pica, A. (2022). Obesity and immune system impairment: A global problem during the COVID-19 pandemic. International Journal of Risk Safety in Medicine 2022 Feb 8(Preprint): 1–6.

[5] Roub´ık, H., Lo˘s˘t´ak, M., Ketuama, C.T., Proch´azka, P., Soukupov´a, J. et al. (2022). Current coronavirus crisis and past pandemics-what can happen in post-COVID-19 agriculture? Sustainable Production and Consumption 2022 Jan 15.

[6] Ali, I., Arslan, A., Chowdhury, M., Khan, Z., Tarba, S.Y. et al. (2022). Reimagining global food value chains through effective resilience to COVID-19 shocks and similar future events: A dynamic capability perspective. Journal of Business Research 2022 Mar 1; 141: 1–2.

[7] Dudek, M. and S´piewak, R. (2022). Effects of the COVID-19 pandemic on sustainable food systems: lessons learned for public policies? The Case of Poland. Agriculture 2022 Jan; 12(1): 61.

[8] Martin, A., Partika, A., Johnson, A.D., Castle, S., Horm, D. et al. (2022). Tulsa SEED Study Team. Both sides of the screen: predictors of parents' and teachers' depression and food insecurity during COVID-19-related distance learning. Early Childhood Research Quarterly 2022 Feb 9.

[9] Yadav, A. and Iqbal, B.A. (2022). Effect of global warming on food security: an Indian perspective. pp. 115–133. *In*: Impacts of Climate Change and Economic and Health Crises on the Agriculture and Food Sectors. IGI Global.

[10] El Bilali, H. (2019). Research on agro-food sustainability transitions: A systematic review of research themes and an analysis of research gaps. Journal of Cleaner Production 2019 Jun 1; 221: 353–64.

[11] El Bilali, H. (2020). Transition heuristic frameworks in research on agro-food sustainability transitions. Environment, Development and Sustainability 2020 Mar; 22(3): 1693–728.

[12] Recanati, F., Maughan, C., Pedrotti, M., Dembska, K., Antonelli, M. et al. (2019). Assessing the role of CAP for more sustainable and healthier food systems in Europe: A literature review. Science of the Total Environment. 2019 Feb 25; 653: 908–19.

[13] Gopinath, R. Perception of ICT in Farming Practices with Special Reference to E-Commerce in Agriculture.

[14] Eitzinger, A., Cock, J., Atzmanstorfer, K., Binder, C.R., L¨aderach, P. et al. (2019). GeoFarmer: A monitoring and feedback system for agricultural development projects. Computers and Electronics in Agriculture 2019 Mar 1; 158: 109–21.

[15] Baldwin, R. (2018). If this is Globalization 4.0, what were the other three. pp. 1–4. *In*: World Economic Forum 2018 Dec 22.

[16] Beardsley, S.C., Enriquez, L., Bonini, S., Sandoval, S., Brun, N.O. et al. (2010). Fostering the economic and social benefits of ICT. Dutta and Mia (2010). The Global Information Technology Report2009. 2010: 61–70.

[17] Walter, A., Finger, R., Huber, R. and Buchmann, N. (2017). Opinion: Smart farming is key to developing sustainable agriculture. Proceedings of the National Academy of Sciences 2017 Jun 13; 114(24): 6148–50.

[18] Zhang, N., Wang, M. and Wang, N. (2002). Precision agriculture—a worldwide overview. Computers and Electronics in Agriculture 2002 Nov 1; 36(2-3): 113–32.

[19] Pierce, F.J. and Nowak, P. (1999). Aspects of precision agriculture. pp. 1–85. *In*: Advances in Agronomy 1999 Jan 1 (Vol. 67). Academic Press.

[20] Cisternas, I., Vel´asquez, I., Caro, A. and Rodr´ıguez, A. (2020). Systematic literature review of implementations of precision agriculture. Computers and Electronics in Agriculture 2020 Sep 1; 176: 105626.

[21] Shafi, U., Mumtaz, R., Garc´ıa-Nieto, J., Hassan, S.A., Zaidi, S.A. et al. (2019). Precision agriculture techniques and practices: From considerations to applications. Sensors 2019 Jan; 19(17): 3796.

[22] Khanna A, Kaur S. Evolution of Internet of Things (IoT) and its significant impact in the field of Precision Agriculture. Computers and electronics in agriculture. 2019 Feb 1;157:218-31.

[23] Patr´ıcio DI, Rieder R. Computer vision and artificial intelligence in precision agriculture for grain crops: A systematic review. Computers and electronics in agriculture. 2018 Oct 1;153:69-81.

[24] Lu Y, Young S. A survey of public datasets for computer vision tasks in precision agriculture. Computers and Electronics in Agriculture. 2020 Nov 1;178:105760.

[25] Tamirat TW, Pedersen SM, Lind KM. Farm and operator characteristics affect- ing adoption of precision agriculture in Denmark and Germany. Acta Agriculturae Scandinavica, Section B—Soil Plant Science. 2018 May 19;68(4):349-57.

[26] Say SM, Keskin M, Sehri M, Sekerli YE. Adoption of precision agriculture technologies in developed and developing countries. Online J. Sci. Technol. 2018 Jan;8(1):7- 15.

[27] Cao K, Liu Y, Meng G, Sun Q. An overview on edge computing research. IEEE access. 2020 May 1;8:85714-28.

[28] Xiao Y, Jia Y, Liu C, Cheng X, Yu J et al. Edge computing security: State of the art and challenges. Proceedings of the IEEE. 2019 Jun 19;107(8):1608-31.

[29] Sitto´n-Candanedo I, Alonso RS, Corchado JM, Rodr´ıguez-Gonza´lez S, Casado- Vara R et al. A review of edge computing reference architectures and a new global edge proposal. Future Generation Computer Systems. 2019 Oct 1;99:278-94.

[30] Chen M, Wang L, Chen J, Wei X, Lei L et al. A computing and content delivery network in the smart city: Scenario, framework, and analysis. IEEE Network. 2019 Mar 27;33(2):89-95.

[31] Velasco L, Gifre L, Ruiz M. Autonomic content delivery network service. In2019 21st International Conference on Transparent Optical Networks (ICTON) 2019 Jul 9 (pp. 1-4). IEEE.

[32] Nishimuta H, Nobayashi D, Ikenaga T. Adaptive server and path switching scheme for content delivery network. In2019 IEEE Pacific Rim Conference on Communications, Computers and Signal Processing (PACRIM) 2019 Aug 21 (pp. 1-6). IEEE.

[33] Li H, Ota K, Dong M. Learning IoT in edge: Deep learning for the Internet of Things with edge computing. IEEE network. 2018 Jan 26;32(1):96-101.

[34] Pahl C, El Ioini N, Helmer S. A Decision Framework for Blockchain Platforms for IoT and Edge Computing. InIoTBDS 2018 Mar (pp. 105-113).

[35] De Donno M, Tange K, Dragoni N. Foundations and evolution of modern comput- ing paradigms: Cloud, iot, edge, and fog. Ieee Access. 2019 Oct 15;7:150936-48.

[36] Alonso RS, Sitto´n-Candanedo I, Garc´ıa O´, Prieto J, Rodr´ıguez-Gonza´lez S et al. An intelligent Edge-IoT platform for monitoring livestock and crops in a dairy farming scenario. Ad Hoc Networks. 2020 Mar 1;98:102047.

[37] Shen W, Sun Y, Zhang Y, Fu X, Hou H et al. Automatic recognition method of cow ruminating behaviour based on edge computing. Computers and Electronics in Agriculture. 2021 Dec 1;191:106495.

[38] Krpalkova L, O'Mahony N, Carvalho A, Campbell S, Corkery G et al. Decision-Making Strategies on Smart Dairy Farms: A Review. Interna- tional Journal of Agricultural and Biosystems Engineering. 2021 Dec 2;15(11):138- 45.

[39] Sitto´n-Candanedo I, Prieto J. 'Livestock welfare by means of an edge computing and IoT platform. InAmbient Intelligence-Software and Applications: 11th Inter- national Symposium on Ambient Intelligence 2020 (Vol. 1239, p. 156). Springer Nature.

[40] O¨ ztu¨rk M, Alonso RS, Garc´ıa O´, Sitto´n-Candanedo I, Prieto J. Livestock Welfare by Means of an Edge Computing and IoT Platform. InInternational Symposium on Ambient Intelligence 2020 Jun 17 (pp. 156-165). Springer, Cham.

[41] Mahmud, R. and Buyya, R. (2019). Modelling and simulation of fog and edge computing environments using iFogSim toolkit. Fog and Edge Computing: Principles and Paradigms 2019 Jan 30: 1–35.

[42] Trilles, S., Torres-Sospedra, J., Belmonte, O´., Zarazaga-Soria, F.J., Gonza´lez-P´erez, A. et al. (2020). Development of an open sensorized platform in a smart agriculture context: A vineyard support system for monitoring mildew disease. Sustainable Computing: Informatics and Systems 2020 Dec 1; 28: 100309.

[43] Oteyo, I.N., Marra, M., Kimani, S., Meuter, W.D. and Boix, E.G. (2021). A survey on mobile applications for smart agriculture. SN Computer Science 2021 Jul; 2(4): 1–6.

[44] Ammoniaci, M., Kartsiotis, S.P., Perria, R. and Storchi, P. (2021). State of the art of monitoring technologies and data processing for precision viticulture. Agriculture 2021 Mar; 11(3): 201.

[45] Sassu, A., Gambella, F., Ghiani, L., Mercenaro, L., Caria, M. et al. (2021). Advances in unmanned aerial system remote sensing for precision viticulture. Sensors 2021 Jan; 21(3): 956.

[46] Morais, R., Silva, N., Mendes, J., Ada˜o, T., P´adua, L. et al. (2019). A comprehensive data management environment to improve precision agriculture practices. Computers and Electronics in Agriculture 2019 Jul 1; 162: 882–94.

[47] Patel, J., Patel, R., Shah, S. and Patel, J.A. (2021). Big Data analytics for advanced viticulture. Scalable Computing: Practice and Experience 2021 Nov 20; 22(3): 302–12.

[48] Goddek, S. and Vermeulen, T. (2018). Comparison of Lactuca sativa growth performance in conventional and RAS-based hydroponic systems. Aquaculture International 2018 Dec; 26(6): 1377–86.

[49] Kashyap, M., Sharma, V. and Gupta, N. (2018). Taking MQTT and NodeMcu to IOT: communication in Internet of Things. Procedia Computer Science 2018 Jan 1; 132: 1611–8.

[50] Placidi, P., Morbidelli, R., Fortunati, D., Papini, N., Gobbi, F. et al. (2021). Monitoring soil and ambient parameters in the IoT precision agriculture scenario: An original modeling approach dedicated to low-cost soil water content sensors. Sensors 2021 Jan; 21(15): 5110.

[51] Deekshath, M.R., Dharanya, M.P., Kabadia, M.K., Dinakaran, M.G., Shanthini, S. et al. (2018). IoT based environmental monitoring system using arduino UNO and thingspeak. International Journal of Science Technology Engineering 4(9).

[52] Evison, D.C. (2018). Estimating annual investment returns from forestry and agriculture in New Zealand. Journal of Forest Economics 2018 Dec 1; 33: 105–11.

[53] Aguiar, A.S., dos Santos, F.N., Cunha, J.B., Sobreira, H., Sousa, A.J. et al. (2020). Localization and mapping for robots in agriculture and forestry: A survey. Robotics 2020 Dec; 9(4): 97.

[54] Datta, S.C. (2021). Wildlife conservation act as future clinical-medical-images-case-reports of COVID-19 model: enriched forestry-horticulture-agriculture-environment-health-biodiversity-medical-science-technology-communication-application-issues! Journal of Clinical and Medical Images, Case Reports 1(1): 1033.

[55] Kok, M.T., Alkemade, R., Bakkenes, M., van Eerdt, M., Janse, J. et al. (2018). Pathways for agriculture and forestry to contribute to terrestrial biodiversity conservation: a global scenario-study. Biological Conservation 2018 May 1; 221: 137–50.

[56] Pendrill, F., Persson, U.M., Godar, J., Kastner, T., Moran, D. et al. (2019). Agricultural and forestry trade drives large share of tropical deforestation emissions. Global Environmental Change 2019 May 1; 56: 1–0.

[57] Neumann, G.B., De Almeida, V.P. and Endler, M. (2018). Smart Forests: fire detection service. pp. 01276–01279. *In*: 2018 IEEE symposium on computers and communications (ISCC) 2018 Jun 25. IEEE.

[58] Avgeris, M., Spatharakis, D., Dechouniotis, D., Kalatzis, N., Roussaki, I. et al. (2019). Where there is fire there is smoke: A scalable edge computing framework for early fire detection. Sensors 2019 Jan; 19(3): 639.

[59] Sungheetha, A. and Sharma, R. (2020). Real time monitoring and fire detection using internet of things and cloud based drones. Journal of Soft Computing Paradigm (JSCP) 2(03): 168–74.

[60] Singh, S.K., Carpio, F. and Jukan, A. (2018). Improving animal-human cohabitation with machine learning in fiber-wireless networks. Journal of Sensor and Actuator Networks 2018 Sep; 7(3): 35.

[61] Chang, Z., Liu, S., Xiong, X., Cai, Z., Tu, G. et al. (2021). A survey of recent advances in edge-computing-powered artificial intelligence of things. IEEE Internet of Things Journal 2021 Jun 14.

[62] Susithra, N., Santhanamari, G., Deepa, M., Reba, P., Ramya, K.C. et al. (2021). Deep learning-based activity monitoring for smart environment using radar. pp. 91–123. *In*: Challenges and Solutions for Sustainable Smart City Development. Springer, Cham.

[63] Gupta, M., Abdelsalam, M., Khorsandroo, S. and Mittal, S. (2020). Security and privacy in smart farming: Challenges and opportunities. IEEE Access 2020 Feb 19; 8: 34564–84.

[64] Bhuyan, B.P., Tomar, R., Gupta, M. and Ramdane-Cherif, A. (2021). An ontological knowledge representation for smart agriculture. pp. 3400–3406. *In*: 2021 IEEE International Conference on Big Data (Big Data) 2021 Dec 15. IEEE.

[65] Cathey, Glen, James Benson, Maanak Gupta and Ravi Sandhu. (2021). Edge centric secure data sharing with digital twins in smart ecosystems. pp. 70–79. *In*: 2021 Third IEEE International Conference on Trust, Privacy and Security in Intelligent Systems and Applications (TPS-ISA). IEEE.

[66] Gupta, Maanak, Feras M. Awaysheh, James Benson, Mamoun Alazab, Farhan Patwa et al. (2020). An attribute-based access control for cloud enabled industrial smart vehicles. IEEE Transactions on Industrial Informatics 17(6): 4288–4297.

[67] Gupta, Maanak, James Benson, Farhan Patwa and Ravi Sandhu. (2019). Dynamic groups and attribute-based access control for next-generation smart cars. pp. 61–72. *In*: Proceedings of the Ninth ACM Conference on Data and Application Security and Privacy.

[68] Tomar, Ravi, Hanumat G. Sastry and Manish Prateek. (2020). A V2I based approach to multicast in vehicular networks. Malaysian Journal of Computer Science, 93–107.

[69] Sihag, V.K., Abhineet Anand, Ravi Tomar, Jagdish Chandra, Rajeev Tiwari et al. (2014). Detecting community structure based on traffic at node in networks. pp. 1–9. *In*: 2014 IEEE Students' Conference on Electrical, Electronics and Computer Science. IEEE.

Chapter 11

Taxonomy of Edge Computing Driven by IoT

Anuj Singh Naruka[1] and *Jagdish Chandra Patni*[2,]*

Edge computing and IoT have gained huge importance in recent years due to their benefits and wide range of use cases. So, in the second chapter, i.e., Edge Computing and IoT we are going to discuss all the major components related to Edge computing and IoT along with their architecture, use cases, benefits and at the end we'll cover two important topics which are IoT edge computing (IOT and edge together) and three laws related to IoT. Everything that we use has some sort of IoT application in it these days whether it is GPS, fitness watches, self-driving cars or voice assistants like google home. IoT has played a significant role in simplifying our tasks.

1. Introduction

As the years have passed by, a lot of virtual data has been generated, analyzed and collected. So, in order to access this data from any location via the internet we have a centralized system, cloud computing, however, issues like latency, bandwidth and security hinder the process of smoothly accessing the data and hence a need for a decentralized infrastructure was felt which led to the introduction of edge computing.

IoT has become one of the major contributors in the amount of data produced by organizations.

[1] School of Computer Science, University of Petroleum and Energy Studies, Dehradun India.
[2] School of Engineering and Technology, Jain (Deemed to be University) Bengaluru, India.
Email: 500082307@stu.upes.ac.in
* Corresponding author: patnijack@gmail.com

1.1 Edge Computing

Modern organizations and businesses produce an ocean of data that provides them with valuable insights as well as real time control on various operations that are carried out [1]. The data, especially the real time data, can be collected from various sensors and IoT devices that provide it from different remote locations and areas where it is impossible to set up an operating environment. This virtual flood of data has brought changes in ways in which organizations are handling computing. Traditional forms of computing which are built on a centralized system/centralized data center and internet are inadequate for endless flowing data. It presents a lot of challenges related to latency, bandwidth and other factors which we'll discuss in the coming sections. Therefore, organizations require a form of computing that allows them to move some part of data processing and data storage out of the centralized data center. This is where edge computing comes into play. Edge brings the services of the cloud close to the location where data is being generated.

Edge computing can be defined as a process of moving data processing closer to the source of data generation. The main aim of edge computing is to establish a decentralized and hierarchical paradigm that supports the operations as well as the development of distributed systems. What this practice does is that it breaks down the centralized computing issues and send all data to a centralized system where whole data processing takes place. Instead of transmitting the raw data to the data center it gets processed and analyzed at the place where it is actually generated. Data related to real-time insights and predictions requiring review and human interference is sent to the centralized data center.

Fig. 1. Edge Computing.

1.2 *Components of Edge Computing Ecosystem* [2]

1. *Cloud* - It acts as a repository for the container-based workloads like ML models and applications. It also acts as a destination for other nodes to get any form of data [15].

2. *Edge Device* - It is a piece of equipment that is integrated into the device and has computation capacity as well.

3. *Edge Node* - Generic way of referring to any edge device, edge server or edge gateway on which edge computing can be performed.

4. *Edge Gateway* - It is an edge server which in addition to edge server functions performs network functions like wireless connections, firewall and more.

5. *Edge Server* - It is a computer that is located in a remote operations facility like a hotel or retail store. It has hundreds of GBs of local storage. It is used to run application workloads and shared devices.

1.3 *Architecture of Edge Computing* [2]

Edge computing consists of three main nodes. These are -

1. *Device Edge* - Part of architecture where the edge devices are present. Devices such as sensors and other physical devices gather and interact with the edge data. The important part is to maintain the applications of these edge devices like real time data processing [18].

2. *Local Edge* - This part of the architecture includes infrastructure to support applications and the network workloads. Components

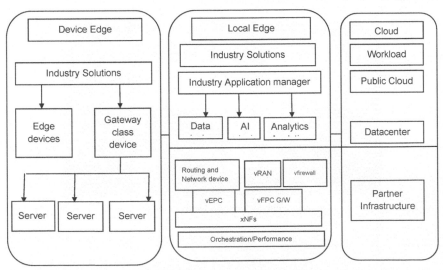

Fig. 2. Architecture of fog computing.

required to manage these applications are present in two sub layers of the architecture -

- *Network Layer* - This layer includes router, switches and other networking components which are an essential requirement for running the local edge [19].

- *Application Layer* - Applications which do not run at the device edge due to large footprints are run here, e.g., video analytics.

3. *Cloud* - This layer is the source of workloads that include both application and network workloads which are deployed at different edge nodes.

1.4 Benefits of Edge Computing [2]

Benefits of implementing edge computing are as follows -

1. *Performance* - Edge lowers the latency which allows quick computation and analysis of data thus increasing the performance. For those who are unaware about the term latency, it is the lag in communication between networks and devices. As we are progressing in the field of networking with upcoming cellular networks like 5G communication speed will increase even further enabling businesses and organizations to cope with the ever growing customer demand.

2. *Security* - One of the key features of edge computing architecture is that the data never leaves the physical area where it is gathered for processing and analysis. Thus the data remains more secure and only edge nodes need to be primarily secured.

3. *Availability* - Systems which are very important need to operate continuously irrespective of the connectivity. The current centralized systems have lots of drawbacks or points of failure related to the company's core network and security risks along network paths and many more. With edge computing the communication is majorly between the device and the consumer and the local edge node. This enhances and increases availability of systems.

1.5 Uses of Edge Computing [2]

- *Cloud gaming* - Cloud gaming is a new era of gaming which streams live feeds to devices. The game is hosted and processed in data centers and thus is very highly dependent on latency. Cloud gaming companies have been eyeing building edge servers in close proximity to gamers which helps in reducing the latency issue and providing a better responsive gaming experience.

- *Smart Grid* - Edge computing will enable enterprises and organizations to manage their energy consumption in an effective manner. Sensors and IoT devices which are connected to factories and offices are used to monitor energy use and analyzing consumption in real time which helps them with strategies to manage energy utilization.

- *Patient Monitoring in Hospitals* - The field of healthcare has a lot of edge opportunities. For example, currently monitoring devices such as glucose monitors and other sensors have a lot of unprocessed data which needs to be stored on a third party cloud. This increases security concerns related to the health data of healthcare providers. Implementing edge in hospitals allows the maintenance of data privacy and also helps in incorporating AI (Artificial Intelligence) which helps in analyzing the medical history of patients from earlier data sets and provides notifications if any unusual behavior is observed on comparing current and past datasets.

- *Video Surveillance* - Video surveillance is a brilliant technique used across the globe by all domains such as industries, businesses and houses. Edge computing nodes which consist of smart cameras can be used at the primary level to analyze data and recognize the targets or entities of interest.

2. IoT

IoT stands for Internet of Things. Kevin Ahton coined the term internet of things in the year 1999 [3]. It can be defined as a concept which involves connecting devices to the internet and to other devices. It is a humongous network which collects data and shares the way in which it can be used in the environment of interest. It includes a large range of objects of all sizes and shapes starting from self-driving cars, whose sensors detect any object in their path to fitness devices that measure parameters such as oxygen level, heart rate, distance covered and calories burnt. All these

Fig. 3. IOT.

sensors are connected to an Internet of Things platform that analyzes this data to provide valuable insights. This information can then be used to track the process to detect possible issues by studying the observed trends uncovered by these insights.

2.1 IoT System

IoT system incorporates four distinct components which are -

1. **Sensors/Devices** - The primary and most important function of a sensor is to collect data from its environment. Sensors can be part of devices that perform various other operations apart from sensing things. For example, our tabs and phones have GPS, compass and camera, however, these are not the only functions they perform [4, 5].

   There are different types of sensors like those for temperature and humidity. Although these sensors prove to be quite effective the major challenges posed by sensors are - cost, battery life and size. It is difficult to design or find a sensor that is small in size, cheap and has a long battery life.

2. **Connectivity** - The data being gathered by the sensors need to be sent to the cloud for which it needs a way. Sensors/Devices can be connected to the cloud via a variety of methods like Bluetooth, Wi-Fi and satellite [6].

   A perfect connectivity option will be the one that has least power consumption, a huge range and the ability to transmit large amounts of data, i.e., it has higher bandwidth. These characteristics of connectivity are impossible. There will always be a difference in connectivity in terms of characteristics as it might be good in some areas but not in some and hence the purpose for which IoT is being used defines the type of connectivity [12, 13].

   - *LPWAN* - LPWAN stands for Low power wide area network. It sends small amounts of data intermittently/multiple times in order to lower the power consumption. The characteristics of LPWAN are :

FEATURES	LPWAN
Range	High
Bandwidth	Low
Power Consumption	Low
Costs	Low

   - *Cellular* - All of us are quite familiar with this type of connectivity. It's used by our mobile phones for sharing data. Although cellular connectivity is a reliable option which provides communication over a long range, it is relatively costly and has a high power consumption. This type of connectivity due to its high-power consumption is not suitable for the majority of IoT use cases but can be used for keeping track of expensive goods like shipping containers which tend to travel over huge distances.

FEATURES	Cellular
Range	High
Bandwidth	High
Power Consumption	High
Costs	High

- *Satellite* - This type of communication has a high range and bandwidth but high power consumption. As it works all over the globe it is the most suitable form of communication for tracking goods or any other form of activity anywhere on earth.

FEATURES	Satellite
Range	High
Bandwidth	High
Power Consumption	High
Costs	High

- *WiFi & Bluetooth* - Reliable and effective over short ranges of communication. Power consumption is lower in comparison to cellular and satellite communication.

FEATURES	WiFi, Bluetooth
Range	Low
Bandwidth	High
Power Consumption	Low
Costs	Low

* **NOTE -** There might be cases where we'll skip the connectivity. The major reason behind skipping the connectivity is to avoid the problem of latency. For example, let's assume that an individual is sitting in an automatic driving car and has to avoid an accident for which the car needs to make immediate corrections. If we wait for the data to be sent to the cloud it might lead to a huge catastrophe.

3. **Data Processing** – The best explanation for data processing is, unorganized data is the input and the output is organized information. This information can be audio, visual or in a text format.

The data processing cycle is composed of three stages which are input, processing and output [7].

- *Input* - This is the initial stage of the data processing cycle where the collected data is converted into machine readable form which allows the computer to process it. Being the initial step, it is quite important as the input provided to the computer will determine its output.

- *Processing* - At this stage the data gets transformed into a more organized and meaningful format which is called information. This transformation is performed by using different data manipulation techniques such as classification and sorting.

- *Output* - Once the processing stage is over the processed data is converted into human readable form and hence provided to the user as useful information.

4. **User Interface -** We have been discussing collection, connectivity, and data processing. Now the final step is to deliver the information to the user. This is done via the user interface (UI). Screens and icons are the features of the user interface through which a user interacts with the computer system. A television remote also has a user interface that consists of buttons [8].

2.2 *Applications of IoT*

1. In the manufacturing industry, smart sensory data helps in requirement analysis, preventing abnormal breakdowns. IoT solutions also allow manufacturers to reduce time in the areas of large-scale customization.

2. In the field of home automation IoT along with machine learning has already developed various devices like google home. The IoT home automation environment allows us to control lights, TV and fans.

3. In healthcare, IoT devices provide different solutions for different issues. Wearable IoT devices allow hospitals to monitor their patients through real time data while they are at home. It also helps hospitals to predict and prevent the occurrence of upcoming dangers. In hospital premises smart beds allow the staff to keep a tally of the number of beds which are free and booked. Sensors also help in detecting any abnormal medical condition that a patient might be going through, i.e., fainting or experiencing a heart attack. These are lifesaving IoT applications behind IoT gaining so much popularity [9].

2.3 *IoT Edge Computing*

After understanding edge computing and IoT, it is important to analyze the relationship between them. According to the discussion that we had earlier in this chapter it is very clear that IoT performs well on having a computer power source close to the physical device or data source that actually exists [10]. So, quick responses of IoT devices for tasks or for mitigation of error edge come into play. IoT devices can be analyzed by edge computing instead of following the approach where it had to travel to a centralized location in order to get the analysis done.

In terms of the relationship between edge and IoT, edge can be defined as a local source that fulfills the storage of data and data processing needs of an IoT device. Let's enlist some of the benefits of using IoT and edge computing together: -

- The latency of communication between IoT devices and the central IT networks is reduced
- System operations can continue in offline mode if there is a loss in network connectivity
- Better network bandwidth
- Operational efficiency also increases

2.4 Three Laws of IoT

Amazon, which is a big tech giant as well as one of the leaders in the field of edge computing, has laid out three basic laws that govern/guide its edge computing and IoT development [11, 14]. These laws are quite helpful in understanding the limitations to IoT and edge computing which on a combined basis can bring about changes to stay realistic [16, 17].

1. *The Law of Physics* - This law states that physical limitations should be considered including technological ones while developing IoT projects. In the case of autonomous devices which need real-time responses some IoT devices need some degree of local computation in case of data transfer limitations, especially those which are concerned with safety. For example, self-driving cars can't afford even a millisecond delay and hence just can't depend only on real time data but also must have the ability for local computation as well.

2. *The Law of Economics* - The second law emphasizes on taking financial feasibility into account. IoT devices tend to produce a large volume of data and it is quite expensive to keep everything connected via service providers. Therefore, sending less data over network devices is financially viable for an IoT project.

3. *The Law of The Land* - This law discusses the legal and geographical restrictions which may hamper the data collection and transfer processes. Moreover, some regions in the world do not have the infrastructure to support basic IoT connectivity.

Summary

- Edge computing focuses on decentralizing the infrastructure that helps in resolving issues related to latency and bandwidth presented by the centralized infrastructure. It is a process of bringing the cloud close to the data generation source.
- Edge computing ecosystems are made up of different components like clouds and edge devices.
- There are three main nodes of edge computing architecture which we covered in detail in Section 2.3.
- Implementing edge computing brings its own set of benefits and use cases which have attracted the attention of various organizations.
- In Section 2.6 we begin the discussion related to IoT (Internet of Things). IoT is a concept of connecting devices to the internet and other devices in order to form a large network that allows them to collect, analyze and share the data according to the environment in which they work.
- An IoT system has in total four major components which are sensors/ devices, connectivity, data processing and user interfaces.
- It is applicable in various industries like manufacturing, healthcare, agriculture and home automation.
- Combining edge and IoT is very useful and effective which we have discussed in detail in Section 2.10.
- At the end we have covered the laws or the set of laws that Amazon follows in the field of IoT. These rules have been made by AWS on the basis of their observations and deep analysis in the fields of edge computing and IoT.

References

[1] Edge Computing, [online] [Available]: https://devops.com/wp-content/uploads/2020/05/Edge-Computing-1280x720.jpg [accessed 12 Apr 2022].

[2] Jason Gonzalez, Jason Hunt, Mathews Thomas, Ryan Anderson, Utpal Mangla et al. Edge computing architecture and use cases, [online] [Available]: https://developer.ibm.com/articles/edge-computing-architecture-and-use-cases/ [accessed 22 Apr 2022].

[3] IOT, [online] [Available]: https://www.bbva.ch/wp-content/uploads/2021/10/recurso_aplicaciones-de-IoT.jpg, [accessed 17 Apr 2022].

[4] Introduction to IoT, LEVEREGE, [online] [Available]: https://www.leverege.com/iot-ebook/how-iot-systems-work#:~:text=However%2C%20all%20complete%20IoT%20systems,processing%2C%20and%20a%20user%20interface [accessed 03 Apr 2022].

[5] Anni Junnila, How IoT Works - Part 1: Sensors, trackinno, [online] [Available]: https://trackinno.com/iot/how-iot-works-part-1-sensors/ [accessed 03 June 2022].

[6] Anni Junnila, How IoT Works - Part 2: Connectivity,trackinno, [online] [Available]: https://trackinno.com/iot/how-iot-works-part-2-connectivity/ [accessed 21 Apr 2022].

[7] Anni Junnila, How IoT Works - Part 3: Data Processing,trackinno, [online] [Available]: https://trackinno.com/iot/how-iot-works-part-3-data-processing/ [accessed 30 Apr 2022].

[8] Anni Junnila, How IoT Works - Part 4: User Interface, [online] [Available]: https://trackinno.com/iot/how-iot-works-part-4-user-interface/ [accessed 03 May 2022].

[9] John Terra, 8 Real-World IoT Applications in 2020, [online] [Available]: https://www.simplilearn.com/iot-applications-article [accessed 27 May 2022].

[10] What is IoT Edge Computing, [online] [Available]: https://www.redhat.com/en/topics/edge-computing/iot-edge-computing-need-to-work-together [accessed 14 Apr 2022].

[11] Jeff Alexander, The Current State Of Edge Computing, [online] [Available]: https://www.freshconsulting.com/insights/blog/state-of-edge-computing/ [accessed 17 May 2022].

[12] Hitesh Kumar Sharma, J.C. Patni, Prashant Ahlawat and Siddhratha Sankar Biswas. (2020). Sensors based smart healthcare framework using Internet Of Things (IOT). International Journal of Scientific & Technology Research, volume 9, issue 02, February 2020.

[13] Hitesh Kumar Sharma, Khushwant Singh, *Dr Md Ezaz Ahmed, Jagdish Chandra Patni, Yudhvir Singh and Prashant Ahlawat. (2020). IoT based automatic electric appliances controlling device based on visitor counter. International Journal of Psychosocial Rehabilitation, Vol 24, Issue 10.

[14] Sharma, H.K., Taneja, S., Ahmed, E. and Patni, J.C. (2019). I-Doctor: an IoT based self patient's health monitoring system. 2019 International Conference on Innovative Sustainable Computational Technologies (CISCT), Dehradun, Uttarakhand, India, pp. 1–6.

[15] Abhishek Gupta and Jagdish Chandra Patni. (2015). A theoretical comparison of job scheduling algorithms in cloud computing environment. 1st International Conference on Next Generation Computing Technologies (NGCT), IEEE, pp. 278–282, 4–5 September 2015.

[16] Gupta, Maanak and Ravi Sandhu. (2018). Authorization framework for secure cloud assisted connected cars and vehicular internet of things. pp. 193–204. *In*: Proceedings of the 23nd ACM on Symposium on Access Control Models and Technologies.

[17] Bhatt, Smriti, Thanh Kim Pham, Maanak Gupta, James Benson, Jaehong Park et al. (2021). Attribute-based access control for AWS internet of things and secure Industries of the Future. IEEE Access 9: 107200–107223.

[18] Tomar, Ravi, Hanumat G. Sastry, Manish Prateek et al. (2020). A V2I based approach to multicast in vehicular networks. Malaysian Journal of Computer Science, 93–107.

[19] Sihag, V.K., Abhineet Anand, Ravi Tomar, Jagdish Chandra, Rajeev Tiwari et al. (2014). Detecting community structure based on traffic at node in networks. pp. 1–9. *In*: 2014 IEEE Students' Conference on Electrical, Electronics and Computer Science. IEEE.

Chapter 12
Recent Trends and Challenges in Cloud Computing

Anuj Singh Naruka[1] and *Jagdish Chandra Patni*[2,*]

Storing, managing and accessing huge amounts of data have been major concerns for organizations which have been resolved by cloud computing. In the first chapter, we'll discuss recent developments in cloud computing in terms of deployment and service models being used by it, its advantages and challenges, and a lot more. In this chapter we will dive deep down into the realms of cloud computing and understand them in detail.

1. Introduction

Organizations these days are producing GBs, or I must say TBs of data and it is impossible for them to carry it everywhere as they might need it for analysis or processing. So, to simplify this issue cloud computing came into being. A cloud is basically a service that provides a platform to store data in audio, video or text form. It ensures data security and allows the user to get access to their data from any place in the world. The only thing we need to ensure is an active internet connection. Cloud computing has gained a lot of importance in the last 10 years especially.

1.1 Cloud Computing

Cloud computing has been a buzz word for quite some time now. In a layman's terms it is like a store where every individual and organization can

[1] School of Computer Science, University of Petroleum and Energy Studies, Dehradun India.
[2] School of Engineering and Technology, Jain (Deemed to be University) Bengaluru, India.
Email: 500082307@stu.upes.ac.in
* Corresponding author: patnijack@gmail.com

Fig. 1. Cloud computing [1].

store or dump their data so they don't have to worry about carrying massive memory disks or drives from one place to another. In a more technical sense, cloud computing is a centralized system where information of all sorts is stored which effectively allows the general public, MNC's and other organizations access to their data from any place at any given time using the internet on any device. Cloud helps in easing out the unprecedented amount of burden put by customers on the companies' IT infrastructure to meet their demands related to reliable and fast services [12].

Some popular cloud service providers are -

1. Google Cloud Platform
2. Microsoft Azure
3. Amazon Web Services (AWS)
4. IBM Cloud
5. Vmware
6. DigitalOcean

Cloud computing has seen numerous developments in recent years. These developments have been majorly driven by increasing customers for cloud services. In the years gone by there has phenomenol development in various areas of cloud computing like data security, amount of storage space being provided to consumers and the overall handling of the databases of organizations and giving them uninterrupted data access. Let's look at the development that has taken place in the last 10–12 years in the field of cloud computing [2].

- A major step was taken in 2010 by tech giants like Google, Microsoft and Amazon in launching their cloud divisions.

- This helped the masses to have access to cloud spaces and domains. This has been followed up by a large bunch of companies getting their systems on cloud as a result. The main reason behind this has also been the security features that have improved over time.

- Cloud computing led to the establishment of numerous software-as-a-service (SaaS) companies globally.

- In India, 55 SaaS companies were established in the year 2017. Cloud also led to the laying of foundations for many startups in the duration, 2015–2016.

- The major area of growth through cloud computing and services has been infrastructure-as-a-service (IaaS). This is quite obvious since the systems around which the companies were built had a traditional infrastructure which had to be completely modified in order to adapt and implement cloud computing.

- As recent as 2018, the infrastructure market was heavily dominated by five providers namely, Google, Microsoft, Amazon, Alibaba and IBM.

1.2 Advantages of Cloud Computing [14]

1. Reduced hardware and software capital costs.
2. Recovery of data is a lot cheaper and much quicker. Both these traits suit and work best for the business community.
3. Enhanced security.
4. Provides more flexibility within the working infrastructure of an organization.

1.3 Cloud Deployment Models

A cloud deployment model defines the locations and controllers of different servers that we utilize. The deployment model is chosen on the basis of the cloud's nature, ownership, purpose and scale [3].

1.3.1 Public Cloud

In this cloud deployment model all the cloud infrastructure services are present over the internet that can be accessed by people or major organizations. The infrastructure that is being used is owned by the cloud service provider. Features such as data retrieval services and storage backup are provided to customers either free or by system subscription. Examples of public clouds are – Gmail and Google Drive [13].

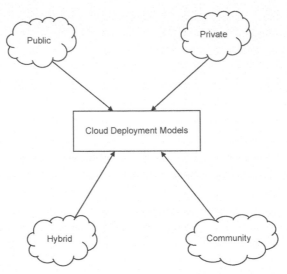

Fig. 2. Cloud deployment models [4].

The advantages of public cloud are that no maintenance cost is paid by the user. It is paid by the service provider and also as it follows the pay-as-per-use service model it is best suited for organizations that require immediate access to resources.

1.3.2 Private Cloud

The private cloud deployment model is a one-to-one environment for a single customer. Basically a single organization uses the cloud. Unlike the public cloud the hardware is not shared with anyone else. Private cloud provides a lot of control over cloud services. It is also called internal cloud because of its ability to access and inspect different services within a company or an organization. The cloud platform is protected by firewalls and is kept under the supervision of the IT department of each organization respectively.

Examples of private cloud are - Microsoft Azure Stack and Amazon AWS Outposts.

Some advantages of a private cloud include customization, control and privacy. In a private cloud, users can modify or design new solutions to meet its specific needs. In the case of a private cloud owned by an organization/user allows complete control over policies, IT operations and more.

1.3.3 Community Cloud

Community cloud deployment model resembles private cloud model with the only difference being in the number or set of users. In private cloud only one company owns the server but in community cloud organizations with similar backgrounds share the infrastructure of community cloud.

The organizations that participate in community cloud can enhance their efficiency if they tend to have uniform requirements in terms of security, performance and privacy.

1.3.4 Hybrid Cloud

A hybrid cloud deployment model encompasses the best features of public, private and community deployment models. This model allows companies to modify and mix these distinct models according to their requirements.

Improved security and privacy, better flexibility and reasonable price are some of the benefits of the hybrid cloud deployment model.

1.4 Cloud Computing Service Models

There are three service models offered in cloud computing where each service model satisfies a unique set of requirements [5]. These models are -

1.4.1 IaaS

IaaS stands for infrastructure as a service. It is an on-demand access cloud to cloud hosted computing infrastructure that is composed of servers, network resources and storage capacity [7]. The computing and hardware resources are maintained by the cloud service provider at its own data center. IaaS customers use the hardware with an internet connection and pay through pay-as-you-go basis or via a subscription model [11].

Benefits of IaaS are -

1. Improved performance due to lower latency. IaaS achieves this as IaaS providers have their data centers in multiple geographical locations.
2. Data centers are protected by a high level of security on site along with more security that is established via encryption.

Uses -

- IaaS is a great boon for startups as they get access to enterprise class data center capabilities without making a huge upfront investment in IT infrastructure.
- It is helpful in IoT and AI (Artificial Intelligence) as it makes it easier to set up different computing resources and storage capabilities for the applications.
- Generally, at the time of sale or festive seasons we clearly observe a lot of traffic on e-commerce websites. IaaS is a great option specially for online retailers to deal with such spikes in traffic.

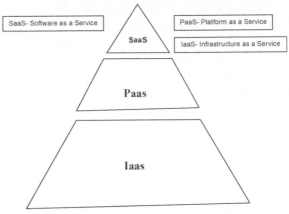

Fig. 3. Cloud computing models [6].

1.4.2 SaaS

SaaS stands for Software as a Service and is sometimes referred to as cloud application services. It can be defined as a software model where different applications are hosted by the cloud service provider [7]. Here the application along with the whole infrastructure that includes servers, application software, and storage are managed and hosted by a SaaS vendor. The job of the vendor is to ensure a level of security, availability and performance which is part of SLA. SLA stands for service level agreement which defines the level of service expected by the client from the supplier and measures the services according to the metrics to which the agreement was made.

In our daily life we use some form of SaaS applications while using a phone like social media, email or any cloud storage platform like Dropbox.

Benefits of SaaS are -

1. SaaS vendors handle infrastructure and application management along with security and storage [20]. This removes the burden from users and all they have to do is create an account, pay for it and start using it.
2. It increases productivity as we can use SaaS apps anytime and anywhere on any device having a browser and an internet connection [21].

1.4.3 PaaS

PaaS stands for Platform as a Service. It provides a cloud-based platform for running, developing and managing applications [7]. All the hardware and software included in the platform like servers, Oss and databases are managed and maintained by the cloud services provider.

Examples of PaaS solutions are Microsoft Windows Azure and Google App Engine.

The main benefit of PaaS is that it allows users to build, test and deploy the applications cost effectively and more quickly compared to the process of building and managing their own platform along with simplified collaboration as it provides a shared software development environment.

Uses of PaaS are -

1. PaaS enables teams to easily develop, run and manage APIs for data sharing.
2. IoT application development requires languages such as Java, Python, Swift and PaaS that support these programming languages which enhances the development and data processing.

2. Trends and Challenges in Cloud Computing

In this section we are going to discuss the different trends and challenges in the areas of cloud computing and high-performance computing.

2.1 Trends [8]

1. **Serverless Function -** Serverless computing has shown promising results to organizations, made possible by cloud. It promises a pay-as-you-go model which means that the organization pays for only those services being actually used. This helps companies to expand their infrastructure as per the requirement of the applications without making any significant capital investment.

2. **Edge Computing -** Edge computing has drawn significant attention as it has a decentralized computing infrastructure, reduces latency and improves performance application. Edge computing is highly preferrable for time-sensitive data and increases operational efficiency significantly and will be implemented on a huge scale in the near future.

3. **AI in Cloud Computing -** AI and cloud computing are dependent on each other as AI is responsible for effective implementation of cloud computing whereas cloud services play a key role in the deliverance of AI services. For organizations implementing AI and cloud together is quite cheaper than implementing them separately. Moreover, AI manages the cloud computing data and the cloud provides a constant data backup and recovery in a virtual environment.

4. **Multi-Cloud Infrastructure** – The multi-cloud model allows companies to choose different cloud services which are best suited for their business, administrative requirements among others. In the

coming years organizations will switch to multi-cloud infrastructure which will remove their dependence on one cloud service provider.

2.2 Challenges

Although cloud computing has shown great promise since its introduction there are few challenges which still haven't been resolved [9]. These challenges are -

1. **Cost -** Although cloud infrastructure follows a pay-as-you-go model which reduces the overall cost of the resources being used, sometimes as the servers might not be fully used or if any resource is not fully utilized it adds up to hidden costs. This means that we are paying for a service that we are not utilizing completely at that moment.

2. **Network -** Cloud has high dependence on the network. A high-speed network ensures smooth transfer of data to and from a server. Organizations need to ensure a high bandwidth internet along with zero network outages for uninterrupted functioning of the cloud or it might lead to huge business losses [15, 16]. Hence this poses a major challenge specially for small organizations to maintain a network bandwidth as it is quite costly to implement.

3. **Performance -** In the case of cloud computing the factor that affects the performance of cloud-based solutions is latency [17]. There can be many reasons for having high latency like the inability of the system to decide where to allocate resources which cause delays in output visibility to users [18, 19]. This degrades the quality of user experiences leading to huge profit losses as usage of cloud services stop.

3. Applications of Cloud Computing

CSPs or Cloud Service Providers provide many cloud services and have tried to touch every sector by providing different cloud applications related to their use case [10]. Some of the real-world applications of cloud computing are: -

1. **Data Storage -** As technological advancements are taking place at a rapid pace, the amount of data being generated is also huge and thus storage is a big issue. This is where cloud comes into play as it stores data and provides users the flexibility to access it from any place at any time.

2. **Big Data -** The traditional methods of data management systems make it impossible for an organization to store a large volume of big data. Cloud computing resolved this problem by storing the organization's data on cloud so that the worries related to physical storage would

no longer prevail. Moreover, cloud computing provides facilities and tools to not only store but also to analyze it which is a critical part of big data.

3. **Education** - Online education made a huge leap in terms of popularity during the pandemic. Cloud computing has played an important role in the education sector by providing e-learning and developing portals for storing student/academic information and more.

4. **E-commerce** - Cloud based e-commerce allows quick responses to opportunities and traffic management on these platforms which might suffer from congestion during festive season sales. The companies preferring cloud based e-commerce spend a lot less and have their platforms set up quickly and efficiently. As the cloud also provides facilities to analyze the data, companies can analyze their customers buying behavior and come up with suggestions and recommendations for each customer with the help of some machine learning techniques.

5. Many entertainment applications like Netflix and video conferencing apps like Zoom use cloud computing. These companies or industries try to adapt and work with a multi-cloud strategy.

6. **Social Applications** - Social cloud applications enable users to connect with each other via social networking applications like Facebook, Instagram, Twitter and LinkedIn.

Summary

- Cloud is a service that has enabled many organizations and individuals to store their data in a safe and easy to access manner. The data can be text, image, video or of any other format.

- Big tech giants like Google, Microsoft and Amazon have their own cloud service providers which are Google Cloud Platform, Microsoft Azure and Amazon Web Services respectively.

- Section 1.3 discusses the cloud deployment models like public and private cloud followed by Section 1.4 which covers the cloud computing service models that are made to fulfill a unique set of requirements.

- Trends define the direction which people are preferring in a particular field. Section 1.5 covers trends in cloud computing.

- At the end we learn about some challenges of cloud computing along with some applications of cloud computing.

References

[1] Cloud Computing, [Online] [Available]: https://info.cgcompliance.com/hubfs/cloud.jpg, [accessed: 22 May 2022].

[2] Gilad David Maayan, How the Cloud Has Evolved Over the Past 10 Years, DATAVERSITY, [Online] [Available]: https://www.dataversity.net/how-the-cloud-has-evolved-over-the-past-10-years/#, [accessed: 13 June 2022].

[3] Yuliya Shaptunova, 4 Best Cloud Deployment Models Overview, [Online] [Available]: https://www.sam-solutions.com/blog/four-best-cloud-deployment-models-you-need-to-know/, [accessed: 13 May 2022].

[4] Cloud Deployment Models, [Online] [Available]: https://cloudcomputinggate.com/wp-content/uploads/2020/11/cloud-deployment-models.png, [accessed: 01 June 2022].

[5] IBM Cloud Education, IaaS vs PaaS vs SaaS, [Online] [Available]: https://www.ibm.com/in-en/cloud/learn/iaas-paas-saas#block-ibm-cloud-content, [accessed: 07 June 2022].

[6] Cloud Computing Examples, [Online] [Available]: https://cloudcomputinggate.com/wp-content/uploads/2022/02/SaaS-vs.-IaaS-vs.-PaaS-Differences-Pros-Cons-and-Examples.jpg, [accessed: 04 June 2022].

[7] IBM Cloud Education, IaaS versus PaaS versus SaaS, [Online] [Available]: https://www.ibm.com/cloud/learn/iaas-paas-saas, [accessed: 11 May 2022].

[8] Brandi Jaylin, 2021 Trends in Cloud Computing, OTAVA, [Online] [Available]: https://www.otava.com/blog/2021-trends-in-cloud-computing/, [accessed: 21 May 2022].

[9] 12 Cloud Computing Risks & Challenges Businesses Are Facing In These Days,datapine, [Online] [Available]: https://www.datapine.com/blog/cloud-computing-risks-and-challenges/, [accessed: 23 May 2022].

[10] Satyabrata_Jena,Real World Applications Of Cloud Computing,GeeksforGeeks, [Online] [Available]: https://www.geeksforgeeks.org/real-world-applications-of-cloud-computing/, [accessed: 30 May 2022].

[11] Jagdish Chandra Patni, Souradeep Banerjee and Devyanshi Tiwari. (2020). Infrastructure as a code (IaC) to Software Defined Infrastructure using Azure Resource Manager (ARM). International Conference on Computational Performance Evaluation (ComPE-2020) at North-Eastern Hill University, Shillong, Meghalaya, IEEE, pp. 575–578, DOI:10.1109/ComPE49325.2020.9200030.

[12] Jagdish Chandra Patni. (2020). Centralized approach of load balancing in homogenous grid computing environment. ICCMB 2020: Proceedings of the 2020 the 3rd International Conference on Computers in Management and Business, Hosei University, Tokyo, Japan January 2020 pp. 151–156. https://doi.org/10.1145/3383845.3383877.

[13] Akshay Sharma, Asif Riaz Ahmad and Jagdish Chandra Patni. (2016). CloudBox – A Virtual Machine Manager for KVM based virtual Machines. 2nd International Conference on Next Generation Computing Technologies (NGCT), IEEE, pp. 588–594, 14–16 October 2016, 10.1109/NGCT.2016.7877403.

[14] Abhishek Gupta and Jagdish Chandra Patni. (2015). A theoretical comparison of job scheduling algorithms in cloud computing environment. 1st International Conference on Next Generation Computing Technologies (NGCT), IEEE, pp. 278–282, 4–5 September, 2015.

[15] McDole, Andrew, Maanak Gupta, Mahmoud Abdelsalam, Sudip Mittal and Mamoun Alazab. (2021). Deep learning techniques for behavioral malware analysis in cloud iaas. pp. 269–285. *In*: Malware Analysis using Artificial Intelligence and Deep Learning. Springer, Cham.

[16] Kimmell, Jeffrey C., Mahmoud Abdelsalam and Maanak Gupta. (2021). Analyzing machine learning approaches for online malware detection in cloud. pp. 189–196. *In*: 2021 IEEE International Conference on Smart Computing (SMARTCOMP). IEEE.

[17] Yadav, Anuj and Madan Lal Garg. (2019). Monitoring based security approach for cloud computing. Ingénierie des Systèmes d'Information 24(6).

[18] Yadav, Anuj Kumar, Ritika Ritika and Madan Lal Garg. (2020). SecHMS-A secure hybrid monitoring scheme for cloud data monitoring. EAI Endorsed Transactions on Scalable Information Systems 8(30): e8.

[19] Yadav, Anuj Kumar and Madan Garg Ritika. (2021). Cryptographic solution for security problem in cloud computing storage during global pandemics. International Journal of Safety and Security Engineering, 193–199.

[20] AnujKumar, Yadav, Ravi Tomar, Deep Kumar, Himanshu Gupta et al. (2012). Security and privacy concerns in cloud computing. International Journal of Advanced Research in Computer Science and Software Engineering 2(5).

[21] Guo, Jianli, Korhan Cengiz and Ravi Tomar. (2021). An IOT and Blockchain approach for food traceability system in agriculture. Scalable Computing: Practice and Experience 22(2): 127–137.

Index